# PCs FROM SCRATCH

# PCs FROM SCRATCH

**Designing and Assembling
Your Own Custom PC**

**Tom Badgett**

**Corey Sandler**

**Wade Stallings**

**BANTAM BOOKS**
NEW YORK · TORONTO · LONDON · SYDNEY · AUCKLAND

*PCs FROM SCRATCH: DESIGNING AND ASSEMBLING YOUR OWN CUSTOM PC*
*A Bantam Book / October 1990*

ISBN 0-553-34963-5

*Published simultaneously in the United States and Canada*

Bantam Books are published by Bantam Books, Inc., a division of Bantam Doubleday Dell Publishing Group, Inc. Its trademark, consisting of the words "Bantam Books" and the portrayal of a rooster, is Registered in U.S. Patent and Trademark Office and in other countries. Marca Registrada, Bantam Books, Inc., 666 Fifth Avenue, New York, New York 10103.

*PRINTED IN THE UNITED STATES OF AMERICA*

0   9   8   7   6   5   4

# ACKNOWLEDGMENTS

The authors note with thanks the contributions of some of the people and companies who helped with this book.

Thanks to Bill Gladstone at Waterside Productions for his capable agentry; to Bantam Books for publishing the book; and to the many people who answered questions and provided valuable material, especially John Pope at CompuAdd Corporation, John Jaser at Logix Microcomputers, and Dan Dotterweich at Charis Computers.

Thanks to our families for their understanding and cooperation. Any vocation you pursue at home—but perhaps writing more than some—is a group effort.

We also wish to acknowledge the valuable assistance provided by a number of major hardware and software companies. We commend their products to your attention.

This book was researched and prepared using equipment and software that included the following:

Austin 286-16. Austin Computer Systems, 10300 Metric Boulevard, Austin, TX 78758. 800-752-1577.

CompuAdd 80386-20 microcomputer. CompuAdd Corporation, 12303 Technology Boulevard, Austin, TX 78727. 800-627-1967.

Hijaak and InSet software for image capture and conversion. Inset Systems, 71 Commerce Drive, Brookfield, CT 06804. 800-828-8088. 203-775-5866.

Fujitsu RX7100 PS printer. An LED technology Postscript printer with HP emulation. Fujitsu America, 3055 Orchard Drive, San Jose, CA 95134-2017. 408-432-1300.

Lanlink Version 5.0, serial network for printer and file sharing. The Software Link, Inc., 3577 Parkway Lane, Atlanta, GA 30092. 404-448-5465.

LGX386 25-MHz 80386 microcomputer with 15-ms 670-MB Micropolis hard drive and high-performance VGA1000 video adapter and Idek VGA monitor. Logix Microcomputers, 375 Morgan Lane, West Haven, CT 06516. 800-248-2140.

NEC Silentwriter LC-890 PostScript LED printer. NEC Information Systems, Inc., 1414 Massachusetts Avenue, Boxboro, MA 01719. 508-264-8000.

Swan 386/20 computer. A 20-MHz 80386 microprocessor with 0 wait state memory, shadow bios, and 150-MB hard drive. Tussey Computer Products, 3075 Research Drive, State College, PA 16801. 800-468-9044.

WordPerfect Version 5.0 word processing software. WordPerfect Corporation, 1555 N. Technology Way, Orem, UT 84057. 801-227-4288.

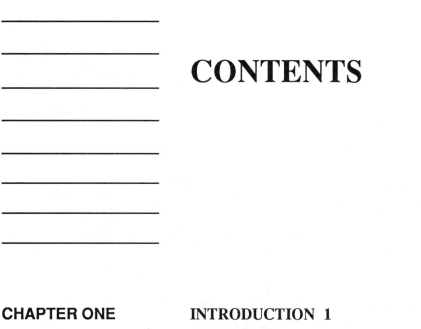

# CONTENTS

# CHAPTER ONE    INTRODUCTION

The earliest personal computers were hand built, because that was the only way to obtain one. You bought chips and a breadboard and a soldering iron and a schematic. The early personal computer programs were laboriously punched out on paper tape.

And, after hundreds of hours of work, the first builders were rewarded by a few tentative flashes of light on a control panel. Video displays came later.

The next step in the evolution of the PC industry came when companies such as Altair, Apple, and Ohio Scientific offered kits of boards and parts. But still only the most dedicated, the most skilled, the most intrepid sampled these early wares.

But by the beginning of the 1980s, the industry rapidly moved to the world of the computer as a "plug-and-play" appliance, with the arrival of PCs that could be purchased anywhere and hooked up as easily as a microwave oven or stereo. That lowered the price, increased the software base, and gave millions of people new access to computer power.

Still, there are those who aren't satisfied with off-the-shelf configurations. It may be because of the need to solve a particularly unusual need, a simple desire for a custom design, or a need simply to save money.

Whatever the reason, today's builder benefits from the standardization of PC components. In today's open market you can assemble components from a wide variety of sources and put them together into the computer system of your dreams. And, best of all, it no longer takes the skill of an engineer, the drive of an explorer, and the patience of a monk to build your own PC from scratch.

Anyone can do it, and this book will show you how.

Why would you want to build a PC from scratch? We consider building a computer from the ground up the ultimate customization. Only by carefully considering your needs, shopping for the components, and putting them together yourself are you guaranteed of a system that fits your needs precisely.

## WHAT IS *PCs FROM SCRATCH*?

This book covers the fundamentals of computer components and shows you how to assemble a computer system from them. By basic components we don't mean chips, resistors, capacitors, and diodes. The term "components" today means keyboards, monitors, the computer box, the motherboard, the power supply, disk drives, and all the other major system pieces.

When you have a sound understanding of what these components do, you can easily design your own computer system. It really is not difficult to build a computer from scratch these days. An inexperienced, nontechnical person can assemble the basic components in a couple of hours. All you need is a few simple tools. In fact, for the vast majority of the PC building tasks, we show you how to do it in this book; all you need is one or two screwdrivers and maybe a pair of pliers.

Even if you are not interested in doing the actual building yourself, but you want to control closely the components used when someone else assembles your system, this book is still for you. The background and reference material provided will help you ensure that you get exactly what you want. We call this the "systems" level of PC building.

On the other hand, you may want to build your own system completely from scratch. This entails selecting and assembling the case, power supply, motherboard, disk drives, keyboard, monitor, and all the associated cards into a working system. We call this the "nuts and bolts" level of PC building. We'll help you with that, too.

If you are uncomfortable with the self-assembly idea, don't worry. You can find instructional video cassettes for about $20 to show you step-by-step how to do it. Such visual material will augment this book and make the job even easier to understand and to accomplish.

And, of course, you'll want to keep this book on your shelf as a reference to answer your ongoing questions about personal computers.

# WHY *PCs FROM SCRATCH*?

There are three primary reasons to build your own PC from scratch. One reason is money. By following the techniques outlined in the chapter "Shopping and Purchasing," you can save at least 20 percent on the cost of your finished system when you design and build it yourself compared to purchasing a retail package.

Perhaps even more important is the ability to get precisely what you need. Although there is a wide choice of systems and vendors today, there still is room for custom system design. When you design and build the system yourself you can select the precise components you want and need for your individual applications.

And, there's the satisfaction of doing it yourself. As the system creator, you will develop a close understanding of how your system works and what it is capable of. As your computing needs change you will have the knowledge and skill to modify and improve its operation.

Assembling computers today is simple compared to years past. Everything today is in modular units that you simply drop-in or plug-in and hook up. Built-in diagnostics and diagnostic software tools reduce to a minimum the amount of technical skill required to test and troubleshoot a system.

Modifying and repairing is also a relatively painless task today. Individual component costs are so low ($70 for a diskette drive, for example) repairing a system is simply a matter of identifying the component to be added or replaced, and then doing it. Labor costs, on the other hand, are high and rising. By learning how basic computer components work and what they do, you can do your own swap-out repairs and save a substantial amount of money.

You really shouldn't have to pay someone else to repair or modify your computer. If you need incentive to try it yourself, compare local labor repair costs to the cost of the items in your computer. You can almost replace the whole system for the cost of one or two visits to the repair shop.

# WHO SHOULD READ *PCs FROM SCRATCH*?

This book is for the beginner and for the experienced user.

For the beginner, it is a tutorial that will take you from ground zero up to a working knowledge level: how the computer works, what programs to use, and computer jargon.

For the experienced user and those who wish to advance beyond the beginner's level, it is a reference book on basic hardware and software descriptions, a tutorial on how to shop and buy computer components and accessories, and a guide on how to assemble your own computer from scratch.

If you know little or nothing about personal computers, this book will be a great way to start your learning process. You will learn what a personal computer is all about.

If you are a typical user who knows software, but who has a limited knowledge of computer hardware, this book will expand your knowledge.

For example, you may know that high-density 5.25-inch disk drives will read and write in both high-density (1.2 MB) and low-density (360 KB) modes, but you never understood why there is a problem in reading the 360 KB generated disks on other machines. This book will answer this question and many more.

This book also is a handy reference for the experienced hardware person. Chapter 6, "Computer Components," is a particularly useful source of information. You should also find Chapter 8, "Shopping and Purchasing," helpful.

## HOW DO YOU USE THIS BOOK?

For the neophyte, the beginning is naturally the place to start. You need to understand first what a computer is all about, then you can progress to how it functions and study the basic components in the system. Next, you get a tour of fundamental software packages.

For the typical user, the discussion of system analysis and design in Chapter 3 may be your starting point. Here you will learn how to translate your needs and wants into the correct computer system configuration for you. Additionally, it will help with your strategic planning of a system that could provide many years of satisfying use rather than something that becomes obsolete within a couple of years.

For the experienced person, Chapter 6, "Computer Components," may be the beginning point. This section gets down to the fundamental description and operation of the various system components. Unless you have an excellent memory, we feel sure that you will find this a useful refresher and reference section.

Finally, the section on Assembly and Test (Chapter 9) and the information on Shopping and Purchasing (Chapter 8) should be of interest to everyone.

## WHAT IS IN THIS BOOK?

Chapter 1 is an introduction to the book.

Chapter 2 describes basic PC components and explains the differences among PC/XT-compatible systems and the newer 80286, 80386, and 80486 machines. You will learn about different bus architectures and receive an introduction to individual computer components.

Chapter 3 covers system operations. Chapter 3 picks up where Chapter 2 left off. Here we present a detailed component-by-component reference. You will use the information in this section again and again as you study product offerings and work to configure your own system. Chapter 3 can also be a long-term component reference as you use and upgrade your system. We pick up this discussion in more detail in Chapter 6.

Chapter 4 covers systems software. This book is primarily about hardware, but your computer is only as useful as the software you run on it. In Chapter 4 we show you how to select an operating system (believe it or not, there are some choices) and explain some of the differences among popular options.

Chapter 5 discusses applications software. In addition to the system-level software that is the housekeeper of your system, you also need applications: word processing, spreadsheets, database, and schedulers and other utilities. Chapter 5 offers a brief overview of the basic considerations in software selection. Choosing the software you need is among the first and most important steps toward designing your system configuration.

Chapter 6 gives you details about computer components. A working computer system is made up of the sum of its parts. Chapter 3 offered a general introduction to the PC component concept. In Chapter 6 we get down to the nitty-gritty of what goes into a system so you can get the functionality you need out of it.

Chapter 7 shows you how to blueprint your computing needs. In the days of room-sized computers, whole teams often worked for months on systems analysis and design before a computer was installed. You need to go through some of the same processes to get the best system configuration for your PC platform. Luckily, the process isn't nearly as complicated as it once was. In Chapter 7 we show you how to decide what functions you need and how to put this information to work for you in planning a computer system.

Chapter 8 guides you through shopping and purchasing. The shopping process is both harder and easier than it was before the days of standardized computer hardware. It is easier because the systems are relatively simple and much of the configuration is done for you in the design of the computer itself. On the other hand, hundreds of vendors are selling systems and components today. How can you sift through this information overload to find what you need? In Chapter 8 we offer some useful hints to get you on your way.

Chapter 9 covers assembly and test of the computer components. After all the planning and decisions, you have to assemble the components you have selected into a working system. That's the topic of this final chapter. We show you how to pull together the various components and test the finished product.

# DON'T WORRY!

You don't have to be a programmer or an electronic genius to build your own personal computer. The basic skills you need to get the computer up and running are easy to master, and the finished product is even easier to use. Most of the software today is very "friendly" and includes onscreen prompts, help systems, and even complete electronic users manuals.

You don't have to own an elaborate set of tools or equipment to build your own personal computer, either. Two or three screwdrivers (Phillips and flat blade), a set of 4-inch or 6-inch needlenose pliers, a magnifying glass, and an adjustable lamp are all that is needed. You may want to consider an IC (integrated circuit) insertion/extraction tool, a handy option for installing and removing memory chips.

Also in the "optional but not necessary" tool category:

1/4-inch nut driver
Penlight flashlight
Tweezers

In fact, if you have ever done any work around the house you probably already have all the tools you really need for a one-time assembly of a personal computer and for maintenance or expansion once it is complete.

As you gain experience with computer building and maintenance you'll evolve your own set of tools and techniques. Always be on the lookout for better ways to do things and ways to use conventional tools and facilities in unconventional ways.

As you study the next sections of this book you might benefit from making some notes about your individual situation to help get you started toward designing a custom computer system and building it yourself.

**CHAPTER TWO**

# PERSONAL COMPUTER BASICS

A complete computer system may contain hundreds or even thousands of individual ("discrete") components. These include integrated circuits, diodes, resistors, capacitors, and more. Luckily, as a system designer and builder you don't have to work with components at this level. Today's systems consist of relatively dense modules with well-defined functions: display adapter, printer interface, keyboard, disk controller, and so on.

As you might expect, there is a wide variety of choices among components with similar functions. Deciding which module functions you need and selecting from among the available options is part of your job as a systems designer.

In this chapter we introduce the concept of system configuration, and we will outline the various system components. This general overview will give you the foundation you need for basic system design and will get you on your way to understanding the design and function of individual components. We'll give you additional hardware details on system components in the following chapter.

## SYSTEM CONFIGURATION

What is system configuration? It is the process of describing the fundamental composition of a computer system. It usually involves specifying the class (size, power) of the computer and the associated peripheral devices (printers, disk drives, displays).

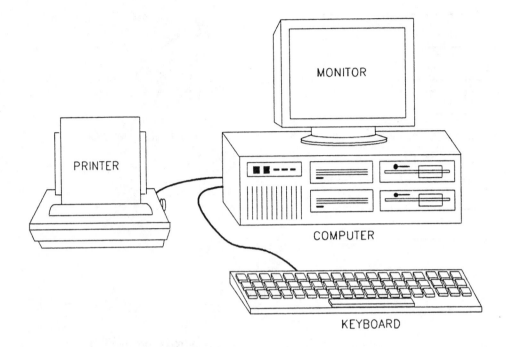

**Figure 2.1**   **Fundamental computer system components**

For example, if someone asks what kind of computer system you have, your first response might be the brand name, or you might narrow down the possibilities for the inquisitor by saying "It is a Mac," or "It is a PC." If you are more in tune with the configuration of your system, your reply might be "A 20-megahertz 80386 system."

If you want to provide more detail on the system configuration, you might describe the memory storage capacity and characteristics of the computer itself, the type of video display, the type of printer, and other unique features of the system.

Consider a basic computer system, as shown in Figure 2.1. In the center of this illustration is the computer itself. This is where all the calculating and data manipulation take place. For communicating to the outside world, the computer uses the video display, keyboard, and printer.

System configuration is the heart of designing and building your own PC. You'll probably start with some specific ideas about how you will use the system, then configure your new PC to fit those needs. You can do a better job of system configuration if you have a basic understanding of individual PC components and how the PC functions as a whole.

# What Is in a PC?

What is inside the computer box or case? The computer can be broken down into basic units. A system-level block diagram is shown in Figure 2.2.

At the center of everything is the Central Processing Unit (CPU), a chip that conducts the actual data manipulation. For short-term memory, the system uses Random Access Memory (RAM), electronic chips that store information as long as the computer is turned on. For long-term memory—usually called storage—a combination of floppy and hard disk drives usually is employed.

To communicate with the outside world, the machine needs input/output circuits to interface to external devices such as the keyboard, a monitor, and a printer.

Finally, it needs a way to link all its internal units together, a central nervous system of sorts, called the system bus. This internal communications link and data highway is composed of two parts, the data bus and the address bus.

The address bus allows the processor (CPU) to identify the system components it wants to talk to. The data bus provides the highway to carry data back and forth between the processor and other internal units.

The processor is the hub around which everything revolves. It interprets and executes instructions, manipulating data based on what it determines is the proper course of action. How quickly it can perform these operations is determined by its "clock speed" and the "data path."

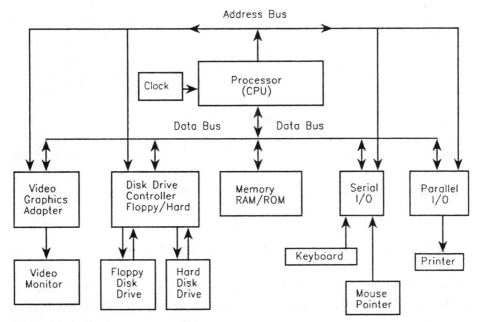

**Figure 2.2**   **Inside a basic 80286 computer system**

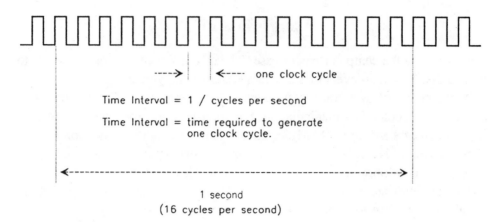

**Figure 2.3**   Curve with timing labeled

## Processor Timing Parameters

The clock speed is the main determinant of "execution time" (how long it takes the processor to perform a task). It is referred to in units of time called cycles or pulses per second. The commonly used name for cycles per second is "hertz," abbreviated Hz, and generally expressed as thousands of hertz (kilohertz) or millions of Hertz (megahertz). Basic timing definitions are shown in Figure 2.3.

Typical clock speeds today are 4.77 MHz, 8 MHz, 10 MHz, 12 MHz, 16 MHz, 20 MHz, 25 MHz, and 33 MHz. The abbreviation  MHz refers to one million cycles per second, so for a 33-MHz clock the heart of the processor must beat 33 million times in one second.

A matching term that goes with clock rate is "time interval," which refers to the duration of one clock cycle. Time interval is the reciprocal of the clock speed:

**time interval = 1/(clock speed)**

It is usually expressed in units call "nanoseconds" (ns). One nanosecond is one billionth of a second.

In addition, remember from high school math that you can express the same formula in terms of clock speed:

**clock speed = 1/time interval**

Why is time interval important? Because the auxiliary components such as memory that are external to the processor must respond in a finite amount of time when the processor makes requests. This finite time interval is called "access time." The amount of time allowed is usually less than one clock cycle, a very small amount of time.

Memory devices are normally rated by access time—how quickly the memory can respond to read and write requests. Typical memory access times are 100 ns or 150 ns. Since access time should be less than one clock cycle, these memory chips could only be used in a computer with a maximum clock speed of 10 MHz or less, as shown by the formula we described earlier:

$$1/100 \text{ ns} = 10 \text{ MHz}$$

or

$$1/150 \text{ ns} = 6.67 \text{ MHz}$$

Also, you should understand that clock speed is an infinitely variable quantity that can be easily changed by the computer designer. And electronic components such as memory devices have a fixed variability called tolerance: in operation the component may actually function faster or slower than the published specification. The design and manufacture of the component establishes this specification.

When selecting the clock speed to use for a computer, the designer has to consider what speed memory (access time) will be used. By knowing what the maximum access time of the memory device will be, the designer knows that the clock speed will have to be less than the reciprocal of the access time.

$$1/(\text{maximum memory access time}) = \text{maximum clock frequency}$$

For example, a memory component will be rated at 100 ns for read and write access time. This description tells the knowledgeable person that it will work with computers that have a clock rate of 4.77 to 10 MHz.

$$1/100 \text{ ns} = 10 \text{ MHz (maximum)}$$

Of course, the inverse of that process also is true and is the important consideration for you, the amateur system designer. In all probability you will first select a system board that has the clock speed you need. When you search the catalogs and magazines to find memory for it, you will need to know how fast the memory must be for it to keep up with the CPU.

Suppose you are considering a "bare" 16-MHz motherboard. To populate it with memory you must find chips with an access time of at least 62.5 ns $(1/16,000,000 = .0000000625)$.

## Execution Time

We have used the term "execution time." What does it mean? Execution time refers to how many clock cycles the processor requires to complete one instruction or to do a particular function.

Why isn't it simply referred to as "execution cycles" instead? While it is true that we say, for example, that it takes 10 clock cycles to do an add instruction, it has no meaning unless referenced back to the clock speed itself. Execution time expressed in time units such as nanoseconds gives a means for comparison against other computers of different designs and clock speeds.

Why bother with execution times? Because every operation of the processor doesn't require the same amount of time. Decision instructions usually require only two to five cycles. Addition and subtraction can require 10 to 20 cycles. Multiply and divide operations can take hundreds of clock cycles. Obviously there is considerable variation in execution times for the hundreds of instructions that a processor can execute.

Let us add one more term to the performance terminology list: "MIPS" or millions of instructions per second. Clock cycles and time interval terms are adequate for describing the instantaneous performance of hardware (physical computer components), but another performance benchmark is needed to measure overall system operation.

To measure the effective computing power of all the parts as a whole, a set of standardized routines for performing a specific function is used to measure how many times the computer can execute the function in one second. This time measure describes the cumulative execution-time effects of all components working as a whole, including the operating system software.

Why would this be important? A 10-MHz computer is a 10-MHz computer, right? Not necessarily. Because of the different processor types, memory access times, and computer hardware designs, cumulative processing times vary. Sometimes the difference in MIPS for different computers is significant.

Of course MIPS is not the definitive way to measure performance. Even though the routines are standardized from a computer language standpoint, the compiler (English-language to processor-language translator), can generate different translations for different types of computers.

Perhaps just as important, a bright programmer who knows the computer's unique features can make subtle changes to the compiled program to improve execution times without altering the program's objective. The result is improved performance that may not truly represent how well the computer will perform when other standard and unmodified software is run.

Ok, let's review. So far we have discussed four ways to measure processor operation. The first three define the timing characteristics of the processor. They are

- Clock cycles
- Access time
- Execution time

The last term, MIPS, gives a subjective overview of the computer as a whole when performing a collection of operational steps (job tasks).

Clock cycles, expressed in MHz, gives a basic description of the processor's capability. It is directly tied to the maximum time specification for the processor's support devices, such as memory. This time specification is referred to as access time.

Access time is expressed in billionths of a second, or nanoseconds. It basically defines the maximum clock speed that a processor can have and still work correctly with the processor support devices.

Execution time defines the number of clock cycles, expressed in nanoseconds, that it will take to execute the various instructions of the processor.

The last term was MIPS. It turns out to be a subjective time measure of the computer as a whole unit instead of the performance of discrete components. It is the general yardstick by which to compare the performance of various computers regardless of the type of processor used.

Frequently when MIPS tests are run, a set of standardized operations is used for the class of machine being tested. The problem with MIPS ratings is the difficulty in comparing machines of a different class or of different architectures. At best, MIPS ratings can only provide a rough benchmark of relative performance; but it is useful, nevertheless.

## Catching the Bus

Now lets look at the other components of processor performance, the "data bus" and the "address bus." These terms are not difficult to understand. They simply define the processor's information highway and the number of different routes data can take in its travels through the system.

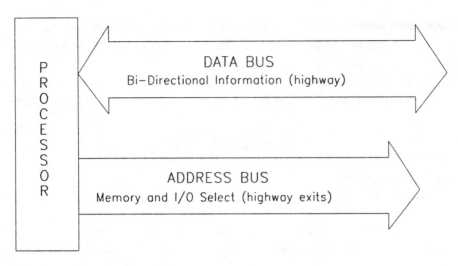

**Figure 2.4**   Data bus diagram

## *Data Bus*

For the processor to do anything, it must have memory to store and read information as well as a means to access other information sources. (See Figure 2.4.) Information passes between the processor and these other devices over the "data bus."

The data bus is defined in terms of discrete units called "bits," the smallest informational unit inside the computer. A bit can only have a value of one or zero.

Data bus widths vary from eight bits to 32 bits for personal computers. The original PCs had eight bit data paths. The original AT class of PCs represented the move to 16-bit data bus computers. Today's new PCs, including the MicroChannel and EISA class machines, have 32-bit data buses.

As you can see, each new generation of computer is increasing its ability to process data by doubling the width of the data bus. This improved capacity is in addition to other improvements in the processor itself. This is why yesterday's eight-bit PCs are pale in comparison to today's machines.

It is easy to see how the data path will affect a computer's performance. The wider the path, the more information that can pass at a time.

Another important factor is "transfer rate." This term describes how rapidly information can move back and forth on the data bus. You can have two computers with the same processor, clock speed, and data bus width, but the data transfer rates will be different. The difference is in the hardware design.

It is like comparing two highways with an equal number of lanes. One highway has potholes, curves, and dips. The other highway is smooth and flat. Obviously the smooth highway moves traffic faster.

### Address Bus

In fact, the analogy of an interstate highway to a computer's data bus is a good one. An interstate is a long, continuous highway with many exits, and so is the computer's data bus. The *address* bus identifies which exit to take. *Exits* from the data bus refer to a particular memory location or a specific input/output device. Just as a wider highway allows more traffic to flow, a wide (8, 16, or 20-bit) address bus allows more exits to be specified.

For example, an eight-bit address bus can specify 256 exits or memory locations; a 16-bit address bus can specify 65,536 locations; and a 20-bit address bus can specify a whopping 1,048,576 memory locations.

For PCs, the first 0–640 KB of memory is assigned to the main memory. The 640 KB is the abbreviated way of stating the actual memory range of 655,360 bytes or individual locations and this memory segment frequently is referred to as "conventional" memory. The video memory occupies the next 128 KB of memory locations. This is followed by the addresses of special ROM memories on the video and disk controller cards. Program code stored in these locations defines how they are to work. At the very end of the address range (F0000–FFFFF or 983,040–1,048,575) is the location of the ROM memories that enable the computer to begin operation on power up, the "boot ROM."

## Memory and Storage

A key component in the system is information storage and retrieval. As mentioned earlier, memory chips are the main short-term storage and retrieval area. The diagram of a basic memory chip is shown in Figure 2.5. The program and data that the processor uses is stored here. When the processor needs new information or needs to store something for future reference or long-term storage, it uses a disk drive.

Memory chips represent fast convenient ways to work with data and instructions. They allow the processor to perform its primary functions; however, when the power is shut off, the memory chips forget everything. These memory chips are said to be "volatile."

Some memory devices don't forget when power is off. These chips are said to be "nonvolatile." The main reason for using volatile memory is cost and speed:

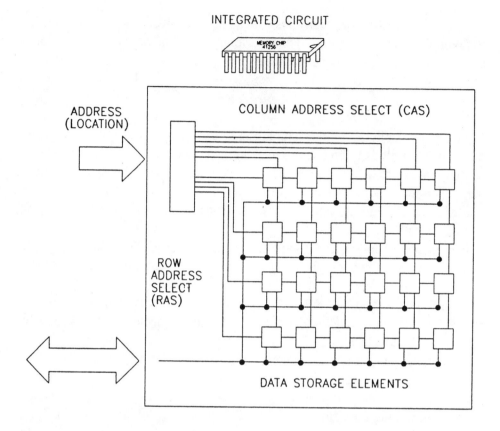

**Figure 2.5**  RAM memory chips

volatile memory chips are very cheap to use and are generally faster than nonvolatile devices.

Disk drives provide a convenient place to store information while executing programs or during times when the power is off. There are two types. The floppy disk drive records information onto a thin, flat, circular, flexible media that can be removed and stored separately from the computer. The hard disk drive uses rigid platters permanently mounted in a vacuum-sealed container.

Floppy disk drives come in various sizes and storage capacities (see Figure 2.6). The 5.25-inch and 3.5-inch diameter drives are the most common. The diameter refers to the diameter of the storage media. Storage capacity ranges from 360 KB (360,000) to 1.44 MB (1,440,000).

Floppy disks are a cheap and convenient way to archive and transport data. A 360-KB 5.25-inch disk sells for as little as $.21 and the 1.44 MB sells for as low as $.89 in lots of 25 disks. If you can use 100 disks of any type at a time, the discounts are even deeper.

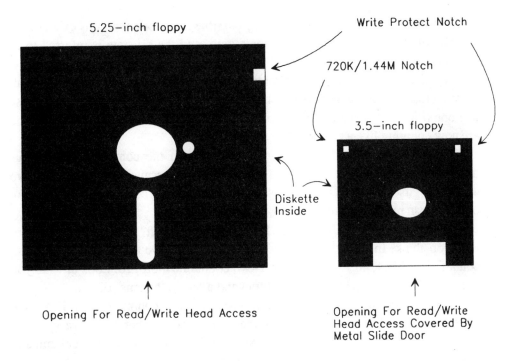

**Figure 2.6**   5.25-inch and 3.5-inch disk drives

Hard disks store tremendous amounts of information that can be accessed quickly. A small 20-megabyte hard disk can store the equivalent of fourteen 1.44-MB floppies or fifty-five 360-KB floppies. They also can access information in a fraction of the time it takes for a floppy disk to retrieve it.

Hard disks are the core component for computer information storage and retrieval. On large mainframe computers and some personal computers, the hard disks can be removed and inserted just as floppy disks can. However, personal computer hard disks usually are mounted permanently inside the computer case. (Though removable hard disk devices for PCs are available and becoming more common as prices fall.) The floppy disks are used to archive information stored on the hard disk in case something happens to the hard disk or the computer. The information from the floppy disks can then be transferred back onto the same or another hard disk, if needed.

## Computer Number System

Today's computers are called *digital* computers, and their principle of operation is based on the binary number system.

In the binary number system only two possible states or conditions exist: off or on. The off state is referred to as a logic zero, and the on state is referred to as logic one.

A good comparison would be holding your hand up in front of you with all fingers closed. This state or condition would be a logic 0 or no fingers. Now raise just one finger. This state or condition would be a logic 1. There you have it; you are now counting like a computer.

This discrete one-digit count is called a "bit" in the computer world. This number counting system is called a base 2 system, because there are only two discrete digits (0 and 1). Humans use a base 10 number counting system, where one digit can represent either 0,1,2,3,4,5,6,7,8, or 9.

If the computer can only count to 1, how can it do math? The answer is simpler than you think. In fact, the computer counts just like we do. Here's how. First, count to 9: 1,2,3,4,5,6,7,8, and 9. Ok. Now, count one more: 10. Look at what you did. You placed a zero in the ones column and a one in the tens column.

Now, see how the computer counts. The computer counts to one: 1. Now it adds one more: $1 + 1 = 10$. This number is not the number 10 as we know it; instead it is the number 1 0 in the computer world: a zero in the ones column and a one in the twos column. That's right, a twos column.

Since humans count in the base 10 number system, our number columns are a multiple of 10. We have ones, tens, and hundreds columns. When the number in a column will exceed 9, we place a zero in that column and carry a 1 to the next column.

The computer's number system is based on the base 2 number system; therefore, its columns are multiples of 2 (1,2,4,8,16, . . .). Thus, when the computer counts to 2 in our way of thinking, it goes like this: 1 then 1 0. First it counted to 1. Next it added one more. Since one is the largest digit it can have, it placed a zero in the ones column and a one in the twos column.

Similarly, binary 4 is expressed as 1 0 0; zero in the ones column, zero in the twos column, and one in the fours column. To add one more to this value, the number 5, simply place a one in the ones column: 1 0 1. One in the fours column plus one in the ones column equals 5: $4 + 1 = 5$. And so it goes. This simple scheme can express any number you desire.

However, in the computer programming world, a workable and equitable counting system had to be found that was acceptable to both humans and computers, and that was easier to integrate into the computer's architecture. The most common is the base 16 number system. This *hexadecimal* system seems strange at first, but the computer has no problems with it since it is a multiple of its base 2 number system.

**Table 2.1**   Counting Systems

| Base 10 Decimal | Base 16 Hexadecimal | Base 2 Binary |
| --- | --- | --- |
| 0 | 0 | 0000 |
| 1 | 1 | 0001 |
| 2 | 2 | 0010 |
| 3 | 3 | 0011 |
| 4 | 4 | 0100 |
| 5 | 5 | 0101 |
| 6 | 6 | 0110 |
| 7 | 7 | 0111 |
| 8 | 8 | 1000 |
| 9 | 9 | 1001 |
| 10 | A | 1010 |
| 11 | B | 1011 |
| 12 | C | 1100 |
| 13 | D | 1101 |
| 14 | E | 1110 |
| 15 | F | 1111 |

Hexadecimal columns are multiples of 16 with the numbers in the columns ranging from 0 to F. Table 2.1 contains the characters found in the ones column of a hexadecimal digit. Adjacent, on either side, are the decimal and binary equivalents.

Each base-16 number column (0–F) has to be represented by four base 2 number columns in the computer world (0000–1111). For example, the decimal number 15 can be represented three ways:

$$\textbf{15} \quad = \quad \textbf{F} \quad = \quad \textbf{1111}$$

**(decimal) 10**     **(hex) 16**     **(binary) 2**

In computer terms, the grouping of sets of binary digits have special meanings:

**Bit:**     A single digit (either 1 or 0)
**Nibble:**  Four bits
**Byte:**    Eight bits
**Word:**    Sixteen bits (or more bits, depending on the architecture of the computer)

As you can see, hex numbers represent nibbles from the computer's viewpoint.

It is only important that you understand that the computer counts in a number system different from base 10. You should recognize that you are looking at a base 16 or hexadecimal number when you see something like FFE0 or 12E3. Also, you need to remember that bytes and words are the computer's way of talking about eight- and 16-bit binary numbers.

Through the remainder of this book, number references will usually be in hexadecimals, bytes, and words.

If you want to know more about computers and the binary-based counting system, look for other books that teach computer basics. Now that you know what to look for in the table of contents, you should have no problem locating just what you need.

# Keyboard

This computer system component, the keyboard, is not hard to describe. This device is what enables you to communicate information to the computer. It is fairly straightforward: you type by pressing keys on the keyboard. The computer interprets each key depression by analyzing the unique code or value the keyboard sends to the computer when each key is pressed. What the computer does with this knowledge depends on what applications you are running.

# Video Display

The computer needs some way to talk to you, and the video display is it. With the display, the computer can present graphical information as well as words in a dynamic mode; everything appears to happen instantaneously in realtime.

Video displays are either "monochrome" (one color on a black or white background) or color (black plus more than one color). The monochrome monitor is the standard for high-resolution text-only displays. For text and graphical information, the color monitor is preferred since discrete items and detail can be easily identified with color. However, not all color displays are alike. More will be said on this later.

The video display represents the last item in the closed loop between human operator and computer. You can talk to the computer, and it can talk back.

# Printer

The main drawback of the video display is that you can only see a limited amount of information at one time, and it is available for viewing only from the computer.

The printer or "hard copy" device allows the computer to give you a permanent record of the requested information.

There are several types of printers. For general-purpose, inexpensive printing the "dot-matrix" type printer is used. For letter-quality printing an "impact" printer is used. If letter-quality and high-resolution graphics printing is required, then a "laser" or other page printer is used.

The dot-matrix and impact printers are usually rated in CPS (characters per second). This measurement refers to the rate the printer can print characters on one line. This measurement ranges from 30 CPS to 300 CPS or more.

This measurement does not accurately define how long it will take to print a specific number of pages. The amount of time it takes a printer to reposition its print head and to advance paper one line at a time varies from printer to printer; therefore, a better measure of performance would be LPM (lines per minute).

This rating is normally used for printers with print speeds in excess of 300 CPS. These printers are capable of printing up to 800 or more lines each minute. A page of print is normally defined as 66 lines.

The dot-matrix printer quality is determined by the number of dots it puts on the paper for each character printed. This number depends on several factors. Some printers can print nine dots at a time while the better ones can print up to 24 dots at once. Another way to improve dot quality is by double-printing a line, with the second printing done a few hundreds of an inch below the first printing. This fills in the spaces between dots, producing better-defined characters.

The laser printer is a modified version of a desktop copier. Instead of copying from a paper placed on top, the computer writes onto the copier's photo drum with a small laser, or uses an LED (light emitting diode) or an LCD (liquid crystal display) light source. The result is an extremely crisp and detailed printed page. Output from these printers is rated in PPM (pages per minute). Eight pages per minute is a fairly common print rate for mid-range units. Low-end devices operate between two and six pages per minute, and more expensive page printers print 10 pages per minute or more.

That is a fairly comprehensive though brief overview of what constitutes a computer system. Hold onto this list of fairly basic but important characteristics and terminology.

In the next chapter, we will discuss how the computer system actually works and provide additional detail on the individual pieces that make up the basic components. Make sure you understand the terms clock cycles, time interval, execution time, data bus, and transfer time. We will use these terms later in this book.

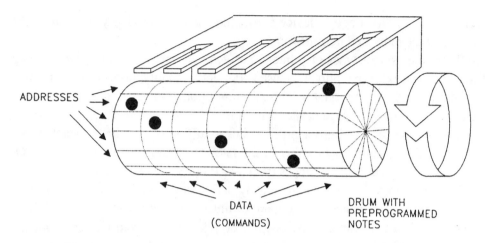

ADDRESSES

DATA
(COMMANDS)

DRUM WITH
PREPROGRAMMED
NOTES

**Figure 2.7**   **A computer program is similar to a mechanical music box**

# HOW DOES A COMPUTER PROGRAM WORK?

Let's take a look at programming or "software." A computer needs a program to make it work. A program provides a series of step-by-step instructions that tell the computer what to do and when to do it. A good analogy is a simple mechanical music box.

A music box contains a cylinder with many tiny bumps or stubbles extending from the surface. This is the program. The varying lengths of metal fingers that rest on the cylinder are the devices to be controlled. As the cylinder turns, the preprogrammed bumps cause one or more fingers to be plucked. The result is music.

The song will continue to play over and over as long as you turn the crank. This is because the beginning of the song follows the ending. In programming terms, this condition would be called a loop because when the program finishes, it jumps back to the beginning to start all over again.

In relation to the computer, the program stored in memory is like the bumps on the cylinder. Look at Figure 2.7. The processor behaves like the metal fingers that generate different vibrations. Instead of vibrating, the processor executes a different sequence of operations for each unique instruction or bump, as in the case of the music box. These instructions are comparable to the location of the bumps along the length of the cylinder, which caused a different and unique finger to be plucked. The rows of bumps going around the cylinder are the memory locations.

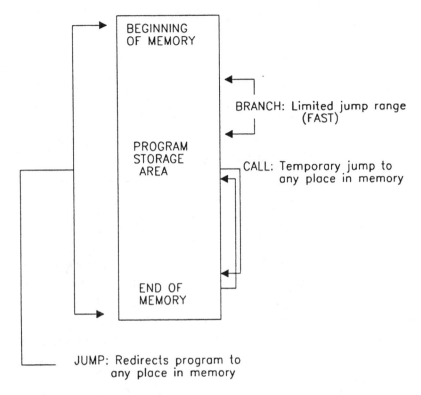

**Figure 2.8**   Special programming commands control the locations of program execution.

Although a program could be made to wrap around on itself, the program would have to occupy the entire memory space of the computer. When the end of memory was reached, the processor would go back to the beginning. This is not practical. Instead, there are programming statements like "jump," "branch," and "return" that cause the processor to move to a particular spot in the program and continue working. Figure 2.8 shows how special programming commands are used.

How does the program know where to jump? Either the last instruction or the instructions prior to the last one contain the memory location or address where the program continuation address is located.

There are three fundamental ways to vector to another spot in a program. You can do a simple jump when the end of a code section is reached. You can make a decision about something and do either a branch or jump to another location. And you can do a return, which is a special type of jump. (See Figure 2.9.)

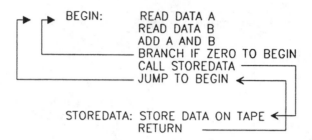

**Figure 2.9**   Direct jump program statement

A straight jump condition occurs when the end of a code section is reached. The last instruction simply says "Hey, move to this location and continue." This type of program statement is called a direct jump.

The second way is a conditional jump. This jump can be executed anywhere in the code section. As the instructions are being executed and data manipulated, the program may require that a decision be made based on the outcome of data manipulation. The manipulated data will be tested. The program will then check through a list of conditional test instructions to determine what to do. When the correct test instruction is found, the program will be directed to the appropriate point in the program.

An interesting point: a conditional jump can turn into a branch automatically under certain conditions. This happens when the specified jump-to location is close to the current location.

Why do we need two ways to do the same thing? The answer is speed. A branch takes about half as long as a straight jump. This is very important because a compiled program will have a fairly high percentage of conditional test statements. If the processor had to do a straight jump each time instead of a conditional branch, the computer program would run very slowly.

The last type of jump is called a return. A return is the end statement of a special section of code that can be used by many different parts of a program. Rather than compiling this section into each section of the program, the compiler puts it off all by itself. It then inserts a CALL SUBROUTINE statement where the code should appear in the main program.

When the program executes the CALL SUBROUTINE statement, the processor goes to the subroutine's memory location to execute the code. When this special section of code is finished, the return statement simply says "Go back to where you came from." The processor then continues executing the main program.

These computer instructions ultimately are produced in the computer's own language, a series of memory locations in an off or on state, the ones and zeros of binary code that we discussed earlier.

The person who wrote the program, however, used a high-level language such as BASIC, COBOL, C, Pascal, or one of the new object-oriented programming systems. This level of programming relieves the developer from much of the worry about the low-level operations of the program.

# THE PROGRAMMER'S JOB

Now let's take a top-level view of the entire situation. In one corner we have the computer system. In the other corner we have you the user. The question is how do we get the two of you to talk to each other. Well, this is the job of the programmer.

The programmer's job is to translate your objectives into a computer program that can be compiled and loaded into the computer so that it will perform the desired tasks. This is not an easy job.

One of the hardest things to do is to clearly detail each particular requirement. This is a long and sometimes painful process. For commercial software people, the success of this phase determines whether their product will make it on the market. Such things as being user friendly (easy to use) with clearly defined screen functions and help menus require a lot of programming by professionals and extensive testing by unskilled operators.

The next most important job of the programmer is deciding on which type of high-level language compiler to use to write the program. Each language has its own unique features that make it best for certain types of applications. Fortran is well-known as the choice of scientists and engineers because of its extensive math library. COBOL is used extensively by the business community, since it is well adapted to plain English descriptions of files and calculations.

But both of these are ancient by today's microcomputer standards and are being replaced by object systems and fourth generation languages that are more conceptual instead of procedural. In other words, with these new, very high-level systems the program can more easily translate the end user's concept into program statements because the programming system itself does more of the work.

Finally, picking a specific language is not totally an answer in itself. Different versions of the same language written by different companies have added enhancements or are custom designed for a particular type of computer. The programmer's job is to understand the characteristics of the computer and to use the appropriate language compiler.

As you can see, the programmer is a vital link between the user and the computer. And, the programmer's job does not end with just writing the code for the computer. The ins and outs of the program must be adequately defined, indexed, and cross referenced.

How can you tell a good program when you see it? The best way to judge the quality of a program is simply to sit down and use it. If you have difficulty in following the choices and options on the video screen (user unfriendly), it very likely will be difficult to use even after training. Furthermore, if sufficient thought wasn't given to the user's interaction with the computer (user friendliness) it is doubtful that the program will accomplish the tasks that you want it to.

Another important characteristic to look for is the documentation. Bigger is not better. Do not judge the quality of the software package by the size of the documentation. Scan through the Table of Contents and the Index. If you can't readily find familiar items, it is doubtful that the documentation will be of any value to you.

Finally, spend some time learning the design concept behind the software you use. Just as your understanding of the basic mechanics of an automobile can make you a better driver, and your understanding of computer hardware can help you design and operate your system, having an awareness of how computer software does what it does helps the programmer produce better code. It also will help you, the computer user, appreciate what is happening inside your system as you use it.

**CHAPTER THREE**

# SYSTEM OPERATION

In this chapter we will begin the next technical level of acquaintance and terminology. We will cover the basic functional units of the computer itself as well as the terms and buzz words required for technical discussion in the chapters to follow.

## WHAT IS IN A COMPUTER BOX OR CASE?

The computer box can be divided into several subsections, as shown in Figure 3.1.

1  The power supply supplies the necessary voltages for all the electrical components.
2  The clock and timing control section ensures that everything marches to the same beat and that each computer component will respond at exactly the right time.
3  The interrupt controller manages requests for processor action by devices such as the printer, disk drives, keyboard, and mouse pointer.
4  The processor and companion math co-processor manipulate data and perform decision instructions.
5  The memory components store the data and programs that are being used by the processor to perform its operation.

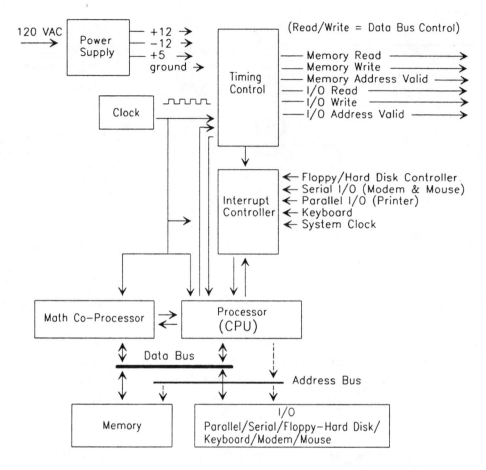

**Figure 3.1**   Computer components

**6**   Storage devices in the form of hard disk, floppy disk, or tape units provide long-term retention of important data and computer programs.

**7**   Finally, "I/O" (input/output) devices perform the various functions of communications with the outside world.

Let's examine what part each component plays in the overall operation of the computer.

## Power Supply

The power supply furnishes the proper electrical power for operation of other components. Its job is to convert the 120 volts AC (alternating current) into several DC (direct current) voltages. The voltages supplied are +5, +12, and –12 volts. The +5 volts is used by nearly every component in the computer box. The +12 volts is used by some of the ICs (integrated circuits) and by the motors on the disk drives. The –12 volts is required for the external interface components and the disk drives.

Another output from the power supply is a "signal good" line. The computer uses this signal to start itself when the power switch is first turned on. When the power switch is turned on, this control line will remain at zero volts until the power supply has sensed that the voltages are stable and correct. It then switches to +5 volts to signal the processor that it is ok to start.

The power supply in today's personal computer differs from those of the past. Previously, power supplies used a transformer to transform the 120 volts AC from the power line into the various computer voltages. Simple filters and regulators were then used to convert the voltage to DC. These supplies were simple both in design and operation. They also were big, weighed a ton, and generated a lot of heat.

Today's power supply uses a complicated charge/discharge switching action to generate the required voltages. The advantage of these supplies is that they are small, lightweight, and they generate little heat. However there are some disadvantages, including their complexity and a minimum load requirement.

Minimum load refers to the need for a minimum amount of power to be used by some device or devices for the switching power supply to work properly. Another problem with these power supplies is that they generate high-frequency noise on the power line that could interfere with other devices, such as TVs and radios.

The advantages of switching power supplies far outweigh their disadvantages, however. If we had to rely on old-fashioned transformer design, personal computers would be bigger and heavier and they would require larger (and noisier) cooling fans.

## Clock and Timing Controllers

One of the most important parts of the computer is the timing and control logic. It supplies the clock, timing, and reference control signals to ensure that everything will work correctly and at precisely the right moment.

To accomplish this task, the circuitry uses the system clock and reference control signals from the processor and some I/O devices as shown in Figure 3.2.

The master input to the timing controller is the clock signal that we discussed earlier. It supplies the heart-beating pulse by which everything is controlled. All

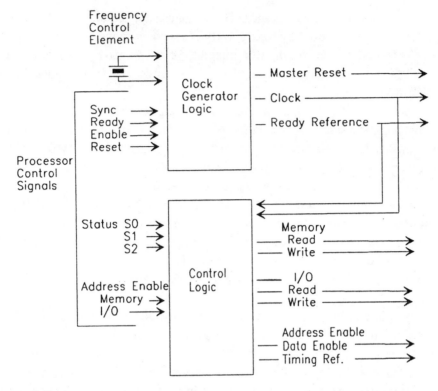

**Figure 3.2**  Clock and timing circuits

components are required to perform their functions either within a fraction of a clock cycle or within some multiple of clock cycles.

The reference control signals govern when the timing controller can generate specific signals. These reference control requests are synchronized by the controller with the clock pulses before being sent out.

For example, when the processor needs to read or write information, it must inform the controller whether it is requesting memory or I/O devices. It must also tell the controller if it wants to read or write information. At the correct moment, the controller will generate the correct signals to the processor and to the desired memory or I/O device so that information transfer can take place.

Not all reference control signals come from the processor. Another device called the "direct memory access controller" will take charge when so instructed. Its job is to move blocks of information very quickly between the main computer memory and an I/O device such as the hard disk. This "DMA" (direct memory access) method is the most efficient method to rapidly move blocks of data.

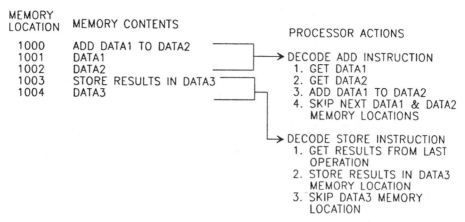

**Figure 3.3** Typical PC Central Processor Unit (CPU)

# Processor and Math Co-Processor

These devices, the processor and co-processor, are the heart of the computer box. As we have already mentioned, the processor (CPU) is the brain of the computer. The processor performs the math and logic operations required for manipulation of numbers and for making decisions.

How does it do this? The CPU execution process is outlined in Figure 3.3. The processor reads the program instructions stored in memory. As each instruction is read, it is decoded into a sequence of steps that the logic functions of the processor must perform.

Some functions require the processor to read or write data from either memory or I/O devices. Other functions direct the processor to compare data stored in either the processor itself, in memory, or within some I/O device. Based on the outcome of the comparison, the processor can go in several different directions in the program.

How does it access memory and I/O devices? The processor uses "address lines" to specify which memory location or I/O device location is required for a read and write operation, as shown in Figure 3.4. It then activates the read/write control line to direct the selected device to either send or receive a piece of data or a program instruction. This data transfer occurs on the "data bus."

For some processors, memory and I/O devices look like one and the same. The I/O devices are "memory mapped." Memory mapping means that the I/O devices are designed to appear to be the same as memory and that they reside in a particular memory address range.

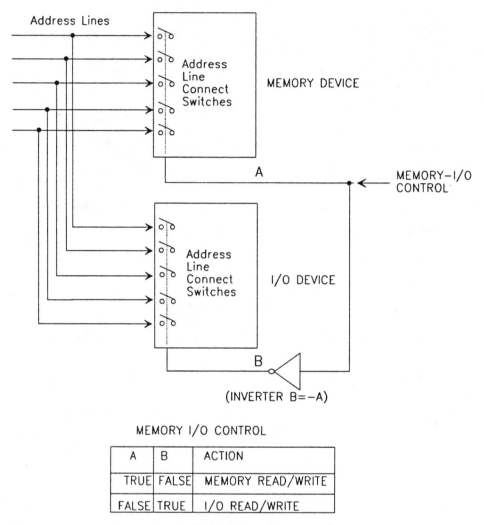

**Figure 3.4**   Address lines specify read/write locations.

For other types of processors, such as the Intel products used in most PCs, I/O devices are addressed separately from memory. The address lines are common to all devices; however, the Intel processor has a control line that identifies whether the address lines are for memory or for I/O.

Regardless of which addressing scheme is used, the data bus remains the same for either. The only variations to the data bus operation is that some I/O devices do not require the total data bus to transfer data. Some devices are 16 bits wide and others are only eight bits wide. If the device's data bus is only eight bits wide, only the lower eight bits (the least significant bits) of the data bus are used.

How does the processor know which is which? When these I/O devices are addressed, they generate a control signal back to the processor that identifies whether the processor is looking at an eight- or 16-bit device. This way the processor is prevented from reading erroneously the most significant eight bits of the 16-bit data bus.

For simple integer math operations such as addition, subtraction, multiplication, and division, the processor is relatively fast. Outside of these functions, it is slow since it must use small programs to generate the desired math functions. The "math co-processor" is a processor-compatible device that works like a pocket calculator.

The math co-processor is an integral part of the processor even though they are two separate devices. When any math function is to be performed, the software (program) instructs the processor to pass off the task of calculating to the math co-processor. The processor transfers the data to it and then requests the desired operation. Once the calculation is finished the processor will retrieve the answer.

How fast is the math co-processor? According to Intel specifications, most programs will run at least five times faster with a math co-processor. This reference is to those programs that are math intensive, including some spreadsheets, graphics and engineering programs, statistical packages, and others.

One last important function of the processor is "interrupt processing." This function is what enables a processor to efficiently operate in conjunction with I/O devices and to do "multitasking" operations. Interrupts cause the processor to stop what it is doing and service a request for a more important operation. Disk I/O is a high-priority operation, for example. An I/O interrupt causes most other operations to cease while it is conducted; however, such an interruption is very brief. You will not even be aware that it is happening.

If you are using a PC as a workstation in a network, you may notice that sometimes your keyboard seems to be sluggish to respond, or cursor movement on the video screen slows to a crawl. The reason behind these mysterious problems is probably due to a network service interrupt request—probably a disk I/O operation. During the disk I/O operation, most or all of your CPU power has been taken over.

## Interrupt Controller

Interrupt processing is a method of controlling and responding to I/O devices. These devices usually have a "response time" that is very slow in comparison to the processor.

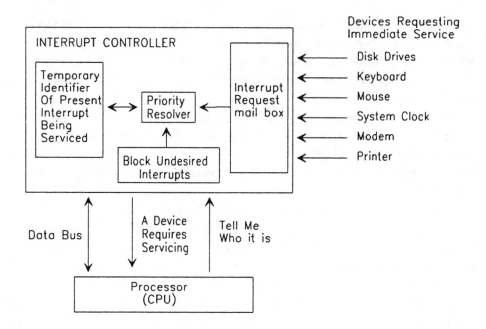

**Figure 3.5**   I/O interrupt processing

If the processor had to wait on these devices to receive or transmit data, the computer would operate at a snail's pace. Instead, the processor will raise a flag, so to speak, on the I/O device to allow it to tell the processor when it is available for use. The processor then goes about its business doing other things.

When the I/O device is ready or when it needs attention, it flags the processor through the interrupt controller. (See Figure 3.5.) Since there are many I/O devices, it is the job of the interrupt controller to sort out interrupt requests from the I/O devices so that the highest priority (most urgent) device is serviced first.

Once it is finished, the next highest priority device is serviced. This process continues until all devices are finished. This method allows everyone to work at maximum efficiency.

# Memory

Two types of memory are used in a computer. One type is called "RAM" for random access memory, and the other type is called "ROM" for read only memory.

RAM memory is used to store programs and data being used by the computer to run the different programs as requested. This memory is usually referred to as

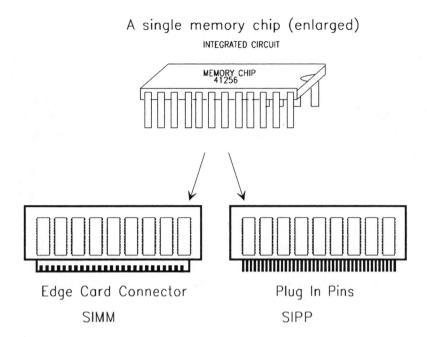

A single memory chip (enlarged)

INTEGRATED CIRCUIT

MEMORY CHIP
41256

Edge Card Connector

SIMM

Plug In Pins

SIPP

**Figure 3.6**   **Various DRAM types**

"main memory," and usually is the 640-KB conventional memory that forms the core of PC application RAM.

This type of memory is usually composed of "DRAM" (dynamic random access memory) memory chips. This type of memory requires constant attention or it will lose its memory contents. This is the reason it is called dynamic.

The memory locations have to be continually read and written to retain its contents. This "refresh" function is done by the memory controller in the timing and control section discussed earlier. The refresh rate occurs at approximately one millisecond intervals (1000 times a second).

Doesn't RAM refreshing interfere with the processor when it wants to talk to memory? No, because the timing and control section makes sure that it doesn't. The whole refresh operation appears totally transparent to the processor.

DRAMs come in different physical and data storage size. The most common type is "DIP" (dual inline pins). This type is the familiar little black bug with legs on each side.

Another type is called "SIMM" (single inline memory module). (See Figure 3.6.) This type has several memory chips mounted on a little circuit board that plugs into a small, elongated edge-connector socket. The last type is "SIPP" (single inline pin package). This type also has the memory chips mounted on a little circuit board, but it has a row of pins along the edge for plugging into a socket.

Another type of RAM memory is called "SRAM" (static random access memory). SRAM does not require refreshing. Once something is written into it, it remains there until changed or until power is removed. SRAM has faster access times than DRAMs; however, it is much more expensive. It also generates a lot of heat.

Both DRAM and SRAM have one big disadvantage. When power is lost, even momentarily, memory contents disappear. ROM type memory does not have this problem.

ROM memory devices have their memory contents permanently fixed. Once information is programmed into them, it stays forever. These devices usually have the slowest access time of the three types of memory devices discussed.

Why do you need ROMs? You can't change their memory contents and they are slow. What good are they? ROMs are used to store the small routines used to get a computer up and running.

When you first turn on a computer, how does it know what to do? After all, its memory is blank.

Here is what happens. After the power supply is supplying the correct voltages and the power-good signal is correct, the processor will, by default, go to a specific memory location and begin execution of whatever it finds. You guessed it. The ROM is located at this memory or address location. Since its contents are permanent, the processor has a program that it can start running immediately.

One of the first things the program does is a "POST" (Power On Self Test). It checks main memory for defects and checks to see what I/O devices are present. It then jumps to the initialization program.

The initialization program determines whether the floppy or hard disk drives have a program to load into main memory. If there is one, the ROM's initialization program will load it and direct the process to begin execution of it.

# Hard Disks

Hard disk drives are the main data storage media used in computers. There are two basic types, fixed and removable. There are advantages and disadvantages to each, but they operate essentially the same.

The fixed hard disk has its data storage media sealed inside the hard disk unit and the hard disk unit is mounted inside the computer box adjacent to the floppy disk units. This type of unit can store from 20 to 620 megabytes or more. It has a good reliability rating since everything is sealed and mounted inside the computer box.

The removable hard disk has its data storage media stored in hard plastic or metal cases that are inserted into the hard disk unit in a manner similar to inserting a floppy disk. The removable media packs usually store between 10 and 40 megabytes. The reliability rating of the units may not be as high as the fixed disk since the hard disk mechanism is sometimes damaged when the disk packs are inserted or removed at the wrong time. The removable hard disk units also cost more.

Why use a removable hard disk unit since it has such limited storage and poor reliability? There are two good reasons.

First, the periodic requirement for making a backup copy of the hard disk contents is reduced. You'll still need a regular, primary backup of all hard disk data, of course, but the need for second and third level backup is reduced somewhat with removable media. You can store your primary backup off site, enhancing the security of your backup data. What happens if all your business records are on the hard disk and someone steals your computer or the building burns? You can simply buy a replacement computer system, insert the hard disk pack and you are back in business.

Second, what happens if something goes wrong with your hard disk unit, and it won't work? Easy, buy a new unit and insert your hard disk pack. You are back up and running in no time.

If the removable is so great, why should the fixed hard disk even be considered? The first reason, as mentioned before, is reliability. The second reason is speed. Access times of removable hard disk drives may be slower than comparable fixed devices. If your applications require large data files you may be disappointed in the performance of some removable drives.

Backing up data from the hard disk onto floppy disks is perfectly OK if you will remember to do it frequently. The trouble is that most people forget to do it before something happens to the hard disk unit. Besides, there are more efficient ways to archive the data, including tape cassettes.

## *Hard Disk Basics*

A hard drive system consists of a number of necessary pieces, including

- Rigid disks coated with magnetic media
- Read/write heads, usually one per platter surface
- A motor and mechanical elements to move the heads

- An electronic interface between the heads and the computer interface
- A computer interface/controller
- One or more cables between the drive and computer

Technology in all of these component areas is changing rapidly. Just a few years ago, for example, a 5.25-inch platter stored 5 MB of data. A 10-MB drive required two platters. Today, drives are moving rapidly to 40 MB per 3.5-inch platter.

The next development is to increase storage density so that 80 MB will fit on a single platter. And, for some applications at least, the size of the platters will get smaller. Already we are seeing a few very light 2.5-inch drives with very low power requirements. These new drives weigh less than half a pound, draw only about 1.5 watts at idle, are just over half an inch tall, and store 20 MB or more.

Putting more data onto fewer platters also decreases disk drive size, letting you put more storage into a smaller space. And it points toward a new desktop storage standard. The majority of AT-class systems today are sold with 40 MB of storage. Soon the majority of AT-class computers will go to users with 80-MB drives. As you reduce the number of platters you also reduce the number of read/write heads required. Each platter generally uses two heads.

## *Hard Disk Mechanics*

The disk storage surfaces are sealed into an enclosure that includes a set of filters to keep dust from landing on them. The drive motors—usually one to spin the disk platters and one to position the read/write heads—are mounted outside of the drive enclosure to isolate the disk from their heat.

The disks themselves are rigid metal platters, eliminating the "floppy" instability of the original floppy drives.

Mechanical and electronic tolerances of hard disk drives are also tighter than those of floppy drives. A hard disk drive typically spins about 10 times as fast as a floppy disk drive, usually about 3600 rpm (40 to 60 times per second).

Both sides of each platter generally are used to store data, and there will be one read/write head for each side. Therefore if a drive has two platters, it will have four read/write heads and four data surfaces. In this case, the servo information that tells the drive where data is stored and how to access it will be written with the data. This scheme is called an embedded servo.

Drives with one less data surface use a dedicated servo. One entire platter is dedicated to storing the servo information, and a special read/write head is used to access it. You can tell if a drive uses a dedicated servo when the number of data surfaces is one less than the product of the number of platters and two.

Dedicated servo models may be faster than embedded designs, but under severe conditions the embedded servo can provide better data integrity. That's because head positioning information is stored on the same surface with the data. If environmental changes occur on the surface, all the required information—data and instructions—change together.

Two general kinds of head positioning techniques are used in today's drives, stepper motors and voice coil positioners. A stepper mechanism moves the read/write head in fixed increments across the disk surface. The voice coil mechanism uses servo track information to determine where to move the head in precise increments. Drives with voice coil positioners usually cost more than stepper motor models, and they can achieve faster seek times. A drive that provides better than 28 ms access time probably is using voice coil technology.

### *Read/Write Heads*

The main element of a standard read-write head is a magnet made from one or more turns of copper wire on a ring of ferrite. The ferrite core has a hairline gap on the side facing the disk.

When current is passed through the coil, the disk surface under the gap is magnetized and a bit is written to the disk. The direction of the magnetization, from North to South or South to North, depends on the polarity of the current. The disk controller causes the polarity to change between a 1 or a 0 bit.

Unlike most floppy disk drives, a hard disk drive's head does not touch the surface of the disk, but instead uses a set of tiny aerodynamic wings to fly a few tens of millionths of an inch above the media on a cushion of air generated by the spinning disk.

Drives typically have opposing read-write heads, one on each side of each disk platter, with the heads moving in and out together. Some very high-performance, high-capacity drives have several heads on a head assembly, with each head covering a smaller "zone."

### *Encoding Methods*

Data is stored on magnetic media by electrically changing the state of the magnetic material to store binary information (1s and 0s). In addition to data, hard drives also frequently store extra information for data checking to ensure accurate storage and retrieval. The amount of additional information, and the distance between pieces of data, are among the factors that determine how much information a given hard disk can hold.

Most ST-506 drives use MFM (Modified Frequency Modulation) data encoding. This is a relatively efficient and reliable technique, but it is rapidly being replaced by more efficient RLL encoding schemes.

RLL (Run Length Limited) encoding reduces the amount of data checking information that must be stored and uses fewer flux reversals (media changes) for a given amount of data. With RLL encoding you can put at least twice as much data on the same surface as with MFM encoding and, because the data is stored closer together, the transfer rate jumps from about 5 mbits per second on MFM to 7.5 mbits under RLL.

Most IDE (intelligent) drives use RLL encoding and many new bus-level controllers will support it, but if you add an RLL controller you should also add an RLL-compatible drive. The increased data density of RLL requires magnetic surfaces designed and certified for this type of service. You might be able to use an RLL controller with your conventional drive, but the chance of having problems is greatly increased.

This is analogous to the difference between high-density floppy diskettes and standard 360-KB diskettes. As you probably know, you can format a 360-KB diskette for 1.2 MB and you may even be able to get reliable data storage and retrieval from it. But there also is a good chance that the format program will find an unusually large number of bad sectors, and it is probable that somewhere along the line you won't be able to get some of the data back.

## *Drive Electronics*

How does the processor get and store information on the hard disk? First, the processor communicates to the special controller chip on the hard disk interface card. (See Figure 3.7.) It tells the controller to look at a particular spot on the hard disk that contains a kind of table of contents called "FAT" (file allocation table). It also tells the controller where to store the retrieved information in main memory. The processor will then say "Go get it."

The hard disk controller then issues the proper commands to the hard disk unit. First it positions the read/write heads over the correct spot on the hard disk platter. This is exactly like placing the pick-up arm of a turntable over the exact spot on a record album. The amount of time required to position the head is known as access time. It is similar to read/write access times for memory chips with the exception that it is measured in milliseconds (thousandths of a second).

The access time that is specified for a hard disk is usually the averaged time, since the time varies according to how far the head has to move to find the desired information.

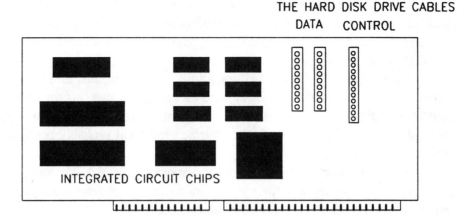

**Figure 3.7**   Hard disk interface card and controller chip

Published access times may or may not include other factors that affect how long it actually requires the drive to retrieve data from the disk. Generally, vendor specifications for access time are actually seek time, the time required to position the head over the correct spot on the disk.

In addition to seek time, a certain amount of "settling" time is required for the mechanical head assembly to become stable over the disk location and get ready to retrieve information. And latency, the time required for the desired piece of data to rotate under the head, must also be added to seek time to arrive at a realistic "time to data" figure.

With most current hard drives you can estimate 8.33-ms latency and figure settling time as negligible. Therefore a good average access time is the sum of the published seek time and the 8.33-ms latency.

To read information from the disk, the disk electronics sense the current caused by the passage of the magnetized sections of the disk as it spins beneath the gap. The electronics can also sense the changes in polarity that represent the difference between a 1 and a 0.

The signal pulses are amplified and converted from ill-defined analog signals to precise digital pulses. Next the drive electronics must separate the data pulses from the clock pulses. A clock signal is a string of precisely spaced pulses that serve as timing references for other signals. Clock signals form part of the overall drive control signals used for head positioning and other tasks.

The sector address is examined, and if it matches the address the computer is looking for, the processing continues. If not, the data is ignored.

If the sector is correct, the drive electronics—in many interface designs—then checks for errors in blocks of data by computing an error-checking value that is compared to the value that was recorded along with the original data. If an error is detected, the controller will try again.

Errors that are caused by temporary conditions—a piece of dust or a bump to the drive or a tiny fluctuation in power—are called "soft errors." If the error is caused by actual damage to the disk or the information on it, it is called a "hard error" and the controller will notify the system, which will probably notify the user with an error message.

Once all has been determined to be as expected, the data-bit stream is deserialized and converted into full bytes of information that can be transmitted on the computer's 8, 16, or 32-bit bus in a parallel fashion.

Part of this process calls for the controller to issue a DMA (direct memory access) request to the memory controller so that it can take control of the main memory. Then, at the speed of light, the controller zips the data from the hard disk platter directly into the main memory area specified by the processor. Finally, the controller releases the DMA request, and the processor resumes control of the memory.

The processor can now scan the retrieved information to locate where the desired information is stored on the hard disk. It will then instruct the hard disk controller to go to these locations and retrieve information just as it did for the table of contents (the FAT).

## Controllers and Interfaces

For the computer to use information from a hard drive and to write information back to the drive, there must be a way for the two entities to exchange information. This is done through a separate hard disk controller interface.

The interface plugs into the system's address and data bus and attaches through a cable to the electronics that are part of the hard disk unit. In this way, information inside the computer intended for the hard drive can be processed and passed to the disk; data from the disk intended for the computer can be read, processed, and passed to the CPU. (See Figure 3.8.)

A number of common controller technologies are in use today.

### IDE Controllers

The newest hard drive technology is the intelligent drive interface (IDE), sometimes called imbedded drive electronics or intelligent drive electronics. This

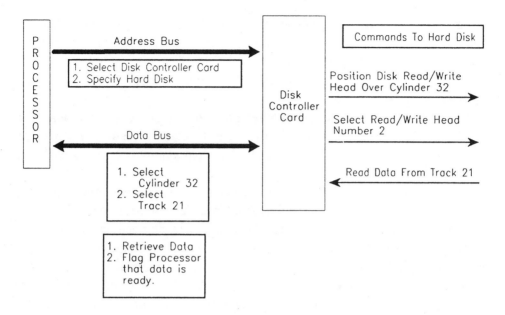

**Figure 3.8**  **Hard disk interface and disk drive block diagram**

term, coined by Western Digital, is not a standard and may mean slightly different things to different manufacturers. However, any drive that contains the control and conversion electronics that normally reside on a bus-level board, is an "intelligent" drive.

These drives have the controller electronics built into the drive instead of on a separate board that plugs into the computer bus. Obviously, to get all of the drive control electronics inside the drives, designers have to use the latest surface mount and VLSI technology. As the drives get smaller and capacity goes up, the technology involved in these devices gets even more interesting and complex.

IDE drives interface to the computer through a 40-pin connector rapidly becoming part of all new PC motherboards. Although pin assignments and some signals are different for different classes of computers, the concept of a motherboard-level interface for drives is a significant technological advance.

As long as you make sure the drive you are considering is designed for your class of machine, you don't have to worry about encoding techniques or controller compatibility. Because most of the operation of the drive is conducted onboard the drive itself, you can pick the features you want, shop for price and availability, and the unit should plug and play.

Presently, vendors are supplying two main IDE standards, AT-compatible drives and XT-compatible drives. That's why you'll find "AT" and "XT" designations scattered among vendor's interface offerings along with ESDI, SCSI, and ST-506. Strictly speaking "IDE" could refer to ESDI or SCSI drives because both of these interfaces put much of the controller electronics onboard the drive. But they usually require a bus-level controller board, and they do not use the new 40-pin motherboard connector.

Therefore, "IDE" has evolved as a separate drive interface that can adhere to the AT-compatible 40-pin connector or to the XT-compatible 40-pin connector. These two connectors look the same, but some pin assignments and signals are different.

IBM has its own 44-pin IDE interface unique to their low- and mid-range PS/2 products, with another proprietary 72-pin interface for high-end machines. Other vendors in the industry have not adopted the IBM PS/2 interface standard.

IDE drives offer several advantages over conventional controller technology. Nearly every IDE drive uses RLL encoding, for one thing, which results in more dense storage and faster data transfer. Besides, when a single manufacturer designs a drive-electronics package to work together, performance and reliability can be improved.

In addition, intelligent drives allow broader selection of features because you don't have to worry about some of the controller specifics. And if your motherboard includes one of the 40-pin connectors, you can free up an expansion slot that normally would be taken up with a hard disk controller card.

Even if your computer doesn't have one of the new IDE, 40-pin interfaces, you can purchase a short "paddle" board that plugs into your AT or XT expansion slot. The 40-pin drive cable plugs into this paddle board.

## ST-506/412 Controllers

The most common hard drive interface to this point has been the original ST-506, now coupled with a later standard, the ST-412. Today when a vendor offers an ST-506 drive, it usually incorporates the additional features of the later ST-412 standard.

You will find ST-506 controllers on smaller, lower-performance drives for existing computer hardware. The newest computers include built-in interfaces that provide better performance.

## ESDI Controllers

The Enhanced Small Device Interface (ESDI) is an enhanced ST-506 interface that provides improved performance, higher capacity and, usually, higher cost.

ESDI moves the encode-decode functions off of the bus-level controller and onto a board that is an integral part of the drive itself; but it is not a full, IDE design.

ESDI was developed by a group of drive manufacturers to achieve higher drive performance. Unfortunately, there can be various implementations of ESDI, which produces potential incompatibilities among interfaces and hard drives. When you buy an ESDI drive you probably should purchase the vendor's matching interface card, or select a package put together by a reputable reseller. This will ensure full compatibility and maximum performance.

## SCSI Controllers

The SCSI (Small Computer System Interface, usually pronounced "skuzzy") is a relatively high-speed, parallel I/O bus popular in workstations and other high-end machines, but it only recently has begun moving down to the PC level. There are many advantages to using SCSI hard drives in your system, and a few disadvantages.

The most obvious disadvantage is that SCSI is not the interface you find in packaged AT-class systems. These dual controllers usually contain a floppy disk and a hard disk interface on a single board. If you already have a machine with a combined controller installed and if you add a SCSI drive, you will have to replace the controller as well.

There aren't as many SCSI controllers to choose from as with other interfaces, nor do all manufacturers of PC-class drives have SCSI models.

In a one- or two-machine installation, these considerations aren't too important. However, if yours is a shop with dozens of existing PCs, you have built-in spare parts and trouble shooting help. If you install a new machine with a SCSI interface, you lose that backup support for the new machine and it doesn't fit into the loop to become a help to you in supporting existing machines.

Although SCSI is a high-speed I/O bus that can provide excellent disk performance, it requires a separate bus-level interface card. If your PC motherboard already contains one of the new 40-pin IDE intelligent drive interfaces, you'll be paying extra for the convenience of SCSI; but if performance and flexibility are high on your list of needs, SCSI is probably worth the price.

SCSI lets you do some things you can't do with conventional interfaces. It supports multiple devices, including disk drives, tapes, CD ROMs, network interfaces, printers, plotters, or almost any I/O device.

A single SCSI interface usually can support up to seven devices in a daisy chain configuration. In addition, SCSI offloads some of the I/O tasks usually performed by the CPU. This can result in better I/O performance and reduced load on the central processor.

Two SCSI designations currently are seen: SCSI and the newer SCSI-2, which includes ANSI extensions that increase bandwidth to a 16- or 32-bit wide bus and raise data transfer rates to as high as 40 Mbps. Standards work on SCSI-3 already is underway. The enhanced performance, increasing acceptance, and broad base of existing installations portend a strong future for this intelligent interface in the micro world.

## Storage Capacity

Ordinary hard disk drive read/write heads and magnetic media now permit as many as 1700 data recording tracks per inch on the disk platter surface. Standard floppy disk drives squeeze just 48 or 96 tracks per inch for 40-track (Double-Density) and 80-track (High- or Quad-Density) drives. Going in the lateral direction, disk drive manufacturers have won tremendous increases in the number of bits that can be packed into each inch of the circular track. Most disk drives are in the range of 10,000 to 30,000 bits per inch, compared to typical floppy disk drive bpi ratings of 5000 to 6000.

Be aware that drive capacities may not be stated precisely. A "40-MB" drive, for example, may actually store 43.5 MB or 44 MB. That's because the drive is really a 50-MB drive or larger, but after the storage surfaces are formatted—after control information for a given computer system is written to the platters—the available storage is reduced. In addition, the formatting process probably will identify some sectors of the drive that cannot store data reliably, further reducing available storage.

Although most manufacturers quote formatted capacities when they advertise a given drive, there still are occasional products that are promoted with unformatted capacities. A "110-MB" drive, for example, may really by a 90-MB drive after it is formatted for your system.

You should only be concerned with formatted capacity as you plan your computer storage needs. Although it may seem that a drive with a formatted capacity very close to the unformatted capacity is preferable, this ratio is generally irrelevant. After all, it is the actual storage you have at your disposal after formatting that is important to your application. And it is this figure that helps you determine the relative cost of drives from different sources.

## Floppy Disk Drives

Floppy disk drives are probably the most common means of transferring programs and storing data. They are cheap, available everywhere, and most importantly, they will work in any brand of computer that runs the same type of DOS (disk operating system). This commonality of exchange has only existed since about 1982.

Before the advent of the IBM Personal Computer, every brand of computer used its own proprietary DOS. It was virtually impossible to take a floppy from one brand of computer and use it in another brand. The reason the IBM Personal Computer made it so big is because other brand name computers were designed so that they could use the same operating system. For the first time, different brand machines could exchange programs and information easily.

Up until several years ago, the standard floppy disk media was a 360-K, 5.25-inch disk. Then came 1.2-M, 5.25-inch disks followed by 720-K, 3.5-inch disks. The 3.5-inch diskettes were primarily for laptop computers because of the small size requirements; however, the small size and convenience of the 3.5-inch disks made them very popular, even for desktop machines. In addition, 1.44-M 3.5-inch floppies are used regularly. For general computer use, the 3.5-inch floppy is rapidly becoming the standard.

Technically the floppy drive works almost identically to the hard disk. The basic difference is that the floppy disk controller has to turn on the drive motor and get the floppy media spinning at the correct speed before it can read or write data from it. The controller then positions the read/write head over the media, just as the hard disk controller does on the hard disk unit.

The read/write process and head-positioning operations for floppy drives typically are much slower than for a hard disk. One reason is the slower rotational speed of the media itself. A floppy diskette may turn 10 times slower than a hard disk. When you consider that the information is read from the spinning disk surface as it passes under the head, you can see why slower rotational speed means slower data transfer.

Remember that the information stored on your floppy and hard disk media is volatile. It can be erased or damaged through any number of careless actions. Smoking, liquids, and magnets are dangerous to the health of all magnetic media and to all other computer parts.

# I/O Devices

Any device that enables the processor to communicate to the outside world is an I/O (input/output) device. The disk drives are I/O devices, but they are not usually called by that name. Basically, when people speak of I/O devices, they are referring to video monitors, keyboards, printers, modems, mouse pointers, and other types of human interface devices, or they refer to output to a plotter or printer.

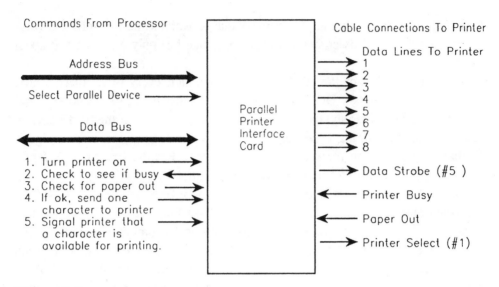

**Figure 3.9**   **Parallel interface**

## *I/O Devices: Parallel*

A parallel interface is a high-speed communications method normally used to talk with external devices such as printers. A parallel interface consists of eight data lines (eight bits) and various control lines. The control lines enable the processor and external device to inform each other as to their status (busy, not-busy, paper ready, etc.). They also allow the eight data lines to be bi-directional. The processor and the external device can exchange information by controlling the direction of data flow over the data lines, as shown in Figure 3.9. The signals on all these lines will be either zero volts or 5 volts in representation of a logic 0 or logic 1.

For most PCs, the parallel printer interface is frequently called a "Centronics interface." This is a standard established many years ago by the Centronics printer company. It defines what pins will perform specific functions. The standard connector is a 36-pin device called a Centronics connector; but the PC has by default changed it to a DB25-pin female connector, as viewed from the back of a PC. These connectors are shown in Figure 3.10.

How does the processor talk to the parallel interface card? Unlike the hard disk and floppy disk controllers, the parallel interface card has no controller. The processor has to select the desired parallel I/O card via the I/O address lines. Now it can either enable or disable the various control lines depending on whether it is

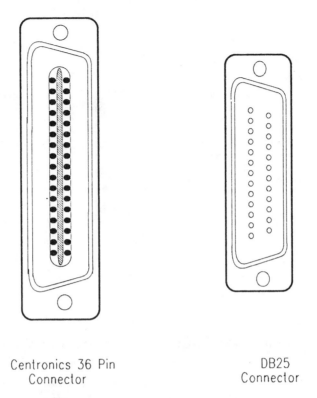

Centronics 36 Pin
Connector

DB25
Connector

**Figure 3.10**   **36-pin Centronics connector DB25 connector**

sending or receiving data. The processor has to repeat this process for each byte of data information transferred.

One problem with parallel interfaces is that cables connecting the I/O interface card with the external device should be no longer than 15 feet because of technical problems such as interference and signal degradation.

## *I/O Devices: Serial*

A serial interface is very similar to a parallel interface with the exception that data is exchanged one bit at a time instead of one byte at a time.

Why bother with a serial interface since it is eight times more restrictive in transferring data? Probably the most important reasons are that it can tolerate long cable runs and it requires fewer wires for interconnection. It is also one of the oldest and most common ways of connecting different types of devices to a computer. Some of the first applications were video terminals and modems.

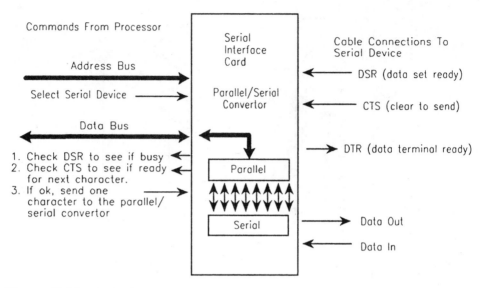

**Figure 3.11**   **Serial interface diagram**

The most common serial interface for PCs is the RS-232C interface. Just as with the Centronics parallel interface, it has been around for a long time. It has control lines just as the parallel interface; however, it has a separate read and write data line. They are not shared as in the parallel interface. Figure 3.11 is a diagram of a serial interface.

The voltages on the data and control lines will normally be between −12 and −3 for a logic 0 and +3 to +12 for a logic 1. This large voltage swing with the plus and minus polarities is the reason that large cable distances can be tolerated. The susceptibility to interference is greatly reduced.

The serial interface is very similar to the parallel interface with the exception that the processor will write a byte of data into the parallel/serial converter device on the serial interface card. It will then instruct the converter to send it. While the converter sends the data out one bit at a time, the processor goes off to do other things. When finished, the converter will signal the processor via the interrupt controller that it is ready for more.

If the processor is receiving data through the serial interface, the process is reversed. The converter receives the data one bit at a time until it has all eight bits. It then notifies the processor via the interrupt controller that it has a byte of data. The processor then reads the data from the serial I/O card.

So which is better, parallel or serial? There is no clear winner. Each has its benefits and drawbacks. The parallel is fast, but a lot of other devices use the serial interface. It is not a matter of which is best. Rather it is choice of the right tool for the right job.

## *I/O Devices: Keyboard*

The keyboard is a special serial interface device. Since it is a vital part of the computer, there is a special connector and hardware interface built on the "motherboard" (main computer board) just to talk to it.

The keyboard is a self-contained communications device. It has a built in microprocessor that scans the keys and sends the correct key requests to the processor when a key is depressed. Since it is important to the processor, a dedicated interrupt controller line is used just for the keyboard. When a key is depressed, the interrupt line is activated. After acknowledgment by the processor, the keyboard microprocessor will send the key code or codes.

## *I/O Devices: Video*

The last I/O device is the video adapter. The display adapter plugs into the computer bus just as the parallel or serial interface adapters and disk controllers do. This card provides output from the computer system to a compatible video display.

There are many different video graphics display modes.

MDA: Monochrome Display Adapter (text only)
HCG: Hercules Graphics Adapter (text and graphics)
CGA: Color Graphics Adapter (color text and graphics)
EGA: Enhanced Graphics Adapter (color text and graphics)
VGA: Virtual Graphics Adapter (color text and graphics)

The MDA and CGA modes are disappearing fast from computer programs. The trouble with MDA is that it won't support graphics, but its text display is great. CGA does graphics and color, but its range of colors and resolution of text display are poor.

The HCG mode has good text display resolution and a high-resolution graphics capability. It has become the alternative choice to the more expensive EGA and VGA graphics modes. The limitation of HCG is that it is a monocolor mode of operation.

The EGA mode is the popular high-resolution color text and graphics display modes; however, VGA is rapidly replacing it. VGA yields higher resolutions and more colors than EGA does. The reason it is replacing EGA graphics adapters is the small difference in cost between the two.

This was not the case when VGA came out a few years ago. The cost differential was hundreds of dollars. Today some vendors offer VGA display adapters at lower prices than comparable EGA adapters. When upgrading to a color graphics display it may make little sense to select EGA unless you already have an EGA-compatible monitor.

The operation of the video graphics card is a little complicated to explain. First, it uses a dedicated area of memory right on the graphics card itself to hold the electronic image being displayed on the video monitor. A video graphics controller is constantly scanning the memory and the video screen in unison. As it scans along, it transfers the digital information in the memory to color dot signals for display on the monitor. The scanning rate depends on what video mode you are in (EGA, VGA, or another mode).

In addition, the processor has direct access to the video memory just as it does the main memory. In fact, the video memory is memory mapped at a location just above (higher address value) the main 640-KB memory. When the processor wishes to change the video display, it simply alters the correct video memory location with the correct data for either color, text, or graphics display.

Doesn't the video controller and the computer's processor interfere with each other when they happen to access the same video memory location? Yes, in the past that was a problem. Today's video graphics controller is able to work with the processor's requests so that this conflict does not arise.

# SYSTEM CLASSIFICATION

When the microcomputer revolution started back in the 1970s, life was simple. There was the Intel 8008 and the 8080 microprocessors, the Motorola 6800 microprocessor, and other lesser known microprocessor types. Although they differed in how they operated, they had one thing in common. They all used an eight-bit data bus and a 16-bit address bus. Thus, memory and I/O devices standardized to eight-bit data transfers and the 16-bit address bus established the familiar 64-KB base memory addressing scheme. Back then, these parameters seemed tremendous. A program that required 20-KB or more of memory was considered a monster.

Boy have times changed! With the continual procession of next generation microprocessor, we now have the Intel 8086, 8088, 80186, 80188, 80286, 80386, and 80486 followed by Motorola's 68000, 68010, 68020, and 68030, and each representing increasing data and address bus sizes for larger and faster data processing. When will it end! Let's hope it doesn't, because it means better and cheaper products for us all.

So how do you sort out all these processor types into something you can understand? Well, first of all we will only be looking at the Intel series, since they are the basis of the IBM Compatible Personal Computer market as it is known. The Motorola processors find wide acceptance in the industrial and military markets, and the Apple Macintosh Series of computers is also based on the Motorola processor. We are primarily interested in being able to buy pieces and parts of a computer system and assembling them into a working system. Thus, we narrow our focus to the IBM Compatible Personal Computer market.

# XT Systems (8-Bit)

## *Background*

Some of you who may be knowledgeable about the present computer market may ask why even bother discussing eight-bit computers since everything today is 16-bit and 32-bit. It is true that the eight-bit systems are like dinosaurs who just don't want to go away, but millions of these systems are still out there just humming along totally indifferent to what is going on.

Why not! Most of them are used to do just one or two specific jobs like word processing, simple data filing, and small spreadsheet applications. They are cheap, and they continue to get cheaper every day. They are ideal for students on low budgets. Therefore, they may be slow and out of date, but they are not going away anytime soon.

## *The Birth of PCs*

The original IBM Personal Computer was built with the Intel 8088 microprocessor and 64 KB of user memory for programs. It could potentially address up to 1,048,576 bytes of memory with a data bus size of eight bits. Designers usually refer to this in a shorthand of 1 MB. It had the BASIC language available from ROM on the motherboard.

The entire computer was built onto one main board with five expansion sockets for accessories such as video display cards, floppy disk controllers, serial interfaces, and other items. This revolutionary "motherboard" was unlike any other because up until then, a motherboard was simply a circuit board with connectors into which everything plugged, including the microprocessor boards.

Although the original PCs came ready for use with a cassette tape recorder as the primary means of data storage and retrieval, provisions were made in the case for the addition of floppy disk drives for those who could afford it. The cassette tape method disappeared very quickly and the standard system soon came equipped with one 360-KB floppy disk drive.

For a video display there was only one choice, monochrome text only. The video graphics or adapter card (it's called by either name) was able to display quality text in an 80-column by 25-line format. It was something for its day. The card also included a parallel printer port.

This basic system of 64-KB memory, one floppy disk drive, and a monochrome monitor sold for about $3000. A simple Epson MX80 (80-cps) compatible printer with the IBM logo would run you another $700. Today, the same basic unit as purchased from the local retail store or magazine would cost only about $400, but it would come with 512 KB of RAM and a monochrome Hercules text/graphics display.

The system would also probably use a clock speed of 10 MHz instead of the IBM's original 4.77 MHz clock speed, and if you are lucky, it would have NEC's V20 microprocessor instead of the Intel 8088. This chip offers approximately 15 percent improvement in operation with little or no incompatibility problems when using software written for the 8088.

## *Now to the Present*

The eight-bit personal computer systems of today are referred to as XTs because when IBM added a 10-MB hard disk to the original PC they called it the XT (Extended Technology) model. The name has stuck ever since.

You will also see references to a "Norton SI" rating of 1.7 or 2.1 next to these new "Turbo" XT listings. The SI (system information) program is part of a suite of utility software from Norton Computing. It is a popular measure of the computer's ability to execute a set of standard processor instructions such as math and data movement. The SI rating shows a computer's performance relative to a standard such as the PC/XT or PC/AT. The "turbo" designation comes from the computer's faster clock speed, 8 or 10 MHz instead of the original 4.77 MHz. The reference is 1.0 for a 4.77 MHz 8088-class machine.

For the 16-bit class of machines, the Norton rating will be 20 to 30. This means they can do the same job 20 to 30 times faster. Another comparable rating is the "Landmark AT Speed" test. A number of these system-testing utilities are available from a variety of suppliers.

The XT motherboard can contain all 640 KB of the main memory right on the motherboard without having to add additional memory boards, as in the past. Most motherboards will accommodate a variety of memory chip types such as 64K by 1 bit, 256K by 1 bit, and 256K by 4 bits. You would need eighteen 64Ks and eighteen 256Ks to make 640K of memory. If you haven't noticed, we specified eighteen 64K and eighteen 256K by 1-bit memory chips; if we were to

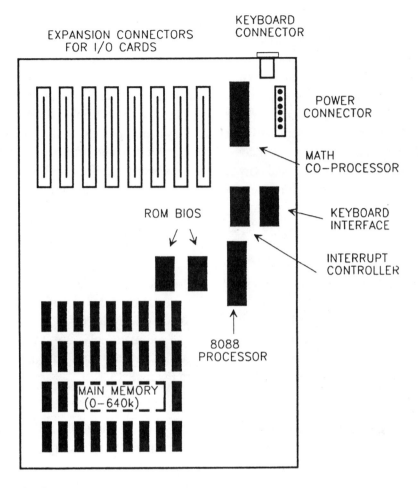

**Figure 3.12** An XT motherboard layout

use chips with larger capacity, the number of chips would be different. A basic XT motherboard layout is shown in Figure 3.12.

Why multiples of nine? Isn't this supposed to be eight-bit memory? Yes it is, but beginning with the IBM PC, "parity checking" was added so that bad memory could be automatically detected.

The parity bit (ninth bit) is set to either a logic 1 or 0, so that the total of the nine bits is always an even number of 1s. If the memory controller retrieves a byte of memory and detects that the total of the nine bits is odd, it will flag the processor that a bad memory location was detected. The operator will then be notified so that the computer can be serviced.

The XTs of today also have eight expansion sockets for plugging in cards instead of the five on the original PC. Normally you will have a video graphics card, a floppy/hard disk controller card, and a multifunction card. This is a minimum configuration of cards.

The multifunction card contains several I/O functions as well as a system clock. The parallel port is for your printer. The serial port is for either your modem or a mouse. A second serial port is usually available on the board with the addition of a few parts and an additional serial cable connector. It will only cost about $10 more to order it with both serial ports. A system time clock is also on the multifunction board, so that you don't have to enter date and time every time you turn the system on. You should now see why this board is called multifunctional.

You have only used up three card slots. You now have five left for adding other gadgets that you may find useful in the future, such as an internally mounted modem or a scanner for use with a paint and draw program.

**CAUTION!** There are restrictions on the size of the cards that you can plug in. When the floppies and hard disk are mounted inside the computer box, they will block two or three of the card slots, so that you can only use the short accessory cards in these slots. Restrictions on expansion card length are shown in Figure 3.13.

One memory chip that is important to know about is the ROM "BIOS." This special memory chip is a read-only device that contains the necessary program for the computer to properly test itself when power is turned on. After testing it searches for a program to load from the floppy or hard disk. This memory chip also contains the special I/O program routines for accessing the floppy and hard disk, parallel/serial ports, keyboard, and clock. Compatibility of BIOS ROMs (ability to run common programs without problems) used to be a problem, but that is essentially nonexistent today.

One last thing to note for XT-class computers is the math co-processor. By all means consider installing a math co-processor. If your applications tend heavily toward spreadsheets and other "number crunching," the math co-processor will speed things up considerably. You can get along without a co-processor, of course, but your system will run noticeably slower.

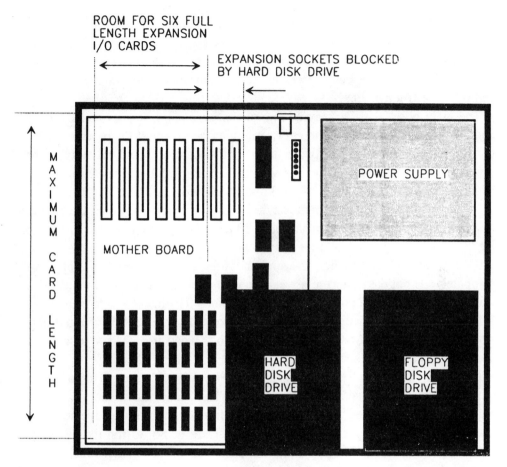

**Figure 3.13** **Expansion card length restrictions**

# AT Systems (16-Bit) and Beyond (32-Bit)

The 16-bit personal computer systems of today are referred to as ATs (Advance Technology). By using the 80286 instead of the 8088 design the ability to use a 16-bit data bus was now possible. Furthermore, the 80286 could address 16 MB of memory instead of only 1 MB for the 8088.

The new 16-bit data bus was a big improvement over the old XT's eight-bit bus. Besides being twice as wide, its data transfer rates were several times higher. There are usually two to three eight-bit-only card sockets on the motherboard just to accommodate eight-bit I/O devices. However, eight-bit devices can be plugged into a 16-bit slot.

How can an eight-bit device work in a 16-bit system? There are two ways. First, the device may be one of those standards in which the software only looks at the lower eight bits of the data bus. Second, the processor has a bus size signal line so that the device being accessed can tell the processor whether it is an eight-bit or a 16-bit device.

The eight-bit I/O device may be one of those standard devices that only use eight bits, such as a parallel printer or serial interface. Even if the processor tried to read or write 16 bits, the software and the interface card would only look at the lower eight-bits. The upper 16 bits would be discarded by the software. This condition would also hold true for the 32-bit 80386 processor.

The other method depends on the device's ability to control the bus size control line. This control line enables a card plugged into one of the expansion sockets to identify itself as either an eight-bit or a 16-bit data device.

Accessing the new memory beyond the first 1 MB on this new class of computer was not easy, since essentially no software could take advantage of it and still run on the then popular XT class machines. The intent was to provide up to 16 MB of program work space; instead it soon became 15 MB of rapid data storage area. This 15 MB of additional memory when used as program work space is known as "extended memory."

Confused? Well, first the 80286 is capable of linearly addressing 0 to 16 MB of memory in what is called a "protected mode." This mode allows for an advance set of instructions for software that can use it; however, the base of the software market was for 8088 machines, which couldn't use it. So, to run the available software, the 80286 would operate in the unprotected or 8088 mode, which meant it could only see, or address, the first 1 MB — just as the XT.

So, was it a wasted design? No. A method called "expanded memory" accessing was developed. This method allowed the additional 15 MB to be accessed through a 64-KB memory window in the first 1 MB of memory space. All a program had to do was select which 64-KB block of the 15 MB memory area it wanted. The restriction to this method is that these 64-KB memory portals are for storing data or temporarily holding programs; the programs could not run or operate while stored there. The great part of this outcome was that XTs could use this method also.

Today, there are programs that will allow full use of the extended memory above the 1-MB barrier of the 8088. Programs such as Microsoft's Windows and Quarterdeck's Desqview allow standard software to work in this memory area. In fact, they allow multiple programs to run at the same time.

An AT-compatible computer of today has an Intel 80286 operating at 12 MHz, 16 MHz, or 20 MHz. One word of caution here. Try to determine that your processor is operating at its rated speed. This is important because some manufacturers of AT 80286 computers will increase the clock speed beyond the rated access time requirements of the 80286 and its components. Although this means more performance, it is risky, since you are forcing the components to operate at the upper limit of their capability. As the components age, the computer will experience strange and nonrepairable problems.

One of the improvements in the motherboard designs is that they will now hold between 1 MB and 8 MB right on the motherboard by using different types of memory chips and/or memory modules such as SIMMs or SIPPs. This means that you can populate the memory according to your pocketbook size. If you have the cash, fill it up to 8 MB.

There are also several other variations in AT motherboard designs. The number of accessory expansion sockets will vary from three to seven with one to three of them being eight-bit sockets. The BIOS will be either the Phoenix, AMI, or another third party version of IBM'S BIOS, since it is not legal to use IBM's BIOS without paying IBM a royalty. The system clock is built into the motherboard, unlike the XT. The AT also doesn't use switches that you have to manually set in order to define the amount of memory, type of video display, and how many disk drives you are using. A basic AT motherboard layout is shown in Figure 3.14.

The real plus of today's AT-compatibles is their motherboards. They are mini-size AT motherboards. This means that you can throw away your old XT motherboard and install one of these mini-size AT motherboards, plug your old XT cards back in, and you are in business. You may need to replace the keyboard if it is not AT compatible. The upgraded system won't perform as efficiently using the eight-bit XT cards, but it will work a lot faster than what you had before.

The top of the line AT-compatible machines use an 80286 running at 20 MHz with Chips and Technology's NEAT (New Enhanced Advanced Technology) chip set. This chip set replaces a double handful of components used in the old AT designs. They also enhanced the operation of the board.

By using a technique called "interleaving" the motherboard can use lower-speed memory chips without requiring wait states. This translates into reduced memory costs. The memory controller section of the chip set splits the memory area into even and odd areas so that information is accessed on an alternate basis for the majority of memory reads and writes. You can save approximately $20 to $50 per megabyte of memory by using slower memory.

The NEAT chip set also supports "shadow ram" (memory area between 640 KB and 1 MB). This allows the slow ROM memory contents to be copied

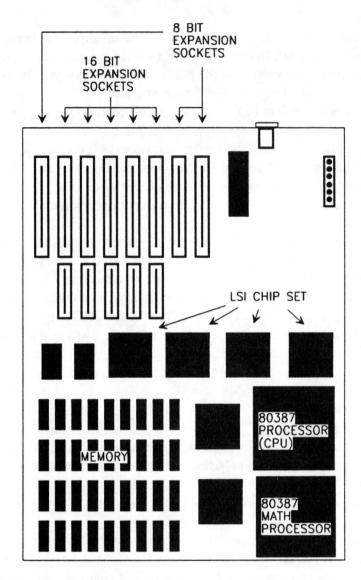

**Figure 3.14**  A basic AT motherboard layout

into faster RAM, so that BIOS operations will run much faster. The ROM contents of the video graphics card can also be copied into shadow ram for faster operation.

This shadow RAM area can also be used for programs. Traditionally, the memory area between 640 KB and 1 MB was reserved for special ROM and I/O functions such as disk controllers, video cards, network cards, BIOS, and other things. The usage of this memory area was unpredictable, since it depended on what you decided to install. The NEAT chip set's shadow ram lets you reclaim the unused areas for use as expanded memory and/or program work space.

And best of all, these mini-AT class machines are not expensive. This 20 MHz, 80286, 8-MB memory, NEAT chip set motherboard sells for as little as $400. The 12 MHz, 80286, 4-MB memory, non-NEAT chip set motherboard sells for as little as $200. These prices reduce the appeal of an 8088-based motherboard.

The next generation of computers has even more to offer. Not only are they totally compatible with present and past software, they also can use the same accessory cards.

The next generation of microcomputers is based on the Intel 80386, 80386SX, and 80486 CPU chips. These processors have a 32-bit data bus with the capability to use eight-bit and 16-bit bus devices. They can address 4000 megabytes of physical memory.

To meet the requirements of these high-power processors, a new system bus is needed. There presently are two contenders. The first contender is IBM's MCA standard (MicroChannel Architecture). It was introduced in April of 1987. The other contender is the EISA standard (Extended Industry Standard Architecture). This standard was decided on by a consortium of the leading PC-compatible manufacturers.

Why two standards? IBM's MCA system bus is a proprietary standard that requires a license from IBM before a manufacturer can use it. To counter this closed system concept, Hewlett-Packard, NEC, Olivetti, Tandy, Wyse, Zenith, AST, Compaq, and Epson derived the open EISA bus standard, which all may use freely without paying royalties. Neither is a clear winner at this point, and other bus standards may yet emerge.

The 80386 series has what is called a "memory management" unit that can shuffle what used to be fixed-location memory blocks to any memory address it desires without requiring any changes to the program. This technique provides the ideal solution to the present 640-KB program area limitation of PCs, since the memory management unit can handle over 6000 640-KB program work areas. This feature is what makes the 80386 so important, because it essentially provides an infinite programming area.

Besides all these enhancements, these new machines are an order of magnitude more efficient. They can "pipeline" several instructions at a time. This means while one instruction is being finished, several more instructions are either waiting or being partially executed to reduce the time required to fully execute these instructions when their time comes.

In addition, these new machines sport even faster clock speeds; 25 MHz and 33 MHz is common now with 50- to 100-MHz machines projected for the future.

This kind of desktop power used to be available only on super minicomputers. These new machines can do some serious computing.

With these high-end microcomputers the MIPS performance rating takes on new meaning, since they are being compared against minicomputers and high-speed workstations. A MIPS is a fairly good method for judging these machines because of the different computer designs, architecture, and processor types. Other performance tests are available, but MIPS is by far the most popular in machines of this class.

With the encroachment of these high-powered microcomputers, the price of high-speed computing is dropping like a rock. Workstations and minicomputers that used to cost $50,000 to $100,000 just a few years ago are now selling in the $10,000 to $50,000 ranges just to stay competitive with an equal $5,000 to $10,000 super microcomputer based on the 80386 and 80486. The next generation of 80586 and 80686 processors will make the desktop competition even more interesting.

So far we have discussed everything but the 80386SX. To coax people to the 80386, Intel developed the 80386SX, a 80386 housed in an 80286's 16-bit world. Now why would you want to restrict it to work as a 16-bit data bus with a 16-MB address limit? The answer is cost. With only minor changes to a 80286 motherboard design, the 80386SX can replace the 80286. From a speed or performance standpoint, you gain little with this change. The real advantage is that you can tap the software power of the 386's world in a 286's hardware environment. Although 80386SXs are presently being targeted at 286 upgrades, the expected future market is for laptop computers.

The 80386SX motherboard costs about half that of a regular 80386 and about twice that of an equivalent 80286. A 16-MHz 80286 will cost about $250, a 16-MHz 80386SX will cost about $450, and a 20-MHz 80386 will run about $700. Although the price differences may seem small (several hundred dollars), the cost of the higher performance memory, math co-processor, and other components will quickly add to the cost differential. Thus, don't be mislead by the initial cost of the motherboard.

In conclusion, the real plus of these next generation computers is that the memory management capability along with the ability to address memory beyond 16 MB brings a virtually unlimited capability to personal and business computing as we know it today. These new functions bring true multitasking and high-performance computing to the individual user, small business, large business, and scientific community. If you want to be ready for tomorrow at a minimum investment, the 80386SX will get you there at only a small sacrifice in performance.

## CHAPTER FOUR

# COMPUTER SOFTWARE

A computer system is more than just the hardware. It is the data that you store and manipulate with it, and the instructions that enable the computer to do its work. These instructions are called "software" and they are grouped together into "programs" for performing specific tasks.

The general levels of computer program include

- System software
- Applications software
- Utility software

The final category, utility software, is considered applications software by some experts and users, and a good argument can be made for this position. We prefer to take the larger view that utility software actually sits somewhere between the system level and the applications level. It is neither fish nor fowl. By the same token, it may be difficult to agree on which programs are utilities and which are full-fledged applications, but we'll try.

## SYSTEM SOFTWARE

System level software forms the basis of any computer operation. It is this set of instructions that tells the computer hardware how to wake up and begin operation.

System software also controls system interaction with applications and utility programs and with such peripheral equipment as communications controllers, printers, and disk drives.

Two basic types of system software drive a PC: ROM-based code that conducts the bootstrap (wakeup) operation to get the computer up and running after it has been turned off, and the disk-based operating system that is loaded as part of the booting process. The operating system gives the system its personality, determines which applications you can run, and conducts most of the low-level functions including keyboard interaction, video display output, sending data to the printer, saving and loading data from storage, and serving as the general interface between the computer hardware and your applications programs.

In the PC-compatible world, the most common operating system is MS-DOS (IBM's version of this software is called PC-DOS), or simply DOS. Although you can run versions of UNIX and other systems on the high-end versions of the PC, relatively few people do so and DOS is what is meant when we talk about the PC operating system.

DOS has undergone a number of revisions since its introduction on floppy-only machines with ROM-based BASIC. As of mid-1990 you could find active machines using versions from 2.0 through 4.01, but the most common versions for new computers was version 3.3 and version 4.01. The 4.x series is the newest version of DOS, but more installed systems probably still are driven by a 3.x version. The major features of these versions of DOS are shown in Table 4.1.

You can use either version with the PC you build from scratch. The cost is very close, and each system has distinct advantages and disadvantages. In the following section we provide a comparative overview of these two versions of DOS.

# DOS 3.3 AND 4.01

DOS 4.x was available for more than two years before it became the default version for most vendors. When you buy a new computer today, chances are you will be supplied with a 4.x version of DOS, if you buy DOS with the machine. As you build your own machine you must decide for yourself which version of DOS to purchase.

DOS 3.3 also is still available from most vendors, but you'll probably have to ask for it. From the standpoint of vendors and users, the trend toward standardizing on a single version of DOS is desirable. With an estimated 45 million MS-DOS users, the fewer versions of a software package out there to be supported, the better for all concerned.

Whether you should be using DOS 4.x or DOS 3.3 depends a little on your particular computing situation. DOS 3.3 is a solid, proven operating system with a long history and follows a traditional, command-driven design.

DOS 4.x, on the other hand, is a rewritten version of the original system. It includes many desirable enhancements, including a "shell" that lets you run programs and perform DOS-level functions from an icon-driven menu instead of with typed commands.

However, because the majority of applications available today were written for DOS 3.x, unless you upgrade your applications software you may notice some difficulties with the newer versions of DOS. If you don't already have a large collection of software that you use regularly, however, there seems to be no reason to avoid using a 4.x version of DOS, particularly if it comes with your new equipment.

By the same token, there certainly is no overriding motivation for you to switch if you already are well established with version 3.3.

Let's look at these two operating systems in detail.

## DOS 3.3

By the time Microsoft introduced DOS 3.3 in April 1987, the concept of large hard-disk drives on PCs was well established; but under DOS 3.2 you could create only a single 32-MB partition on each drive. If your drive were larger than that, some of the space was wasted.

DOS 3.3 solved a part of that problem by introducing support for multiple hard disk partitions of up to 32 MB each. This let users partition a single 100 MB drive, for example, into three 30-MB drives and one 10-MB drive. Information in each partition was accessed as if it resided on a different physical drive. In this example, the single large hard-disk drive would be broken into four logical drives, C:, D:, E:, and F:.

IBM's new machines were using high-capacity 1.44-MB, 3.5-inch floppies, and DOS 3.3 was designed to support them. Laptop vendors and other computer suppliers quickly followed IBM's lead and the high-density microfloppy became quite common as primary storage on laptops and for at least one drive position in desktop machines.

DOS 3.3 also added useful new commands and enhanced some others. The APPEND command in DOS 3.3, for example, is extremely useful. Since early hard-disk versions of DOS, the operating system could seek out executable files in subdirectories other than the currently selected one. APPEND lets DOS find any file, whether or not it is executable, as long as the subdirectory where the file resides is included in a PATH command.

Two other features also were added in version 3.3: the FASTOPEN command and the CALL command.

FASTOPEN works a little like a disk cache routine, except that it builds a disk location table to track recently accessed files in RAM, reducing disk access as files are opened. And the CALL command, used in batch file programs, lets one batch file use the routines from another batch file and return to the original file to continue with other commands. Prior to CALL, when you branched to another batch routine you could not return to the original file.

In addition, the BACKUP/RESTORE routines were enhanced in 3.3 to pack data more densely on the backup diskette, and BACKUP was changed so it could automatically format a diskette during the backup process.

A minor but useful addition to the ATTRIB command also was introduced in version 3.3. The "/S" switch, used with wildcard file specifications, lets you modify or read the attributes of files in all of the subdirectories below the current or specified directory. This is just one more example of the constantly improving DOS recognition of the need for hard disk management.

## DOS 3.3 Strengths and Limitations

Except for obvious bugs, the strengths and weaknesses of a given software product are highly subjective. However, among DOS 3.3's greatest strengths is its longevity. It has been installed on millions of machines, and thousands of software products have been written to support it.

While it is true that some people have reported arcane problems with DOS 3.3, for most users of commercial applications this should be considered a stable product with a high degree of applications compatibility. Microsoft has committed publicly to continue marketing version 3.3 as long as the demand exists.

On the other hand, if you are a new user of PC-class machines, someone with little or no operating system experience, then version 3.3 with its arcane prompt and command structure may be hard to learn and even a little intimidating.

Moreover, as the price-capacity ratio of PC-based hard disks gets better, you may be frustrated by the 32-MB limitation on hard disk volumes under version 3.3. If you maintain very large databases, such as sales and inventory information or remote sensing data, you may need files larger than 32 MB. DOS 3.3 won't let you do it—DOS 4.01 will.

On the other hand, if your applications don't require very large data files, you may find, like many users, that breaking up a large hard disk into multiple 32-MB logical volumes actually is desirable. Such partitioning helps you organize data into logical drives, and, especially if you already are using backup tape equipment, the divisions can make backup easier.

Another overlooked advantage to partitioning a hard disk into small sections is that access time can be improved. Programs and data files are almost never stored together as one continuous spot on the hard disk. A data file for example may be stored as hundreds of file chunks (sectors) scattered all over the disk. By using the entire disk as one volume, the read/write heads would be required to move across the entire surface of the disk to search a data file. By segmenting into smaller volumes, areas for data and program storage will be confined so that the heads will not have to move as far.

# DOS 4.x

Computer users eagerly awaited the release of DOS 4.0, hoping for faster operation, expanded memory support, hard disk volumes larger than 32 MB, and a user-friendly shell. The original release was quickly replaced with version 4.01 to correct a number of bugs and inefficiencies discovered in the field.

DOS 4.01 delivers most of the features users wanted, but with varying degrees of success and utility. Let's look at some of the features and problems of this version of DOS.

## *Menu Installation*

The installation process should be extremely simple, but it may not work out that way. Generally DOS 4.01 is sold only through computer manufacturers (also known as OEMs) who buy it to market with their particular brand of computers. MicroSoft does not sell the product directly.

Although MicroSoft does license "packaged" DOS to OEMs who don't modify it, basically DOS is not meant to be sold by itself. The DOS 4.01 box we received directly from Microsoft during preparation of this book is prominently marked "Not for retail sale except with a computer system."

This means that there are essentially as many different versions of MS-DOS 4.x as there are OEMs selling it, which is 28 as this is written. To ensure total compatibility with all the drivers and utilities supplied with your version of DOS, you should make sure you are using the version of the program that was customized for your computer system. While it is highly unlikely that any OEMs modify the DOS kernel itself, they may supply a number of custom utilities and drivers to enhance operation with their particular hardware.

You can tell what system your version of DOS is designed for by reading the label carefully. In addition to the Microsoft company information, you will find a copyright notice from the company that modified it. This is where you should go for support when you have questions about your version of DOS.

CompuAdd Corporation, the Austin, Texas, PC clone manufacturer, for example, loads a small TSR (terminate and stay resident) program with DOS on PC/XT systems to correct a problem with segment boundaries. Interestingly enough, this change is not required if you use FDISK yourself to configure an XT disk; but if you let SELECT, the DOS 4.x installation program, do it for you, problems can crop up.

In theory you need only put the Install diskette in the A: drive of your computer and reboot the system. DOS is supposed to load, and an included AUTOEXEC.BAT file starts the SELECT installation program.

It didn't work that way for us, primarily because the SELECT program is among the more inflexible pieces of recent software we have seen. Our version of DOS 4.01 was supplied on 3.5-inch diskettes. Except for a V20-based laptop machine, none of the eight other machines in our office have the 3.5-inch drive configured as the A: drive. SELECT won't run from anything but the A: drive, even if you use the DOS ASSIGN utility to change the logical assignments.

Even when we had solved this problem, SELECT kept saying we had the wrong diskette in the A: drive. Microsoft technical support people sent us a replacement set of diskettes to correct this installation problem, but the difficulties persisted. We finally corrected the problem by copying the SELECT.COM file from an OEM version of DOS 4.01 to our install diskette. Neither version of DOS supplied by Microsoft included the SELECT.COM file.

Several computer system vendors and users we contacted as part of our research for this book said they had not experienced similar problems; they felt DOS 4.01 worked fine. We contacted an equal number of individual and large company users, however, who said they had tried DOS 4.01 on some machines and had removed it in favor of the established 3.3.

## *DOS Shell*

The concept of a menu or shell to isolate users from the DOS prompt and its command interface has been popular for some time. Third party products such as The Norton Utilities (Norton Computing) and XTREE (Executive Systems, Inc.) give users hard disk management and program execution help with any version of DOS.

With release 4.0, Microsoft made a graphical shell program part of the operating system shipment. Notice that the shell is not actually part of the operating system. Rather it is a separate set of applications that is executed like any other application from the DOS prompt or from inside a batch file.

The SHELL program offers three basic functions: directory display and maintenance, applications grouping and execution, and DOS utilities access. This utility won't give you the functionality of Microsoft Windows or other GUI, but it is a useful program, nevertheless.

For example, once you have it set up you can point to a database or spreadsheet data file with the mouse, and SHELL knows which applications software to load to give you access to it.

You can customize the SHELL menus, installing about any program you like and by having AUTOEXEC.BAT load the SHELL automatically you have created a menu-driven environment for inexperienced computer users.

However, the version of SHELL we evaluated is a slow program. We tested it on a Swan 396/20D, a 20-MHz 80386-based machine, and a 16-MHz Smart Micro 286 Pro, and still were frustrated with the extremely slow response to mouse clicks and menu selections.

Compared to available third-party products, SHELL from DOS 4.01 lacks functionality. It doesn't include additional utilities, for example, and it is not a developmental or programming environment. If this is your goal, Microsoft Windows, Quarterdeck's DeskView, or even WordPerfect's Library would be better choices.

### Expanded Memory Support

Support for LIM EMS (Lotus/Intel/Microsoft Expanded Memory Standard) is part of DOS 4.01, but mostly with add-in drivers installed through CONFIG.SYS. The supplied EMM386.SYS, for example, can be used to configure expanded memory on 80386-based systems. Unfortunately there is no printed documentation on this driver—even in the appendix titled "Installable Device Drivers." A disk-based READ.ME file does offer additional information on these utilities.

### Disk Partitions Larger Than 32 MB

Larger disk partition support is, in our opinion, the really useful addition to DOS with version 4.x. Prior to this release you could create partitions no larger than 32 MB. Now, the hard disk partition size is essentially unlimited.

If you prefer several smaller logical partitions, as was required under previous versions of DOS, you also can do this with 4.01 simply by creating a primary partition that is smaller than the full disk size, and then creating extended DOS partitions to configure the rest of the available disk space. However, be aware that the current version of DOS 4.01 will access only up to 1,024 cylinders. Depending on individual hard-disk design, you may not be able to use DOS 4.01 alone to configure a single large volume. Before you purchase a large disk drive, determine how many cylinders it uses.

## New and Enhanced Commands

Most of the utility in this version of DOS comes from enhancements to existing utilities. However, there are a few new commands.

A new utility program, MEM.EXE, displays the amount of used and free memory, including allocated and free areas and which programs are currently loaded. This can be helpful during system configuration, but it doesn't actually allocate expanded memory for you.

New features in Debug, a system-level utility supplied with DOS, do let you allocate and deallocate expanded memory; but this program is not for the casual DOS dabbler, and it is not something that can be used to permanently change your system's memory configuration.

There are many subtle differences between DOS 3.3 and DOS 4.x. You'll be pleasantly surprised, for example, to see DOS 4.x provide more information on errors. Suppose you have an incorrect entry in your CONFIG.SYS file. In DOS 3.3 you will see a message:

```
Unrecognized Command in Config.Sys
```

In DOS 4.01, however, the message is

```
Unrecognized Command in Config.Sys
Error in Config.Sys Line 12
```

In this case you have misspelled a command or entered an incorrect command on line 12 of Config.Sys, and DOS 4.01 tells you which line the error is on.

For some time now we have used the BASIC command REM at the head of CONFIG.SYS commands we don't want DOS to implement, but which we want to keep in the file for future use. DOS 3.3 ignores the commands all right, but it feels compelled to tell you about every one of them with the "Unrecognized

Command in Config.Sys" line. DOS 4.01, on the other hand, simply prints the line to the screen without acting on it and without returning an error. Much cleaner!

In fact, with DOS 4.01's enhanced batch file handling, you can precede the REM statement with a commercial AT sign (@) and the echo of that line to the screen will be suppressed.

When you ask DOS to delete all the files in a subdirectory, Version 3.3 asks "Are you sure (Y/N)?" With DOS 4.01, however, the additional message, "All files in Directory will be Deleted. Are You Sure (Y/N)?" Such additional feedback helps you interpret the messages DOS sends and could keep you from making a mistake on the DOS command line.

In addition, later DOS-level error messages are more enlightening. Suppose you enter

```
TYPE READ.ME
```

and DOS can't find the file. In DOS 3.3 you would receive the error message "File not found." In DOS 4.01 the message reads "File Not Found - READ.ME."

Many of the external DOS commands have some changes under Version 4.01. When you FORMAT a disk, for example, this new DOS tells you what percent of the operation is completed instead of displaying the head and cylinder information as in Version 3.3.

The REPLACE command, added in Version 3.3, has a new switch. Now you can tell REPLACE to update only the files in the target directory that are older than those in the source directory. This is an excellent tool for helping you maintain backup copies of certain files or anytime you want to make sure you have the latest version of a file in a given subdirectory.

The BUFFERS, FASTOPEN, and other commands have been enhanced to include additional startup options and switches. With BUFFERS, for example, you can now specify the maximum number of sectors that can be read or written in one I/O operation. The default is 1; you can specify up to 8.

FASTOPEN now includes options to set the number of files to track on each disk, and you can specify that the records it tracks be stored in expanded memory.

Other commands, such as DEL (Erase), have similar enhancements. The new /P switch with DEL, for example, tells DOS to prompt you before deleting the specified files. This is particularly useful when you use a wildcard to delete a range of files. You may want to verify each deletion to avoid removing the wrong files.

## *Strengths and Limitations*

For some users the SHELL will be a valuable addition to DOS, opening up access to the operating system and making applications execution easier. For it to be really useful, however, the SHELL must be customized with the applications and utilities you need to access. In addition, if you run applications from batch files, many of these may have to be modified; otherwise, when an application terminates you are returned to DOS instead of to the SHELL.

Support for large disk partitions will be welcomed by most users, and the enhanced error reporting and user feedback features are desirable.

Although difficult to quantify, DOS 4.x may provide better performance for some applications.

On the down side, this version of DOS is the largest yet, requiring up to 87 KB or so of RAM. Even so, under some configurations—say those with a very large number of buffers—you may actually save memory because these buffers can be placed in expanded memory.

Another potential problem: DOS has been changed enough so that some of the applications you are running now under older versions of DOS won't work properly with the new DOS unless they are modified. Most large software vendors are aware of what is required to make their products compatible with DOS 4.x, and these changes have been made. However, you will have to install the later versions of these packages if conflicts arise.

For example, we use The Software Link's LAN Link serial network as part of our office configuration. When we installed DOS 4.01 we noticed some intermittent problems. It was a simple matter to contact the company for an updated version of the LAN Link, but unless you require the enhanced features of the new DOS it may not be worth the effort to make such a change.

The professional consensus seems to be that the latest version of DOS is a "mature" and "stable" product that should be treated as a natural replacement for DOS 3.3, at least on new systems. Whether users who are successful with DOS 3.3 should upgrade to 4.01 is strictly a personal matter.

Hardware vendors such as CompuAdd Corp. in Austin, Texas, routinely supply the newest DOS to their customers. Version 3.3 is sold only if a customer specifically asks for it. This seems to be the approach of most major hardware vendors.

Again, if you are building your first PC and just now starting to install your own applications base, DOS 4.x is the logical choice. It is the most recent version of the PC operating system, it has more features, and is more flexible with newer hardware configurations. Just make sure as you purchase applications and utilities that they are compatible with the new DOS.

If the PC you are building is to replace an existing machine or to add to your equipment pool and will be running established applications, you might do well to specify DOS 3.3 as the first operating system of choice, at least until you have been able to upgrade all of your applications.

DOS 4.x did not enjoy a groundswell of support, but most industry observers agree that posture likely will change. Vendors are reporting very few end user problems with the product, and Microsoft says it is workable and stable.

The enhancements and new features add significantly to ease of use, error avoidance, and ease of disk management, especially for inexperienced users. (Anybody remember the old days when microcomputer operating systems returned errors such as ER 202? We've come a long way, baby.) Besides, the prospect of establishing a single standard for PC operating systems should promote the acceptance of DOS 4.01 at a relatively rapid pace from here on out.

# INSTALLING DOS: HINTS AND KINKS

If you have trouble with your version of the SELECT install program, or you find yourself with the wrong media, you can still get your system up and running with the following simple procedure. Note that this procedure produces a bootable floppy diskette, leaving the current operating system on your hard drive. This is a safe way to discover any incompatibilities between the new DOS and your applications.

- Boot the system using your present version of DOS.
- Format a diskette in the A: drive.
- Insert the DOS Install diskette in the B: drive.
- Make B: the default drive (Type B:<ENTER>).
- Enter the following commands:

```
SYS A: <ENTER>
COPY COMMAND.COM A:<ENTER>
```

Now you have a bootable DOS diskette. Boot the system with this diskette, enter the correct DATE and TIME when DOS asks for them, or press Enter if they already are correct.

Next, copy the CONFIG.SYS and AUTOEXEC.BAT files you have been using on your hard disk onto the DOS diskette. If you haven't included the full path to any utility or driver files you load with these files, use a text editor to modify the command lines to include paths.

Finally, copy the DOS utilities you need from the Install and Operational diskettes. Among the programs you probably will need are:

- FORMAT
- XCOPY
- DISKCOPY
- SYS
- FASTOPEN
- RAMDRIVE
- APPEND

Here's another hint that may be helpful in running DOS 4.01 from a floppy diskette. Use RAMDRIVE in your CONFIG.SYS file to create a small RAM disk.

When large applications run they pretty much take over your system, using even the space where COMMAND.COM would normally reside. When you exit the application, unless you booted the system from the diskette containing the application programs, DOS prompts you to insert the disk that contains the COMMAND.COM program.

If this extra step irritates you, set up a small RAM disk as the C: drive (or one drive higher than your last local drive) and copy COMMAND.COM over to it. That way, when applications terminate, DOS can load COMMAND.COM from the RAM disk without bothering you for another diskette.

To do this, add the following line to your CONFIG.SYS file. (Use any text editor or word processor in ASCII mode to modify your CONFIG.SYS file.) Use the command line:

```
Device ramdrive.sys /x
```

where x can be either the letter "e" or the letter "a." Use "e" if you want to use extended memory for the RAM disk, or "a" to use LIM EMS expanded memory.

This tells DOS to take over 64 KB of your available RAM and reserve it as a RAM disk. DOS automatically assigns the next available disk drive to the RAM disk. If you have a dual floppy system, for example, the RAM drive will be drive C:. If you are using only a single floppy, then the RAM drive would be drive B:. On a single hard disk system, the RAM drive is drive D:, and so on.

**TABLE 4.1** Major DOS Features

|  | DOS 3.0/3.1 | DOS 3.2 | DOS 3.3 | DOS 4.0/4.01 |
|---|---|---|---|---|
| Announced | Aug. 1984 | Mar. 1985 | Apr. 1987 | Aug. 1988 |
| Major Features | 1.2-MB floppy | 720-KB floppy | 1.44-MB floppy | DOS Shell GUI |
|  | Reduced cluster size | Int'l support | Multiple disk partitions | Partitions >32 MB |
|  | Network support | XCOPY cmmnd | FASTOPEN cmmnd | LIM EMS Support |
|  | VDISK cmmnd | REPLACE cmmnd | Enhanced Cmmnds: | HIMEM.SYS |
|  | Enhanced subdirectories | SHARE cmmnd | ATTRIB | EMM386.SYS |
|  |  | STACKS cmmnd | BACKUP | XMA2EMS.SYS |
|  |  |  | RESTORE | RAMDISK cmmnd |
|  |  |  | FILES | MEM cmmnd |
|  |  |  | APPEND cmmnd | SELECT cmmnd |
|  |  |  | CALL cmmnd | Enhanced cmmnds: |
|  |  |  |  | ANSI.SYS |
|  |  |  |  | BACKUP |
|  |  |  |  | BUFFERS |
|  |  |  |  | CHKDSK |
|  |  |  |  | DEL |
|  |  |  |  | FASTOPEN |
|  |  |  |  | FORMAT |
|  |  |  |  | MODE |
|  |  |  |  | TIME |
|  |  |  |  | TREE |
|  |  |  |  | XCOPY |

You have to do one more thing to make this scheme work. Add two lines to your AUTOEXEC.BAT file:

```
COPY COMMAND.COM C:
SET COMSPEC=C:\COMMAND.COM
```

SET COMSPEC is part of the DOS environment and tells DOS what path to use to reload the command processor when it has to. This parameter is loaded by DOS automatically when the system boots. Obviously, DOS knows where it booted and found COMMAND.COM the first time, and it assumes that's where it should go the next time it is needed.

If you don't have COMMAND.COM, at least, loaded on your boot disk, when you exit an application DOS can't find it. By adding the SET COMSPEC command to your AUTOEXEC.BAT file, you won't have to insert the DOS diskette each time you exit.

These simple steps will avoid the annoying message "Insert Diskette with COMMAND.COM" when you run an application that uses nearly all of your available memory, wiping out the command processor. With these modifications to CONFIG.SYS and AUTOEXEC.BAT you can remove the boot diskette once the system is up and running.

Now use DOS booted from a floppy to run all of your existing applications and take notes on any incompatibilities or problems you encounter. It may be that the provider of any offending software has a later version that will run fine with the newer DOS. If not, you may decide to use DOS 3.3 for some or all of your applications.

You can install the DOS SHELL by copying SHELL.* from the shell diskette supplied with DOS to a hard disk subdirectory. You should get five files:

```
SHELLB.COM
SHELLC.EXE
SHELL.HLP
SHELL.CLR
SHELL.MEU
```

Then use an ASCII editor to create the following batch file:

```
@C:
@CD \SHELL
@SHELLB DOSSHELL
@SHELLC
/TRAN/COLOR/DOS/MENU/MUL/SND/MEU:SHELL.MEU/CLS:SHELL.CLR/
PROMPT/MAINT/EXIT/SWAP/DATE
```

Save the file as DOSSHELL and you can call up the shell with the DOSSHELL command. If you have placed the shell files in a directory other than C:\SHELL, change line two of this batch file to point to the proper subdirectory.

## OTHER OPERATING SYSTEM CHOICES

You can run other operating systems on today's high-end PC platforms, notably UNIX (or Xenix, the Microsoft implementation of UNIX), and OS/2, IBM's multitasking, multiuser DOS for its PS/2 computer line. Depending on your applications, you may want to consider OS/2 or another alternate operating system.

Whether you're using DOS 3.3 or a later version, there are some things you still can't do in DOS. Most notably, you can't do true multitasking (doing more than one job at once), and DOS only supports one user at a time.

There are a number of third-party additions that support some multitasking features—such as DesqView from Quarterdeck and DoubleDOS from SoftLogic Solutions—but true, operating system multitasking is not part of DOS.

DOS 5.0, still a rumor and speculation as this book is written, is said to include more multitasking features and will be married to the Windows GUI.

For now, however, users who really need multitasking support must turn to OS/2, itself an immature multitasking environment because applications for it are new and few, or to a version of UNIX.

UNIX and its derivatives are strong operating system choices for high-end applications on full-featured hardware. It has been around long enough for a large user base to develop, and numerous applications are available for it. On the other hand, UNIX requires a lot of memory and storage. Just to install the basic UNIX system and utilities may take 15 MB or more of hard disk space. And, you wouldn't get much satisfaction out of running UNIX applications without at least 4 MB of RAM.

Too, UNIX can be complicated to configure and use. It is not an operating system for the casual user, unless it has been preconfigured and has applications installed.

All things being equal, for some users there are some strong reasons to move to OS/2, mainly because of its "big machine" features. For example, for all its improvements DOS still does not take advantage of the 32-bit registers in today's high-end CPUs; OS/2 does. DOS is limited to 1 MB of addressable memory, but OS/2 can match today's hardware, which supports 16-MB segments. In addition, OS/2 gives you virtual memory management that spools anything too big for physical memory out to disk, treating the disk like memory. And OS/2 can address up to 4 GB of physical address space (16 MB at a time).

OS/2 also is much easier to use than UNIX and likely will become more popular on PC platforms than UNIX, which is primarily considered a workstation, minicomputer, and supercomputer operating system.

Despite its strengths, OS/2 has not received a groundswell of support. OS/2 was announced in April 1987, amid predictions of OS/2 dominance over DOS by 1992, and the first piece in the four-part OS/2 puzzle shipped in December 1987.

For many, the problem is that OS/2 was three years too late. It is the operating system PC users expected when the PC/AT, 80286-based machine was released in

1984. Users were told, "Just wait. The real power of this machine will come with its new operating system, real soon now."

During the long delay between announcement and shipment, good old DOS was upgraded at least five times and thousands of DOS-specific applications have received wide market acceptance.

In addition, applications developers have been slow to write for OS/2. If you look long enough you can find software to do just about anything you need under DOS. That's not true if you're running OS/2. Together these developments have resulted in slow OS/2 sales. Microsoft reports that all versions of OS/2 have sold about 300,000 copies, while MS-DOS is still selling at the rate of 12 million units annually. The DOS inertia, with about 44 million units installed, is hard to overcome.

By some standards, OS/2's Windows-like Presentation Manager (PM) user interface and programming platform is its greatest strength. PM is designed to give users and developers a standard interface to operating system features and the applications that run under it. (If you think this sounds like a Macintosh strategy, you're quite correct.)

Again, however, PM may have come too late to capture the loyalty of users and the imaginations of developers. Revealed as part of the initial OS/2 program announcement in 1987, it was 18 months later, October 1988, before a version of Presentation Manager hit the streets.

Adding to the confusion is the four-level nature of the OS/2 concept. OS/2 Standard Edition is the version offered by non-IBM vendors, and consists of version 1.0, which is the basic operating system kernel, and version 1.1, which is this basic kernel plus the Presentation Manager. In addition, there are presently two versions of OS/2 Extended edition. Version 1.0 adds a DB-2 compatible database manager and a communications manager to the basic kernel; Version 1.1 also includes LAN workstation software and the Presentation Manager.

The enhancements in the Extended Edition are "value added," provided only by IBM for PS/2 platforms. Although it is possible for other vendors to offer their own extended versions of OS/2—the procedures and architecture are in place for this—so far, they haven't.

So what is the bottom line on OS/2? At the risk of stepping off into the black abyss of predictions, we believe OS/2 will gain broader acceptance among users of high-end 80386 and 80486 machines. This will come as the early problems are forgotten and as multitasking (and perhaps multiuser) applications mature. However, we expect DOS to continue to evolve, and it likely will remain the operating system of choice for the rest of us.

Even with improvements in memory use, DOS takes far less hard disk and RAM space than OS/2, and it costs a third as much as the most basic OS/2 kernel. Coupled with Microsoft Windows, Quarterdeck's DesqView, or other user interface, its functionality rivals OS/2 as far as most users are concerned.

OS/2 is a better software development environment, providing good interprocess communications and the potential for multiuser and multitasking operation. But at this point, it is potential only. Without applications and utility support—and given the very large installed base of DOS—OS/2 is destined to remain in second place as an operating system for PC platforms.

The next chapter offers an overview of major applications software to show you something about the current software trends and what to look for as you begin or add to your software library.

# CHAPTER FIVE APPLICATIONS SOFTWARE

To use your new computer system, you need more than the operating system. You must have at least one application software package for the computer to do useful work. Since the beginning of the personal computer phenomenon, the three most popular applications have been word processors, spreadsheets, and databases. Dozens of other useful and popular applications have been added, but those three remain high on the list of software sales and popularity.

## WORD PROCESSING SOFTWARE

If you do nothing else with your computer, you likely will want to do some word processing. We know casual computer users who have only an ancient Apple II or Commodore 64 and a small printer. They bought the machine to write reports and letters, and that's all they do with it still. The ability to enter text and move it around, check the spelling, and format it for output was an exciting, imagination-capturing prospect when it first became available—and it still is today.

The choices for text editing, word processing, and desktop publishing are extremely varied. Notice the three designations for word management. This is a fairly arbitrary division, but one that will help you visualize the different groups of word processing software available.

# Text Editing

Text editing is a relatively simple process and requires relatively simple software. In the early days of text editing these packages were severely limited. They were line-oriented editors that could display a full screen of text, but required you to redisplay a line—usually by specifying a line number or by searching for text—before you could edit anything.

With these early packages you couldn't move the cursor all over the screen and add or change text wherever you wanted. If you want a reminder of how primative this early software was, try using the EDLIN editor that still is supplied with some versions of DOS. Given user's expectations and experience, software such as EDLIN is an exercise in frustration.

But you have to remember that early microcomputer software was written by and for highly technical people, and the first text editors were used mostly for program development. In fact, that's how we got the early word processors. Programmers developed tools for themselves that would let them enter and change assembly language and higher-level code relatively easily. Then they modified this editor to let them write the documentation to accompany their software.

Finally, other computer users—people who had been wanting text management capabilities from the beginning anyway—saw what the programmers were doing and further refinements were added as the software was marketed to the more general purpose market.

A number of "text editing" packages are still available, and they, too, are targeted at the program developer. Probably the most widely distributed is WordPerfect Corporation's Program Editor that is a subset of the company's full-blown word processing software. PE, like most text editing software, produces straight ASCII files and will load, save, and edit any character in the PC's expanded character set.

You can even turn on a split-screen mode that shows your text in the top of the screen and the control codes and other expanded characters in hexadecimal format on the bottom. This display—the bottom part—is similar to the one you get from the DOS utility DEBUG. It is for specialized applications, but when you need to change a single hidden character in ASCII text, it is one of the best tools around.

For example, you may want to remove the spaces from the .PRN output of a spreadsheet file and replace them with tabs. With PE in split-screen mode you can see each space, tab, and carriage return as different codes displayed in different colors.

Other text-editing offerings may contain task-specific tools. For example, a number of companies offer language-specific text editors that help programmers produce error-free code by recognizing command errors and flagging them. This feature can save a lot of development time, especially when you are programming in a compiled language. If the editor you use doesn't catch errors, you have to compile the program to catch the errors, then load the source code back into the editor to make the change.

Unless you are a programmer you probably will have little need for a specialized editor, and a simple "text-editing" package is so limited, compared to a higher-level word processor, that we don't recommend any of them for general purpose applications. We do recommend, however, that you consider one of the multipurpose ASCII editors as a second text-management utility.

Most word processors are a little finicky when it comes to loading files with special codes or control characters it doesn't use itself. There are times when you may want to view or edit a file created by a spreadsheet, database or other application. Your word processor may or may not be able to load it, but a flexible text editor can.

## Word Processing

The most common form of text management is what we call word processing. This is the level of performance typified by such products as WordPerfect, Microsoft Word, Xywrite, WordStar and many, many others. The products just mentioned are probably the best selling of the word processing packages, and they offer very high-level performance. In fact, WordPerfect and Word, particularly, can do light desktop publishing duties.

Word processing is different from text editing in many respects. The most obvious difference is the level of formatting control they offer. Most full-featured word processing packages let you select fonts, size them, set bold, underline, italics, and other features, and even include graphics and line drawing support.

For many applications, such as business letters or simple reports, the power of these packages may be more than you need. You can obtain reasonably capable word processing software as part of an integrated package, such as Symantec's Q&A, for example, or from vendors whose primary product is in another area. Parsons Technology, for one, is known for its low-cost accounting software; but they also market a low-cost and very capable word processor.

There are probably hundreds of word processor-class packages on the market, and deciding which one to purchase can be difficult. However, our guidelines are relatively simple. For one thing, decide how much you are willing to spend. None

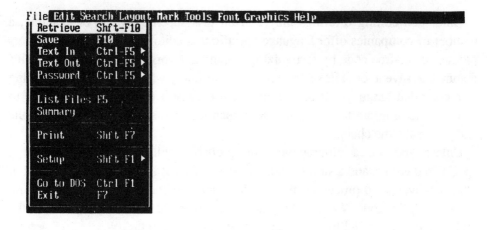

Figure 5.1   WordPerfect version 5.1 is among the most popular high-end word processing programs. It offers pulldown menus and mouse support.

of this software is particularly expensive, yet there are cost clusters that help you make a choice on price.

WordPerfect, for example, has a suggested retail price of $495, but it is readily available from mail order and local discounters for $250 or less. The same is generally true of Word, WordStar, Xywrite, and other high-end packages. Given the amount of word processing power they offer for the price, it is hard to justify buying anything less if you are serious about your word processing tasks.

Examples of word processing screens are shown in Figures 5.1 and 5.2.

On the other hand, if all you ever do is write an occasional business letter and the main part of your computer use is for database or spreadsheet applications, then a less functional, lower-cost package may be in order. The Parsons Technology software, for example, is sold for about $30, and there are even fairly capable packages available free from bulletin boards or for a $5 to $10 fee at your local or mail-order distributor.

If you are unsure about your word processing tasks, you might start with one of these inexpensive offerings, then upgrade later when you find out what you really need.

One more consideration. As always, this industry is driven by standards. By far the majority of serious word processing users have one of the top four or five

**Figure 5.2**   At the low end of the text-handling scale are products such as this word processor that uses simple icon menus.

packages. If you intend to be able to exchange files with a publisher, typesetting bureau, or a contract typist, you're better off with one of these "name brand" products. It may cost more than you really want to spend, and it may have more features than you think you will need; but you can grow into it, and it is compatible with the rest of the world.

## Desktop Publishing

The top-level text management area is desktop publishing. The number of PC users who really need this level of software is relatively small compared to the number who regularly use some form of word processing or text editing, but we expect this market to grow as more powerful computers reach more desktops and as desktop publishing software gets easier to use.

What is desktop publishing? Well, the line between high-end word processing and desktop publishing is merging, but there are still some distinct differences.

Desktop publishing packages such as Aldus Pagemaker or Ventura Publisher can use files output from the popular word processing software, but they go beyond word processing capabilities in page layout, graphics management, font control, and the like.

These packages can be used for the complete production of books, magazines, high-quality newsletters, annual reports, and about any publishing job. The down side is they require high-end computers and, for now at least, they are not easy to use. These publishing packages support only minimal editing capabilities, because they depend on a word processor to produce the bare text; and because of the large number of high-end functions they offer, they are relatively difficult to use.

However, if you need full control of your publishing operation, and you want to be able to work right down to a tight deadline, there is no substitute for doing it yourself.

# SPREADSHEET SOFTWARE

Many people say the spreadsheet application alone is responsible for the growth and popularity of personal computers. Prior to the original release of VisiCalc—the first widely distributed spreadsheet software—users of early Apple and other computers were offered the BASIC programming language and, on some machines, the industry standard COBOL. From there you had to write your own programs.

The third-party applications that were available were rigid, inflexible offerings, frequently written for a specific company or application, then marketed to the general user base. This early software did not often solve the specific problem it was purchased to address.

The spreadsheet was different. This was a program without limits. It allowed you to develop custom applications without having to write programs.

Spreadsheet software presents a blank grid on the screen. Within this grid you can construct ledger sheets, memos, forms, balance sheets, cost projections, almost anything that can be built with formulas and cell relationships.

The spreadsheet grid generally is labeled with alphabetic characters along the horizontal axis and with numbers in the vertical plane. To address an individual cell you specify the two-digit address. A1 is the first cell in the upper left-hand corner of the screen, for example, while D10 would appear about center screen.

By placing data in these cells and writing relatively simple formulas that define the relationships among the information in the various locations, you can build a custom application in real time, following the results of your efforts by watching values change dynamically on the screen.

From the earliest spreadsheet offerings, the market has grown to include several viable vendors. The products offer such enhancements as WYSIWYG ("What You See Is What You Get") graphics displays, programming languages, three-dimensional spreadsheets, and add-on utilities including word processors, communications, and printer enhancements. A spreadsheet screen is illustrated in Figure 5.3.

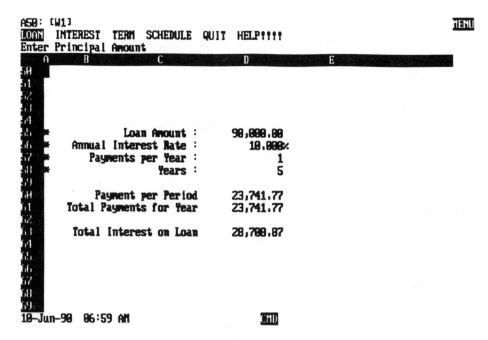

**Figure 5.3** Lotus 1-2-3 Release 2.2 is the mainstay spreadsheet for most users.

Without a doubt the premier spreadsheet product today is Lotus Development Corp.'s 1-2-3, with two versions currently being sold, Release 2.2 and Release 3.0. However, as more users become aware of their need for spreadsheet software, new products are entering the market with some success. Companies such as WordPerfect, for example, best known for its word processing package of the same name, is getting good response from its PlanPerfect offering, a spreadsheet that follows closely the menu and operational structure of the word processor.

Perhaps diversity is the one word that best describes today's spreadsheet market. From "A to Z," automatic recalculation to zero suppression, users are offered a multitude of features. To compare features you have to understand the different spreadsheet concepts for data management. To make a buying decision you have to understand your specific needs—application, user experience, hardware platform, speed requirements, and budget—and you need a sense of how well each individual package meets those needs.

Technology has evolved greatly since the original two-dimensional (2-D) VisiCalc and Lotus Development Corp.'s 1-2-3. Soon linked spreadsheets, like original Multiplan and Surpass, allowed the referencing of external spreadsheet cells. The next concept was to provide a third dimension to give depth to the spreadsheets.

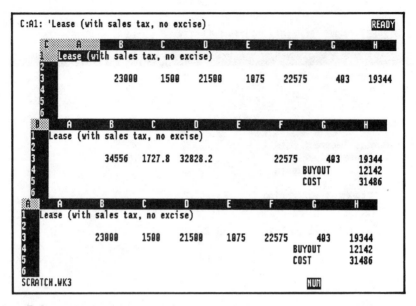

**Figure 5.4**    Lotus 1-2-3 Release 3.0 offers three-dimensional spreadsheet display.

The elusive "3-D" term has different connotations depending on the manufacturer, but most companies are offering some form of it to satisfy user's needs for more worksheet space and more flexibility in worksheet design. Some define 3-D as a spreadsheet with a third dimension or axis ("pages") with cell referencing of three coordinates. 1-2-3 Release 3 is one of these, using a spreadsheet prefix to the standard cell coordinates. You can associate up to 256 spreadsheets in this way, and display three of them on the screen at once, as shown in Figure 5.4.

This "3-D" capability lets you keep calculation detail—such as financial or sales figures from different divisions—in individual spreadsheets, with each sheet related to a master sheet that displays only summaries. Separating data into various worksheets makes the job of organizing, printing, and changing data easier.

Mosaic's Twin Level III allows a similar effect by using global range names and multiple active files in memory.

Lucid 3-D establishes a three-dimensional (3-D) work area by associating another worksheet with a cell in the current sheet. You could think of each cell on the current worksheet as a window into another complete worksheet. The second worksheet can be associated with a third, that one with a fourth, and so on down as many levels as you like. You can have as many as nine sheets open on the screen at a time.

More than three dimensions are provided in relational or multidimensional spreadsheets. A monthly ledger is a realistic example. You would have January's 2-D ledger pages stacked (creating a 3-D effect). Now, if you stack February's ledger pages, you have created a fourth dimension. March would be a fifth dimension, and so forth. VP-Planner allows five dimensions, and TM/1 allows eight.

Although the results are similar, each product approaches the problem of multiple sheets in slightly different ways, and some products may be easier to apply to your particular problems than others.

In addition to the move toward 3-D support, there are other trends in spreadsheet features worth looking for as you select software. Speed is one welcome feature produced by enhanced program design in most of the currently popular offerings. Most spreadsheet programs today provide minimum recalculation to recalculate only those cells that have been modified or referenced since the worksheet's last recalc. If a product does not have this feature, the entire worksheet—all the formulas and cell relationships—must be recalculated each time one cell is changed, even though nothing else was modified.

In addition, a growing number of spreadsheet programs provide background recalculation to allow work to continue on the spreadsheet while recalculation on other cells is done in the background. Together, these features are significant steps toward speeding up data entry without the user having to remember to manually compute a worksheet periodically.

You will appreciate the improved user interfaces available with today's offerings. While it is true that Lotus Corporation continues to drive the market with the horizontal menu approach in its 1-2-3 spreadsheet series, many companies are expanding the user interface to include their own, more flexible designs.

PlanPerfect, for example, supports the Lotus menu, but also is compatible with WordPerfect word processing commands.

Ease of use has become a major vendor concern because of the wide range of user expertise. With the ease of pointing to graph data ranges and use of one-screen "fill in" menus for selecting graph criteria, even the novice can easily produce a quality result with most packages.

Mosaic Twin, among the most Lotus-compatible of the current offerings, adds pulldown menus, color selection, and other features you may like.

Output capabilities are increasing to include more fonts, type sizes, fill selections, and shading patterns. As is apparent in PlanPerfect's support of 450 printers, the trend is toward more printer support, including those using PostScript.

Linking, the ability to exchange information from one worksheet to another, is supported by the majority of spreadsheet software. Before the linking capability you could place calculated values into a destination sheet with a one-time consolidation procedure. Products in the Lotus Release 2.01 era could link at the cell level, sometimes only one cell per spreadsheet. Today's products approach "live links" that keep data continuously up to date across spreadsheet boundaries, and the limits on the number of cells that can be linked have expanded.

Lucid 3-D allows linking of ranges, not just cells, and demonstrates the merging of the "link" and "3-D" concepts. Actually, a sophisticated link creates a 3-D spreadsheet. In Lucid you can display the link in 3-D view. Some other products differentiate between linking and 3-D.

Balancing a tradeoff between performance and worksheet size, modern spreadsheet packages can support very large spreadsheets. Ashton-Tate's Framework III, for example, supports a spreadsheet grid of up to 32-K x 32-K cells. To support these larger sizes, most packages use expanded memory. However, with some 80386 systems, using expanded memory slows system performance—sometimes by only a little, sometimes by as much as a factor of three. You are adding some CPU overhead for the software memory management, for one thing. However, some products seem to be more efficient in memory management than others.

Because of the inherent slowness, vendors have compensated by using virtual memory techniques, math co-processors, and better program designs and features. Be aware that once expanded memory is configured, some packages will always use it even if conventional memory is available. Allays, the Lotus add-in, is an example of this.

If you plan to generate large spreadsheets and assume expanded memory will be needed, look at the differential between your machine's RAM and the amount of memory required for DOS, the spreadsheet, and add-ins. It is possible there could be enough memory available for your applications.

Some general market observations: Only about one-fourth of the available spreadsheet packages are RAM resident; that is, they can be popped up on top of other applications. In addition, most spreadsheet programs will run in 640-KB RAM (even if they also support expanded or extended memory), except Lotus 3.0 and 10 Planner. Both of these require extended memory and 80286 or 80386 CPUs.

Macro support is important as applications get more and more complex. Some packages, such as Smart from Informix and PlanPerfect from WordPerfect, have relatively complete programming languages in addition to cell-level or keystroke-record macros. Many packages have unique "built-ins," such as pulldown menus, color, and sideways printing.

Another approach is to provide a "total" solution for office needs. Integrated packages such as SmartWareII, T/Master, and FrameWork III include word processing and database management with the spreadsheet. Other companies offer a "family" of standalone packages providing similar command structure, menu design, and file compatibility. Using one or more packages, you can meet current office requirements and integrate additional modules as needed. An example of this approach is WordPerfect Corp.'s PlanPerfect, DataPerfect, and WordPerfect group.

The spreadsheet graphics market is evolving. To simplify your buying decision, consider two main areas. First, define the quality level and types of graphs you require. For example, will you need presentation quality graphics, extensive font flexibility, documents merged with graphs, specific graph types, color, or 3-D capability?

Next, determine the hardware needed to support your graphing requirements. Do you need a screen display larger than 25 x 80, EGA, VGA, additional graphics cards, or support for PostScript, mouse, plotter, film output, or specific printer types? After defining your criteria, determine the products that meet your needs.

SmartWare and a few other packages offer "true" 3-D graphics where the $z$ coordinate is maintained with true data integrity. Mosaic's products offer "3-D effects" that allow shading on bar and pie charts to represent a third dimension, but this is not true 3-D.

More vendors today are supporting mixed charts, allowing you to overlay a single chart with multiple types, such as Lotus Release 3.0's support of mixed bar and line. SmartWare II offers composite graphing to display multiple individual graphs on one page.

Executive users should check for text chart support and the ability to merge graphics with word processing documents. These capabilities are found in SmartWare and PlanPerfect, for example.

Most spreadsheet software, including Lotus 3.0, allows direct graphics access from the spreadsheet. A new "hot key" function lets you view a graph with a single keystroke, however, the graph detail varies from package to package. And relatively few packages support simultaneous chart and text display—a handy feature to let you see exactly what the chart will look like before it is printed.

There is a trend toward better database support. Although products like 1-2-3 were never really intended to replace a complete database package, many users did just that, even though database operations inside a spreadsheet are cumbersome at best.

Today, products such as Mosaic Twin include a full-screen database template so you don't have to enter or edit data in the spreadsheet's horizontal format. Lotus 1-2-3 Release 3.0 lets you read and write dBASE and other database files directly, so you can have the database capabilities of one program and the graphics support of the other, for example.

In fact, many programs tout direct read and write of Lotus 1-2-3, dBASE, and other files; in most cases this is not strictly true. It is more accurate to refer to the process as direct read with conversion. While you can specify a 1-2-3 file, say, for direct load, the program converts the 1-2-3 file to its own format during the load.

Now think about the many things you need to consider before purchasing a spreadsheet product.

- Evaluate your needs: What do you plan to do and how do you plan to accomplish it using the spreadsheet?
- Evaluate existing equipment configuration: What hardware and software do you currently have? Are you planning additional purchases?
- Evaluate specific file compatibility: Do you have Lotus files, macros, or templates that will need conversion? Do you have other files, such as word processing, that would need to be compatible?
- Evaluate your existing personnel resources: Is anyone knowledgeable about a particular package? How many people need access to software?
- Evaluate total office automation needs: Will you need word processing, database, or other related capabilities?
- Evaluate corporate needs: Do you need a multitasking environment, networking, or multiuser system?
- And, last but not least, how much can you spend? Prices on today's spreadsheets are as diverse as capabilities. Although it still is generally true that "you get what you pay for," price is not necessarily an indication of power or functionality, but it certainly is one factor that must be considered.

Just as your office has its own personality, each spreadsheet has its strengths and weaknesses. The days are past when everything on the market is a VisiCalc or Lotus clone. Although 1-2-3 compatibility is important in today's market, and most of the software in this survey offers at least some level of compliance features, functionality and ease of use may be more crucial. If you are jumping into the spreadsheet market, or if you are considering a change from your current product, study the available offerings carefully. Remember, you'll have to live with what you select.

# DATABASE SOFTWARE

The third in the list of most popular applications is database software. A database provides a relatively structured environment in which to store information such as inventory, sales figures, company names and addresses.

The two most common database types for microcomputer platforms are flat-file databases and relational databases. The very newest technology, object-oriented database software, is destined to take over most of the microcomputer market. But that won't happen for several years because of the amount of research and development that remains to be done in this area. For now, flat files and relational files are the two most prevalent database types.

A flat-file program stores information much the same way you would put data into a card file or a notebook. Suppose you were keeping track of your sales contacts with a simple 3 × 5 card or Rolodex system. You would write the person's name at the top of the card and fill in such information as company name, street address, city, state, zip, telephone, perhaps the date of your last conversation, and whatever other information is useful to you. If you wish to keep track of more than one person from the same company you probably would fill out a separate card with the same information, filed in the appropriate alphabetical order by that person's last name. An example of a flat-file program is shown in Figure 5.5.

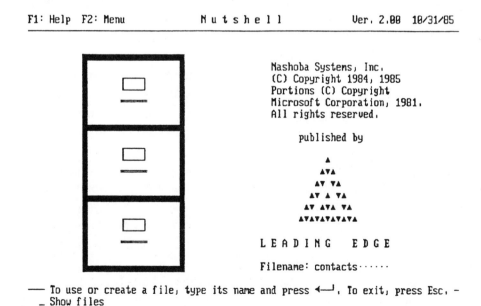

F1: Help  F2: Menu            N u t s h e l l            Ver. 2.00  10/31/85

```
                              Nashoba Systems, Inc.
                              (C) Copyright 1984, 1985
                              Portions (C) Copyright
                              Microsoft Corporation, 1981.
                              All rights reserved.

                                  published by

                                       ▲
                                      ▲▼▲
                                     ▲▼ ▼▲
                                    ▲▼ ▲ ▼▲
                                   ▲▼ ▲▼▲ ▼▲
                                  ▲▼▲▼▲▼▲▼▲▼▲

                              L E A D I N G   E D G E

                              Filename: contacts······
```
── To use or create a file, type its name and press ◄─┘. To exit, press Esc. ─
_ Show files

**Figure 5.5a**   **Nutshell from Leading Edge is a popular database program for novice and experienced user alike.**

```
F1: Help  F2: Menu               Add Records
_____


Last Name       Badgett · · · · · · · · · · · · · · · · · · · · · · · · · · · · · · · · ·
First Name      Jordan · · · · · · · · · · · · · · · · · · · · · · · · · · · · · · · · · · ·
Street          123 New Street · · · · · · · · · · · · · · · · · · · · · · · · · · · ·
City            Anywhere · · · · · · · · · · · · · · · · · · · · · · · · · · · · · · · · ·
State           US · · · · · · · · · · · · · · · · · · · · · · · · · · · · · · · · · · · · · ·
Zip             12345 · · · · · · · · · · · · · · · · · · · · · · · · · · · · · · · · · · · ·
Telephone       900-555-1212 · · · · · · · · · · · · · · · · · · · · · · · · · · · · ·
Comments        This is a sample Nutshell Entry · · · · · · · · · · · · · · · ·





_____

 _ Show index  _ Import from file  _ Ditto  _ Validation
```

**Figure 5.5b**   Designing a database and entering data in Nutshell is a simple, menu-driven process.

A flat filing system may be all the database you need for tracking most of your data, if the file sizes are relatively small and if the amount of disparate data you track is limited. If you follow a wide range of information, if you need that data reported in a variety of formats, and if you want to maximize use of storage space, then a relational system may be more appropriate.

A relational system uses separate files for different types of information and "relates" the different data through a common piece of data, such as a company name or customer number. That way you only store the company name and address once and relate that information to the data about the many individual people who work for that company.

You could set up a similar system with two Rolodex files; in fact, we have seen many handwritten files set up just that way. In one file you would store the information about each company. In another file beside the first you would put people information. When you looked up John Jones in the people file it would tell you that he works for Skunkworks, Inc. If you want to know more about Skunkworks you check out the company card file.

A relational database works that way, except the links between files can be made automatic, and you can tie together several files as easily as two. A third relational possibility, for example, is a list of transactions with each company.

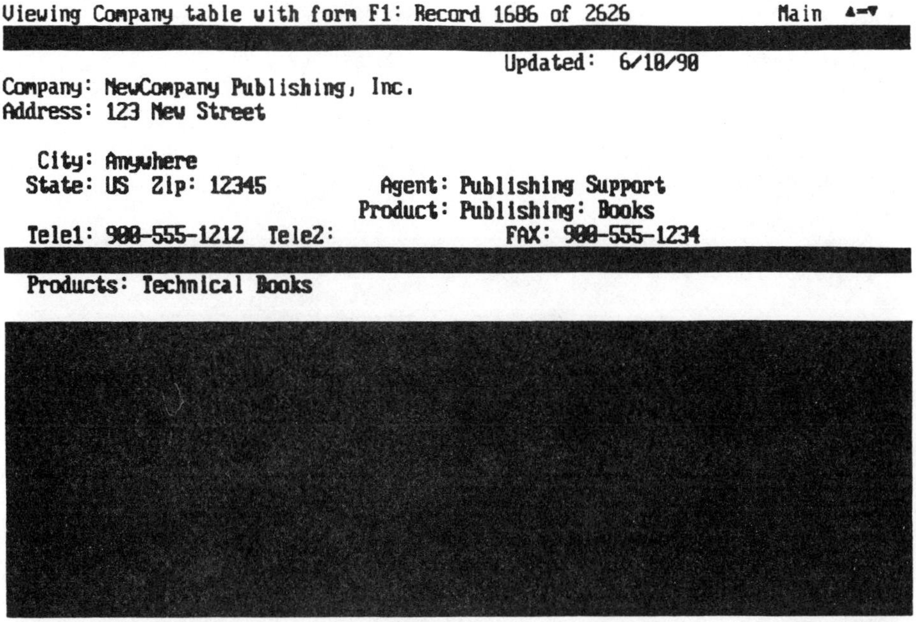

```
Viewing Company table with form F1: Record 1686 of 2626          Main  ▲▬▼
                                        Updated:   6/18/98
Company: NewCompany Publishing, Inc,
Address: 123 New Street

   City: Anywhere
  State: US  Zip: 12345          Agent: Publishing Support
                               Product: Publishing: Books
  Tele1: 900-555-1212  Tele2:           FAX: 900-555-1234

  Products: Technical Books
```

**Figure 5.6a**  Paradox 3 is a popular relational database program that presents data in a spreadsheet format or in custom templates. This is a single-file custom screen display from Paradox 3.

Every time you contact the company or make a sale or receive a payment you enter this data into one or more files related to the company file. Figure 5.6 shows (a) a single file and (b) linked files.

Again, you only have to store the company name or ID with each transaction record—the full company name, address, amount owed, product type, and the like remains in the company file.

Relational databases have become the type of choice for the majority of business-related microcomputer applications. In today's market the base is expanding through improved software design coupled with faster and more capable hardware.

Among the power features offered by most database vendors are built-in networking—which is the ability to put an out-of-the-box software package up on a network for shared data access—and complete programming languages that can be used to develop custom applications, including menus and reports.

Just a few years ago network users were frustrated by the lack of networkable applications software. After the struggle of selecting a network and getting it up and running, adapting single-user applications was anticlimactic. Today that has

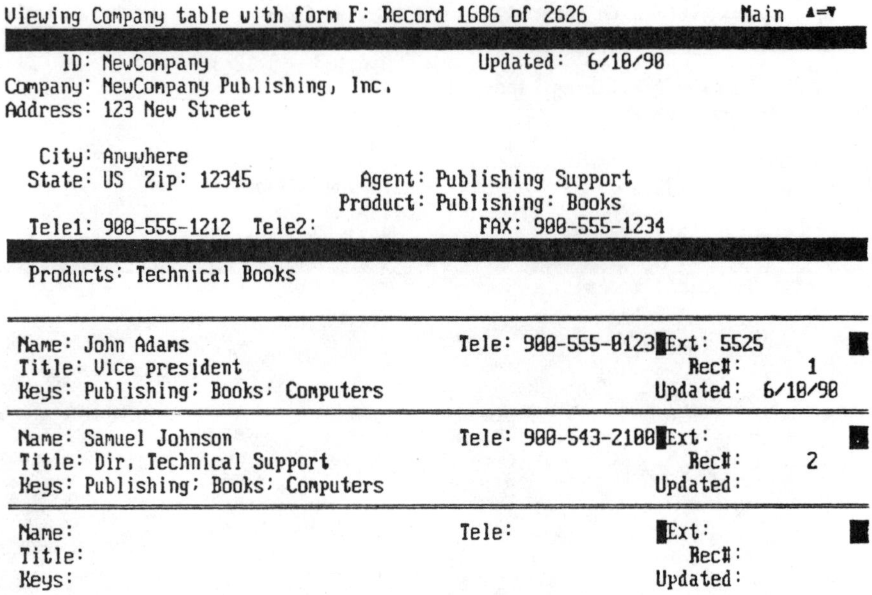

```
Viewing Company table with form F: Record 1686 of 2626          Main  ▲=▼
━━━━━━━━━━━━━━━━━━━━━━━━━━━━━━━━━━━━━━━━━━━━━━━━━━━━━━━━━━━━━━━━━━━━━━━━━━━
     ID: NewCompany                        Updated:  6/18/98
Company: NewCompany Publishing, Inc.
Address: 123 New Street

   City: Anywhere
  State: US  Zip: 12345            Agent: Publishing Support
                                 Product: Publishing: Books
  Tele1: 988-555-1212  Tele2:              FAX: 988-555-1234
━━━━━━━━━━━━━━━━━━━━━━━━━━━━━━━━━━━━━━━━━━━━━━━━━━━━━━━━━━━━━━━━━━━━━━━━━━━
  Products: Technical Books


 Name: John Adams                   Tele: 988-555-8123 Ext: 5525       ■
Title: Vice president                                  Rec#:      1
 Keys: Publishing; Books; Computers                 Updated:  6/18/98
─────────────────────────────────────────────────────────────────────────
 Name: Samuel Johnson               Tele: 988-543-2188 Ext:            ■
Title: Dir, Technical Support                          Rec#:      2
 Keys: Publishing; Books; Computers                 Updated:
─────────────────────────────────────────────────────────────────────────
 Name:                              Tele:             Ext:            ■
Title:                                                 Rec#:
 Keys:                                              Updated:
```

**Figure 5.6b**   It is easy to link two or more files into a custom multifile screen display in Paradox 3.

changed for the better. Database products, particularly, are natural networking applications. Whether the software is used for inventory, purchasing, sales tracking, accounting, or simple name and address tracking, the ability for multiple users across a network to access common data is a boon to productivity.

Some companies provide a two-user capability at no extra cost, but with most databases you will have to purchase a "network pack" or add-on software to enable multiple, simultaneous access. If you have several users with their own standalone versions of the software, however, you can probably design multiuser databases without further investment, providing an excellent upgrade path if you do not now have networking but plan to install a system in the near future.

Whatever your network status, you probably will change it, either through an upgrade or by installing a new network from scratch. Therefore you should work with your supplier to determine what is the best method to purchase database applications. If you don't already have a network, then you will have to buy individual modules. If you do have a network, it probably is cheaper to purchase multiuser versions of the software—but let an expert help you analyze your installation to come up with the most cost-effective and most flexible configuration.

Another important aspect of the new database offerings is that they wrap their power with a series of menus, full-screen editors, and automatic features that make conducting full-featured relational operations relatively easy. Early products, such as dBASE, for example, were command line driven. When you loaded the software the screen cleared and you were presented with a single period on the screen, the "dot prompt."

To do useful work with the software you had to learn a complete set of commands and procedures. This generally limited access to experienced programmers or to people who had applications written for them. This is not true with today's products. End-user demand for database access has prompted software producers to design realistic user interfaces, and recent technical developments—faster CPUs, expanded memory, high- resolution graphics—have helped make the software more "user friendly."

Paradox is a good example of this software friendliness. A few fairly simple menu sequences is all it takes to link two or more tables on a single form, for example, allowing multitable viewing and editing of database information. In addition, a cross-tabulation feature automatically sets up retrieved data for graphing, using the Quattro spreadsheet graphics, now a part of Paradox 3.0.

dBASE, traditionally a command line product, now appeals to a wider audience, while retaining strong developer tools that are well known by a broad base of established programmers. The dBASE QBE (query by example) interface, for example, rivals Paradox for ease of use and the simplicity with which you can join multiple tables.

While menu-driven and user-friendly interfaces are an important feature of new database products—features that can provide relational database power to a broader range of users—programming language support is crucial for custom development and large applications. If you stick with the most popular, big-name products, all have reasonable programming support, although each product has its own personality, flavor, and features.

One area that database watchers are keeping their collective eyes on is support for graphics-type fields. Although none of the really popular microcomputer products support this feature as this book is written, it is only a matter of time, we predict. Serious contenders in the word processor market can now access binary data in a variety of formats, and a few database products can do it.

In the minicomputer world an increasing number of database packages can import files in a standard graphics format and store this data for access through the database tools. You set up a file with one or more fields designated to hold graphics or to point to a specific graphics file. When you access a record with graphics information, the database itself either converts the data for display or printing or it accesses the native graphics tool that was used to produce it in the first place.

The overall software marketplace is moving toward compound document integration that will allow text, numbers, graphics, and images to coexist within a common environment. With the proliferation of drawing and presentation graphics software as well as video capture and image-scanning hardware, computer users need a way to store, catalog, and retrieve this information. A relational database platform is a logical tool to do this.

A mouse input device typifies the graphical user interfaces through various windowing environments that are moving across workstations and PCs to become the standard way for accessing all applications. Current database products are no exception, though they do not support mice and other alternative input devices as broadly as other program classes, it seems. The DOS market is slightly behind larger workstations in this regard, but when the dust of controversy over OS/2, Presentation Manager, and the various windows formats settles, we will see broader support for mice and other alternative input devices.

PostScript support also will take on new importance in increasingly distributed environments where hardware and software products from many sources work together on a network. In a heterogeneous enterprise, broad support for standards such as PostScript will be imperative to ensure compatibility and ease of configuration.

Part of nearly any database discussion these days is the SQL user interface, a query language frequently used to construct reports and manipulate the database. The importance of SQL as a user interface, at least in the PC market, is waning. Even database products that use SQL to query the database don't often use it to capture input from the user. Graphical user interfaces, menus, and object construction is replacing this potentially difficult method of getting to your data.

Although SQL is very much a part of database offerings for minicomputer platforms, its necessity in PC-only environments is questionable. As PCs are integrated deeper into the overall computing enterprise, however, such "large machine" functionality could well take on new importance; but it probably will be encapsulated in a more friendly and functional interface than the standard SQL command prompt.

SQL is another of the spreading standards that provide a common set of tools to access computer-based information. The major stumbling block for widespread implementation is the variance in SQL standards. Although standards exist, most companies choose to implement a superset of SQL functionality to provide better product flexibility. As soon as you program an application in this enhanced SQL,

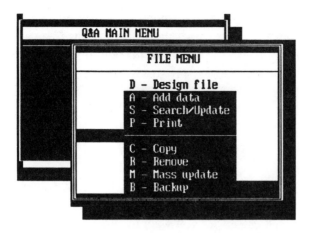

Esc-Main Menu          F1-Description of choices          ← Continue

**Figure 5.7**   Q&A from Symantec is an integrated package that includes database and word processor functions.

it probably is not compatible with the lower standard or with another vendor's enhanced version.

Chances are you will want some form of database program on your computer. You could start with something simple yet easy to use, such as Nutshell from Leading Edge. This is an extremely popular flat-file or relational database that uses simple screen setup and full-screen painting to design the files and produce reports.

Q&A from Symantec is another popular flat filer that has some extras. This integrated package contains a capable word processor in addition to the database facilities, and the "intelligent assistant" module helps you construct English language queries to find and report on the information you have stored in the file. This package has some limitations for serious, big-business database requirements, but for departmental data, personal data, or small-business information tracking, it is one of the more verstaile and easy-to-use packages on the market. Figure 5.7 shows a screen from Q&A.

There also are a number of specialized database offerings that are really flat filers or relational databases prepackaged for a particular task. Several companies offer sales list management or Rolodex maintenance, for example.

Accounting software is a specialized database application, and so is inventory management. You could develop any of these applications in a capable database package, but it probably doesn't make sense for you to spend the time doing it. The price of these dedicated packages is so low that you can better spend your time saving money building your PC or conducting your regular business.

# UTILITY SOFTWARE

Whatever else you do with your computer, you likely will need one or more utility software packages. What is a utility? Just about anything that doesn't fit into whatever predefined categories you want to agree exist. For the purposes of this book, utility software includes "toolbox" type packages that help you manage hard disk directories, diagnostic software, communications, graphics editors, and more.

The utility area is something that continually grows as you use your computer and other software. Whereas you likely will decide fairly early on what database, spreadsheet, and word processing software you need and like to use and stick with it, your utility toolbox will grow and change continually over the years.

You might include in the utility area a relatively new class of software called PIM, for personal information manager. Like other utility software, the PIM designation is wideranging and includes a variety of different software functionality.

This is software that covers a wide range of functions, from hard disk management to personal calendars, from text database manipulation to card files and autodialers. This is sometimes called "productivity" software, and in the minicomputer world variations on this theme have carried the moniker "Executive Information System."

PIM is but the latest trend in a software industry striving mightily to help the computer solve the far-flung information management needs of a wildly disparate audience. PIM is a "buzzword" without firm definition, but it serves well enough to describe a range of personally oriented software designed for individual configuration and application.

You still need to study your own information needs before deciding which package to use, because there is a variety of PIM software available. However, the flexibility and support for custom needs supplied by most PIM software is truly amazing and helps you have the features you need for a particular task.

What tasks can you expect PIMs to handle? The same ones you already are doing with a variety of dedicated packages, but PIMs can consolidate many functions and frequently can work across datafile types, giving you easier access to the variety of data you already have stored.

For example, some PIMs are particularly strong in searching very large text files, one at a time or in groups, looking for specified data or concepts. And they might do this without regard to what word processor created the files, so you can search your WordPerfect, WordStar, Xywrite, and EDLIN files at the same time from a single application.

Other packages are better suited to helping you build very personal data files of sales contacts, telephone numbers, TO DO lists, and appointment calendars. You construct these data files on the fly as you need them, adding and replacing information as your needs change.

Still others are oriented toward helping you locate programs and data files you have distributed all over your hard drives. They can display organized lists of files by directory or type, sort them, perhaps provide custom menus, and run the programs you select.

And, of course, most PIMs consolidate several of these functions into one package. None of them has it all, but with a little study you will be able to find software that contains the particular combination of functions you most need.

Borland's Sidekick was one of the first general purpose PIMs, popular long before the term PIM even existed. This is a pop-up, RAM-resident utility that gives you an appointment calendar, autodialer, text editor, ASCII chart, screen capture, and some other goodies in a reasonably compact, easy-to-use package. SideKick is a good model for newer products in this category, but it is a model only. The basic functionality has been greatly enhanced in most available packages, and there seems to be a trend toward somewhat more specialization. Figure 5.8 shows a screen from Borland's Sidekick.

For example, when you need to manage a large number of text files, perhaps produced with more than one word processor, you need to step into a program that is designed for data organization and data retrieval. This type of product is perfect for writers and reporters, for example, who frequently take notes about articles and research. University researchers, librarians, and students have some of the same needs. Note files, coupled with articles and perhaps E-mail and memos related to various projects constitute a wealthy storehouse of continuing information. The problem is, how do you get to it?

Text-retrieval software such as AskSam from AskSam Systems, or Ize from Persoft, help you access all this information. By building word indexes based on the contents of the original files, such programs give you rapid, direct access to text data. And they frequently can create cross references, proximity searches, and "sounds-like" retrievals.

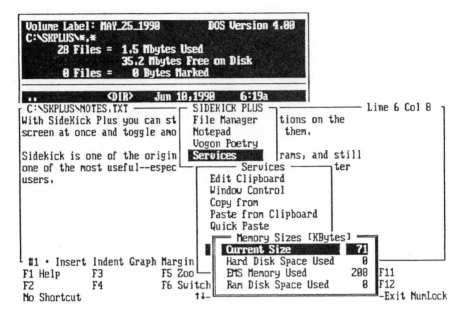

**Figure 5.8**   Borland's Sidekick Plus is the latest version of this multifunction TSR utility.

A text-retrieval PIM is not for the casual user with a few personal notes or memos to manage. But to manage megabytes of disparate data, dedicated text retrieval software will fill the bill.

As hard disks get bigger and bigger, so do the headaches of tracking all that information. PIMs can help you do it, generally by creating custom "views" of the files based on file contents, filename, date of creation, and subdirectory location.

PIMs such as Lotus Development's Magellan or Traveling Software's ViewLink help you launch programs by linking data with applications, using long filenames or tags, and by drawing graphics directories.

Most PIM and other utility software is relatively inexpensive, say under $100. The specialty products, such as high end text retrieval, for example, may cost five times that much. As with any software, you must decide what level of functionality you need and weigh that against how much you are willing to spend. These two criteria together help you narrow down the choice.

So, what software should you install on your newly built PC? No less than you want, no more than you need. And above all, don't hesitate to experiment. The cost of software is low enough today that you probably can afford to try several offerings for awhile until you find one that fits your particular needs and usage patterns.

## CHAPTER SIX

# COMPUTER COMPONENTS

## CASES AND POWER SUPPLIES

Until a few years ago life was fairly simple in regard to case and power supply selection. There was a choice of either an XT case and 150-watt power supply or an AT case and 200-watt power supply. Your selection depended on whether you went with an 8088 or 80286-class computer. Today, your choice of case and power supply depends on your computer needs and your preference for where you want the computer to sit.

Vendors provide the 80286, 80386SX, and 80386 in minimotherboard versions so that they can be used in standard XT computer cases. So, if you have an old XT computer case, you can install one of these new technology boards right inside it. As for the old XT power supply, it should have a minimum rating of 150 watts or else you may experience heat problems after an hour or more of operation. A full 80386SX system (memory, floppies, and hard disk) will operate with a power supply rated less than 150 watts, but you are taking a big chance on a burnout due to overload.

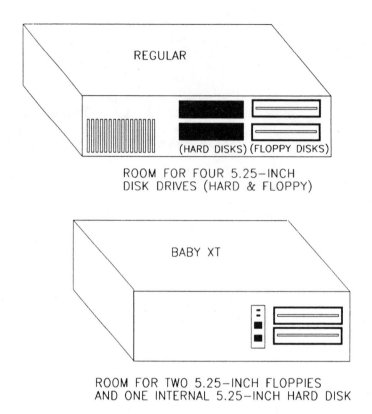

**Figure 6.1**   The regular and "baby" XT computer cases are compared.

# XT Case and Power Supply

The full-size or standard XT case measures 19.5 inches wide by 5.75 inches tall by 16.5 inches deep. A new baby version is now available that measures only 14.5 inches wide. It is nice for those who have a small space for a computer. Both case sizes are designed to take the standard 12-inch by 8.5-inch XT motherboard and the newer mini 80286 and 80386 motherboards. Figure 6.1 illustrates the XT computer cases.

There are two mechanical versions of the cabinet. One version has the top of the case hinged. Remove one screw from each side of the front of the case, and the top opens up for easy access. The other version requires five screws to be removed from the back. The outer case then slides off from the front. This version is more difficult to disassemble and assemble, but it usually is less expensive. Both versions are shown in Figure 6.2.

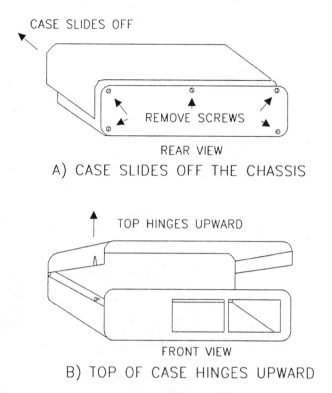

CASE SLIDES OFF

REMOVE SCREWS

REAR VIEW

A) CASE SLIDES OFF THE CHASSIS

TOP HINGES UPWARD

FRONT VIEW

B) TOP OF CASE HINGES UPWARD

**Figure 6.2**  Slide and hinged style XT cases

Both styles have a back plate that will accommodate eight expansion slots. The old style PC case had room for only five expansion slots. The motherboard mounts so that the expansion sockets on it are directly below the back plate. Starting from the outside edge of the cabinet and progressing toward the middle, the first five or six expansion slots probably can be used for full-length expansion cards in most cases. The two or three remaining sockets in the middle of the cabinet may accommodate only short-length expansion boards, since the disk drives probably will get in the way. At the left front of the case, you will find the small speaker that connects to the motherboard for sound generation. (See Figure 6.3.)

On the full-size or standard XT case, there are two 5.25-inch full-height disk drive openings in the front. Since almost all 5.25-inch hard and floppy drives are half-height, this means you will have room for up to four disk drives. On the baby XT case there is room for only three vertically mounted 5.25-inch disk drives.

You are not restricted to using only 5.25-inch drives. You can obtain adapter hardware that will allow 3.5-inch drives to be mounted. This means that you can use the newer 3.5-inch 720-KB and 1.44-MB floppies and 3.5-inch hard disks.

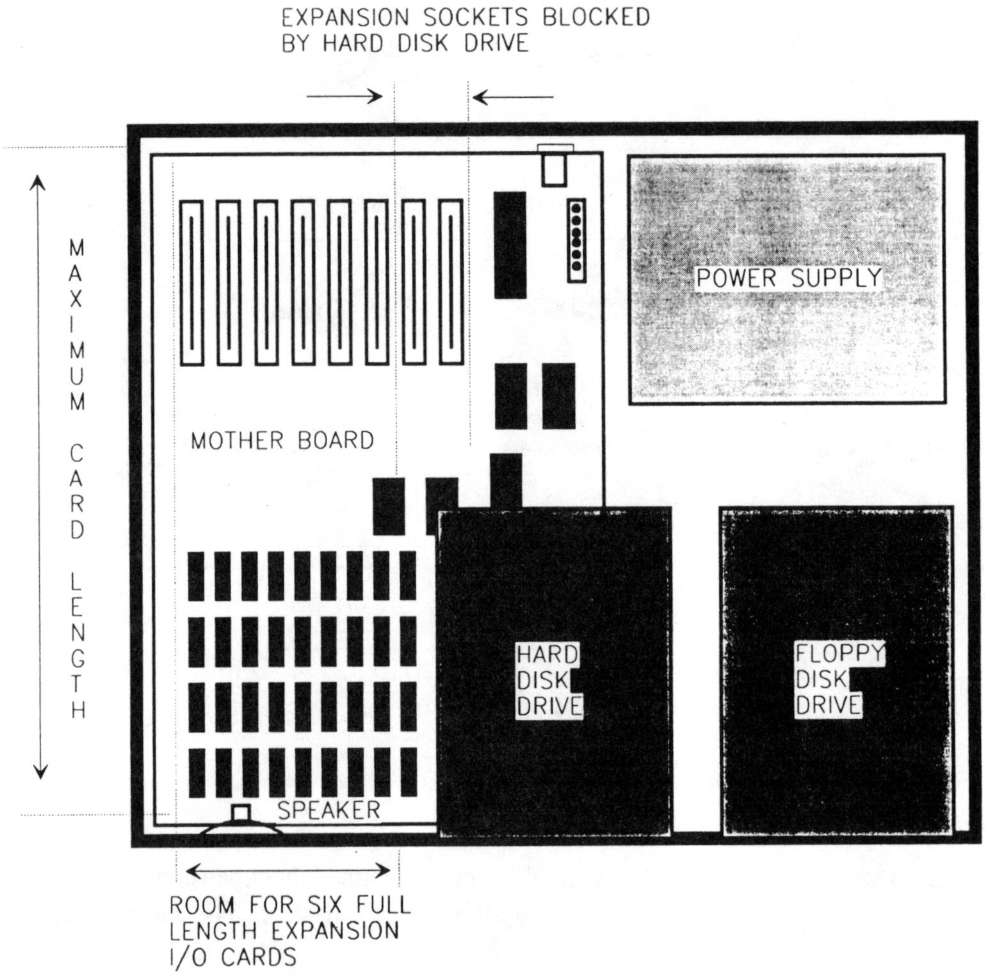

EXPANSION SOCKETS BLOCKED
BY HARD DISK DRIVE

**Figure 6.3** Restrictions on expansion slots

The drives are held in position by mounting screws on the sides of the drives. Screws should be used on both the left and right sides of the drive (especially the floppy disk drives), but you can get away with using only one side.

A new sliding plastic mount is available from some suppliers that lets you slide drives in and out of their mounts without removing screws. This is a useful addition when you need to service a drive, replace it, or if you want to be able to swap drives among machines. The cost is no more than standard screw-in mounts, so we suggest you look for it.

Figure 6.4 shows the two types of floppy disk mountings.

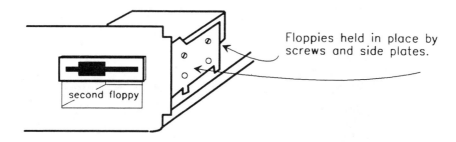

Floppies held in place by screws and side plates.

second floppy

A) XT TYPE MOUNTING PLATE & SCREWS

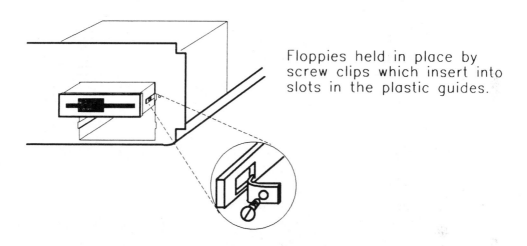

Floppies held in place by screw clips which insert into slots in the plastic guides.

B) AT TYPE SLIDE MOUNTS WITH CLIPS

**Figure 6.4**  **Floppy disk drive screw mountings**

Normally, the floppies are mounted toward the outside edge of the cabinet on the right and the hard disk drive or drives are mounted in the middle openings, as shown in Figure 6.5.

The floppies should also be mounted so that one is directly over the other one because the connectors on the controller cable are made to plug in that way. You can mount them side by side, but you will need a controller cable with widely spaced floppy connectors. The positioning of the hard disk drives follows the same reasoning.

Another nice feature to look for in an XT case is a Turbo Speed select switch and a Reset switch. The Turbo Speed switch lets you change the clock speed of the CPU from the outside without having to open up the case to change jumpers. The Reset switch is very handy for those times when a software problem causes

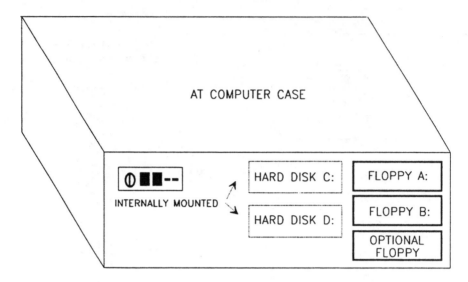

**Figure 6.5**   Normal mounting positions in an AT computer case

your machine to lock up. Instead of having to switch the power off and back on, you can just push the reset button. Quickly cycling the power off and on is a good way to damage the computer.

As for the power supply, there is only one choice today, and that is the 150-watt XT-compatible power supply. The power supply is a box measuring 6.25 inches wide by 6 inches deep by 6 inches high with the power switch protruding out of the side of the box. An AT-compatible power supply will not normally fit in the XT-style cases. It is important to specify a physically compatible XT-size power supply when ordering.

One feature that you can look for among the available XT-size power supplies is multiple floppy and hard drive power connectors. If you can get one with four connectors, you will have all that you will ever need, otherwise you may have to buy a power-splitter cable when you add your third or fourth drive.

## AT Case and Power Supply

The choices of AT case are varied. There are two categories, vertical and horizontal. Within the categories there are full size and mini or baby size. The choices depend on system needs and where you want to place the computer. Both types are shown in Figure 6.6.

The full-size vertical case frequently is called a tower. It measures approximately 7 inches wide by 17 inches deep by 25 inches tall. It normally has

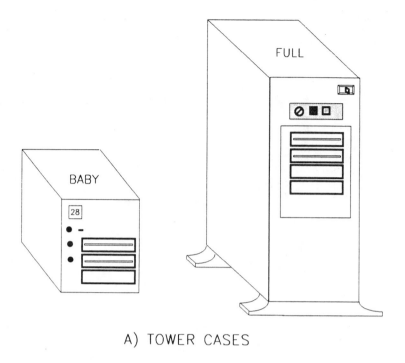

A) TOWER CASES

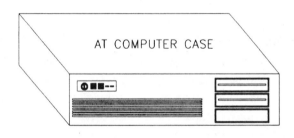

B) STANDARD HORIZONTAL CASE

**Figure 6.6**   **Tower and horizontal AT cases**

some type of support legs or footing so that it can sit on the floor in a vertical position adjacent to a desk.

This hummer is for the serious computer user. No problem mounting a large power supply in this baby. There is room for any size and type of motherboard you plan to use now or in the future:

- Full-size motherboard 12 inches wide by 13.75 inches deep
- Mini-size motherboard 8.5 inches wide by 13 inches deep

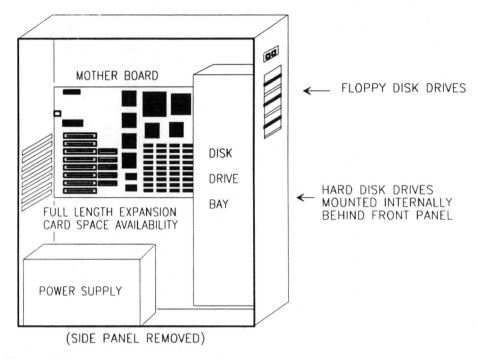

**Figure 6.7**   Disk drive possibilities in tower case configuration

Additionally, there is ample room for eight full-length expansion cards. However, the real reason for the large case is disk drive space. (See Figure 6.7.)

These tower cases can house six or seven 5.25-inch half-height drives. Typically, two 3.5-inch cage inserts will be included so that 3.5-inch drives can be mounted without any fuss. Some cases have all drive bays open so that technically you could install floppies in each bay. Other cases only have three or four bays exposed. The floppies are designed to go into the exposed bays with the hard disks being mounted in the other bays since access from the outside is not necessary or desired. Most users buying this style case intend to have three or more hard disk drives.

The mini-vertical case is a reduced-height (typically about 13 inches) cabinet. This cabinet will normally sit in a very small space on top of a desk and will only accept the mini-size 80286 and 80386 motherboard.

It may not be possible to use full-length expansion boards in all eight sockets of the motherboard, since the disk drive bays may partially block a couple of the sockets. The disk drive bays will be limited to two or three 5.25-inch drive openings and one or two 3.5-inch drive openings.

Why would you want a vertical case? As already mentioned, there is ample room for anything. Another reason is convenient access. The case's cover is easy

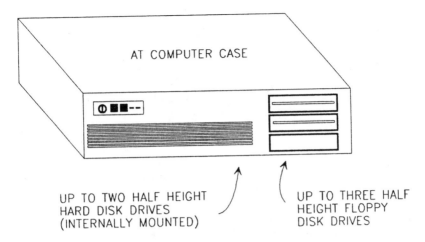

AT COMPUTER CASE

UP TO TWO HALF HEIGHT
HARD DISK DRIVES
(INTERNALLY MOUNTED)

UP TO THREE HALF
HEIGHT FLOPPY
DISK DRIVES

**Figure 6.8**  Configuration of the standard AT case

to remove. Once off, everything is easy to get at. Additionally, with the motherboard positioned vertically, there is less danger of dropping something on it and damaging it.

Why would you want a mini-vertical case? The main reason is that it takes up very little desk space. You can place it off on one side of the desk out of the way. Another convenience of it when sitting on your desk is that the disk drives are up high and thus easy to get to. The horizonal case that sits on your desk will typically have items piled up on the desk in front of the floppy drives.

The horizontal or AT-style case (see Figure 6.8) is cheaper than the vertical style case. The full-size AT case is about 21 inches wide by 17 inches deep by 6 inches high. The mini or baby size AT case is only 17 inches wide. Either one takes up a lot of desk space.

The AT style and baby AT cases have provisions for eight expansion cards with the usual two being blocked by the disk drives. That doesn't mean you can't use these slots, but you'll have to use only short cards in these slots. In addition, you may lose one more slot close to the power supply, either because the disk controller cables get in the way or because it, too, is behind the disk drive bay. You can probably get a very small card, such as a mouse controller, in these slots, or you can use them for a small modem. But you can't use eight full-sized cards in most AT style cases.

The mini case can typically hold only three 5.25-inch drives; whereas the full-size AT case can hold three exposed 5.25-inch drives and two hidden 5.25-inch drives. This is almost as good as the tower case.

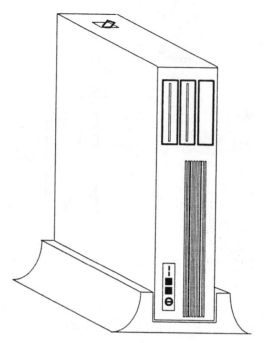

**Figure 6.9** Standard case mounted in clip-on stand

The full-size AT case has the advantage of being able to use either the normal-size AT motherboard or the mini motherboard. The mini case can only use the mini-size motherboard.

Some users find it convenient to place the standard horizontal case on the floor under a desk or beside your operating position. Many companies sell clip-on stands to help stabilize the case in this position. Just be sure the position you choose is secure and that the machine is in no danger of being pushed over. (Under a desk is a good location.) This mounting position (shown in Figure 6.9) also turns your disk drives on their side, which is OK, but some users have reported that for optimum operation they have to reformat the hard drives turned over in this fashion.

Both the vertical and horizontal AT cases come with standard front panel features. There are usually indicator lights for turbo-speed mode, power, and hard disk activity. A reset switch and keyboard disable switch will also be found.

Why would you choose one over the other? Cost is one reason. The full size vertical case with power supply will cost about $250 verses $100 for the full-size horizontal case with supply. Another reason is space. You simply may not have any place to put the computer except on the floor, which means a vertical case is best for you.

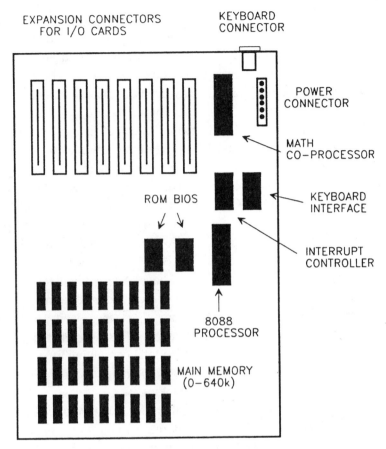

**Figure 6.10**   Basic XT motherboard, showing layout of components

# MOTHERBOARDS

## XT Motherboards

By far the most popular XT motherboard is identified as an 8088 Turbo motherboard with eight 8-bit expansion sockets. Most all operate at 8 MHz and some operate at 10 MHz. They can also operate at the traditional 4.77 MHz, but there is no need since speed-sensitive software has all but disappeared. You can still find a few five-slot XT motherboards that can reside in the very old, five-slot chassis; and there are some CPU options, such as the NEC V20 and V30 series. A basic XT motherboard layout is shown in Figure 6.10.

The BIOS probably will be the Phoenix, AMI, or Award version, which are among the most popular today. However, other companies including Quadtel and ERSO also offer BIOS for microcomputers. Both have a long history of successful operation. When purchasing the motherboard, it may be worthwhile to make sure that your copy of BIOS is legally licensed. Occasionally a vendor will copy a legal BIOS chip and install it in a bare motherboard, avoiding the required royalty payments. You can identify a bogus BIOS chip. The legal BIOS will have a professional label, while a copied BIOS may have no label or a handwritten paper label.

All the motherboards will hold at least 640 KB of RAM. Memory can be populated using either 4164 (64K) or 41256 (256K) memory chips, or a combination. For example, a total of eighteen 4164s and eighteen 41256 will give you the necessary 640 KB of RAM. Most programs of today require a minimum of 512K to run. DOS requires another 60 KB to 70 KB; therefore, 600 KB is a bare minimum of RAM these days, so you'll have to fully populate conventional memory to the maximum of 640 KB because of the memory design.

As for memory speed, 150-ns chips are fine since wait states are not implemented for the XT. When it is time to refresh the memory contents, everything stops. In fact, up to 7 percent of the total computing time is lost due to memory-refresh operations. The AT version of computers performs memory refresh operations when the processor isn't looking.

The math co-processor is a useful addition for some applications such as spreadsheets or a large database. When ordering it, you will need to know the speed of the clock signal supplied to the math co-processor socket. The 10-MHz clock will require an 8087-1 chip, an 8-MHz clock will require an 8087-2 chip, and the 4.77-MHz clock will use an 8087.

XT motherboards are cheap. Some of the older 4.77-MHz-only motherboards sell for as little as $69. The turbo versions are only $15 to $20 more.

## AT Motherboards

### Chip Sets

Today's 80286 motherboards are truly outstanding compared to their earlier counterparts. What makes these boards exceptional is the replacement of 30 to 50 regular logic chips with just a few super chips. These super chips not only do the job of the components that they replaced, they also do neat things like shadow ram, interleaved memory operation, and programmable wait states for memory. The leader of the pack is Chips and Technology NEAT chip set. See Figure 6.11.

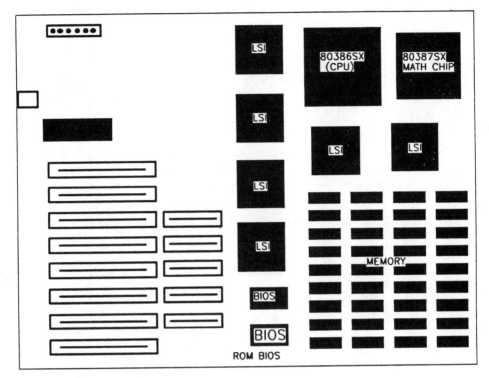

**Figure 6.11**    Key AT components

**Shadow Ram**    Shadow ram involves assigning high-speed RAM to the area of memory between 640 KB and 1 MB which is normally assigned to ROMs used by controllers and by the computer's ROM BIOS. Memory organization is shown in Figure 6.12. During the boot-up process when power is turned on or when the reset button is pushed, the contents of all the ROMs are copied into the faster RAM memory. The ROMs are then isolated by the chip set so that any memory-read operations that would have gone to the ROMs now go to the RAMs instead. The result is faster I/O operations, because the ROMs have slow memory access times.

Another benefit of shadow ram is that those memory locations that are not being used in this 640-KB to 1-MB range can now be utilized as expanded memory and high-memory. You may be able to gain as much as 150 KB of additional memory from this area. If you are using an EGA or VGA video card, this amount will be reduced since these cards will take 128 KB of the area for their use.

By utilizing this area as expanded memory, you can have a disk cache area without eating into your 640-KB main memory base. You can also move some of

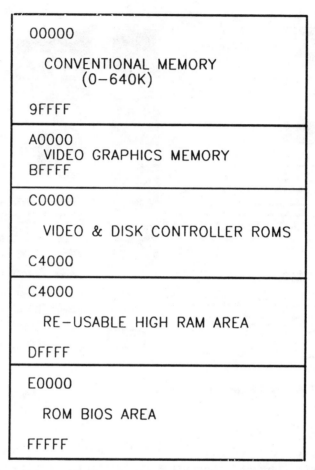

**Figure 6.12**   Allocation of RAM and ROM in high RAM usage area

your TSR (terminate, stay resident) software into this high-memory area and thus free up more main memory for programs.

Another feature of the NEAT chip set is that it supports LIM EMS 3.2 and EMS 4.0 expanded memory operation. This feature plus RAM remapping allows for easy implementation of expanded memory.

Finally, the NEAT chip set supports interleaved memory operation. This function allows slower memory chips to be used without any wait states. For example, the 16-MHz version of an 80286 motherboard would normally require 80-ns memory chips for zero wait states (uninterrupted processor operation). By utilizing the interleave memory concept, 100-ns memory chips can be used.

**Interleaved Memory**   What is interleaved memory? Interleaved memory operations divide the sequential memory banks into even and odd address

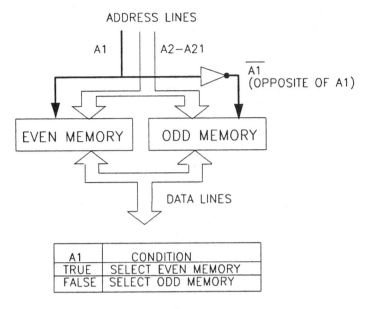

**Figure 6.13**  Diagram of interleaved memory operation

memory banks, as shown in Figure 6.13. When the processor is retrieving instructional information or data, it will be retrieving it from either the even or odd bank. While the memory bank yields its contents, the other bank of memory prepares for the next sequential memory operation in which it will have to respond. When its time comes, the other memory bank will prepare for the next sequential access. By bouncing back and forth between the odd and even memory banks in a sequential fashion, the slower memory chips can keep up with the processor without requiring a wait state (additional cycle of clock time).

Interleaving is not perfect, however. What happens when the operations are not sequential? Well, the memory controller will generate a wait state giving the slower memory a chance to respond. Even though wait states will be generated, they will not have to be generated continuously, as would be the case if interleaved operations were not employed. Overall, you will gain speed since a majority of the memory accesses will not require a wait state.

The NEAT chip set 80286 motherboards come as either 16 MHz or 20 MHz. The clock speeds can be switched down to 8 MHz if needed. They can hold up to 8 MB of memory (4 MB of DRAM and 4 MB of either SIPPs or SIMMs). There are usually 36 sockets for memory chips such as the 41256 (256K) or 41000 (1 MB). This means you will have either two or four megabytes depending on which chip you use. In addition to the DIP sockets there will be provisions for either four SIPP or four SIMM memory modules. You can also get these modules in either 256-KB or 1-MB capacity.

On some of the older 80286 boards, it is possible that the SIPP and SIMM memory modules will not be available. These boards will require their own special memory expansion board.

Non-NEAT chip set 80286 motherboards usually run at 12 MHz, switchable to 8 MHz. They do not perform shadow RAM or interleave memory operations and thus require 80-ns memory for zero wait-state operation at 12 MHz. One wait state is needed for 100-ns memory. These boards will typically hold up to 4 MB of memory using 1-MB DRAM memory chips. There is nothing wrong with these boards except that the performance is not as good when compared to the NEAT chip set boards.

Both types of boards have the built-in clock/calendar chips, the nonvolatile ram scratch pad, and eight expansion slots. The clock/calendar provides the system time and date functions. The clock/calendar is kept alive by a battery mounted either on the motherboard or on the case. The nonvolatile ram is used to store the hardware parameters so that when the computer is powered up, the processor can determine the preset configuration of the computer. Of the eight expansion slots, two or three slots will be for eight-bit expansion cards, such as parallel and serial I/O. The other five or six slots will be 16-bit types for the disk controllers and other VGA video cards.

**Math Co-Processor**   A math co-processor is an excellent addition if you do any serious computing other than word processing. Most programs will run an average of five times faster with the math co-processor installed. The 80286 will require the 80287 co-processor.

You need to determine the speed of the clock signal going to the math co-processor on the motherboard before ordering a co-processor. Just because the motherboard is rated at 12 MHz, 16 MHz, or 20 MHz doesn't mean the math co-processor will run at that speed. Depending on the design of the board, it could run at the system clock speed or slower.

Why not just order a co-processor rated for the clock speed of the motherboard? There is nothing wrong with doing this except that you will pay more for the higher speed. The price differences for co-processors of different speeds is not very much. Here are some mid-1990 comparative costs:

| | | |
|---|---|---|
| 80287-20 | (20 MHz) | $300 |
| 80287-12 | (16 MHZ) | $280 |
| 80287-10 | (12 MHz) | $240 |
| 80287-8 | (8 MHz) | $210 |

One unique thing to mention about the 80286 and its math co-processor is the way the two operate together. Unlike the 8087 co-processor for the 8088 and 8086 processors and the 80387 co-processor for the 80387 processor, the 80286 and 80287 operate asynchronously instead of synchronously.

If there is a math operation to be done by the math co-processor, the 80286 passes the data and instruction for math operation to the 80287 and then tells the co-processor to let it know when finished. The 80286 then proceeds to do something else. When finished, the 80287 signals the 80286 and the math portion of the program is continued. The 8087, 80387, and 80487 all require the processor to hang in limbo while it works. This is why an 80286 16-MHz computer with a math co-processor will appear to work faster than an 80386SX 16-MHz computer when doing extensive math operations.

# 80386 Motherboards

Much of the excitement at the start of 1990 was with 80386-based computers. High-performance VGA video graphics adapters, SCSI controllers and disk drives, and high-power software will run like molasses on a cold winter day without a fast and efficient CPU and memory architecture.

The 80386 motherboards are finally providing the computing power to do complex tasks in a near real-time mode. By using a 32-bit bus, interleaved or paged memory, and high-speed SRAM cache memory, they can perform awesome computations at lightning speed.

### Memory Management

The built-in memory management function offers the ultimate in memory resource allocation. No longer does the 640 KB of program memory have to reside at physical location 0–640K. The memory manager can place it anywhere it wants in the four gigabyte address range. In fact, it can create thousands of these 640-KB program areas and thus create a true multitasking computer.

The 80386 and the series to follow open the door to unlimited computing as we know it today. Memory bounds are essentially gone because these processors can reach out to 64 terabytes (64,000,000,000,000,000 bytes) of virtual memory. Presently, 33-MHz machines are common with 50 MHz and higher versions just around the corner.

Just as in the 80286, the Chips and Technology NEAT chip set is present in the 80386 machines. The same shadow ram, interleaved memory operations are present. A paged-mode memory operation is also available with the Chips and Technology CS8230 chip.

Unlike interleaved memory operations, which divides conventional memory into even and odd address banks, paged memory operations treat memory as blocks or chunks. This pagination scheme requires special DRAM memory chips that can be addressed as pages. Another name for this type of memory is static-column RAM.

## Paged Memory

A page is a small continuous section of memory. As long as the processor is reading and writing to this small section of memory, no wait states are necessary since the setup time required to access the next memory location is small. Should the processor need access to another page, a condition similar to the nonsequential access of the interleaved memory occurs (a wait state).

How does paging work? A DRAM's internal memory contents are accessed by specifying a RAS (row address select) and a CAS (column address select). Each time the processor requests something from memory, a RAS and CAS have to be generated. (See Figure 6.14.) The DRAM combines these two address directors internally to determine the correct page and the location within the page.

The special DRAMs minimize access time by remembering the RAS value. When a new memory request is made, the DRAM compares the new RAS value with the stored one. If they match, the DRAM only has to update the CAS value thus saving time. Should the memory request contain a different RAS than the one stored, the memory will work like conventional memory by combining the RAS and CAS and then accessing the location. Therefore, as long as the RAS remains constant (same page area), the DRAM requires less setup time to access its contents and thus a faster access time with no wait states.

## Memory Caching

Probably the most important onboard memory feature, the one that will make the most difference, is memory caching. Memory caching is like the print buffers for printers. The memory cache acts as a kind of buffer between the processor and the main memory. Its job is to provide the processor with what it needs from memory. Should it not have what the processor needs, it gets it from memory, passes it to the processor, and makes a copy for itself in case the processor asks for it again.

Why do we need a cache? Well, guess what memory speed you would need for a 33-MHz 80386 machine. How about 30-ns memory! You can't get DRAM that

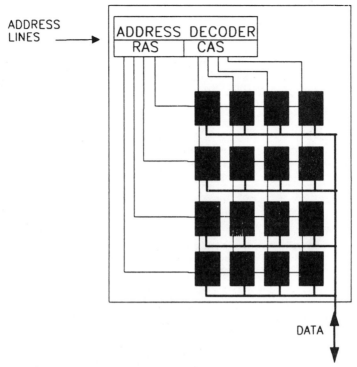

**Figure 6.14** Organization of paged memory

fast, and if you could, you would have to sell your car just to buy a few megabytes of it. A memory cache is a small 1-KB to 64-KB area of high-speed SRAM (static random access memory) that can meet these speed requirements. Its job is to allow the processor to operate unimpeded by memory constraints.

A special type of memory cache controller is needed to make everything work. When the processor requests a memory location, the cache controller examines the address to see if it already has that address tagged (address is contained in its reference table). If the address is tagged, the cache controller will allow the processor to access the cache memory. Should the tag not exist, the controller will generate the required wait states so that the information can be retrieved from the slower 60-ns or 80-ns main memory. As the information is being passed to the processor, a copy is stored in the cache memory. The corresponding address location will then be tagged for future reference should the processor request the same location. This type of caching is called "fully associated caching," as illustrated in Figure 6.15.

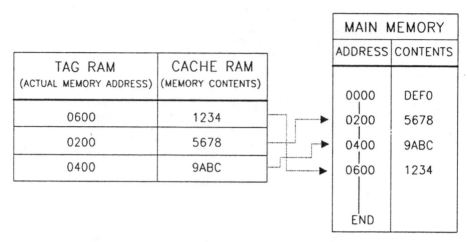

**Figure 6.15**   Operation of basic fully associated caching

When the tag address reference table is full, the controller uses a prioritizing scheme to decide which tag address is the least used. When a new tag address is required, the controller discards the selected tag and replaces it with the new tag.

Another type of caching control is called "direct-mapped caching." No tag addresses are used. The main memory is divided into sections equivalent to the memory cache. If the cache size is 32K, then the main memory is divided into 32-KB sections. The cache's memory locations corresponds exactly with the associated location in the presently selected 32-KB main memory section.

When a processor makes a request of memory, the controller looks to see if the information is in the cache. If not, it gets the contents of the location specified in the 32-KB main memory section, passes it to the processor, and stores a copy in the associated 32K memory section of the cache for future use. This operation is illustrated in Figure 6.16.

The problem with direct-mapped caching is that when a request from just one location outside of the 32-KB block is made, the entire 32-KB cache memory is flushed in preparation for the new 32-KB block. If the processor is bouncing back and forth between 32-KB memory boundaries, memory access times rise dramatically due to the constant flush and reload of the cache. Thus, the cache is ineffective or even detrimental. This problem is solved with a two-way associative cache. Here, the cache is split in half with one half handling one 32-KB boundary block and the other half handling another 32-KB boundary block. This division of boundaries reduces the number of occurrences of flush and reload.

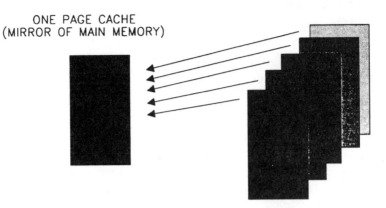

A COMPLETE MEMORY PAGE IS COPIED INTO THE CACHE.

**Figure 6.16**   Basic direct-mapped cache operation

As a note, the access time to main memory is longer than it would normally be when a memory cache section is present in the system. Normally, only one or two wait states would be added to each memory read or write operation to allow the slower memory to work with the faster CPU. If caching is used, not only will you have the normally required wait states, but you will also incur additional delays as the information passes back through the cache memory and controller. Thus, memory accesses outside of the cache memory will be slower than normal. To minimize this time penalty, the cache memory must be of a minimum size.

How big a cache do you need? A 2-KB cache will meet the 60-percent minimum "hit rate." Intel has an 8-KB cache built into its new 80486 processor. An 8-KB cache should get you in the 80-percent range. Larger caches will get you closer to the 90-percent point, but remember that this memory is very expensive so you will be paying a lot to gain a little increase in hit rate.

Hit rate is a measure of the cache's performance. Hit rate is determined by the ratio of the number of cache memory accesses versus main memory accesses. An 80-percent hit rate would imply that the processor was able to get what it needed from the cache's memory 80 percent of the time. To be effective, the hit rate should be 60 percent or more; otherwise, you will be spending half your time waiting on the slow main memory.

$$\text{HIT RATE} = \frac{\text{cache memory accesses}}{\text{main memory accesses}} \times 100$$

Most of the 80386 motherboards have either the direct or two-way associative cache. The fully associative cache is complex and more costly to build into the boards. You will only find it on a few high-performance 80386 motherboards.

Motherboards with memory caching will cost about $400 or more than a motherboard without caching. It is certainly nice to have, but as to whether it is justifiable, only you can decide based on the quantity and intensity of the computer's expected operation.

## *Math Co-Processor*

One important feature to look for on 80386 motherboards is the math co-processor support. As in the 80286 motherboards, clock speed at the math co-processor's socket has to be determined to choose the correct math co-processor. For the 80287 the price differences were relatively small. For the 80387 the price differences in mid-1990 were more noticeable:

| | | |
|---|---|---|
| 80387-33 | (33 MHz) | $650 |
| 80387-25 | (25 MHz) | $500 |
| 80387-20 | (20 MHz) | $400 |
| 80387-16 | (16 MHz) | $350 |

There are a couple of 80386 motherboards that will accept an 80287 math co-processor. The intent was to offer an economical choice for a math co-processor.

Ideally, the motherboard should support both the 80387 math co-processor and the Weitek 3167 or 1167 FPU math processor. The Weitek math processor can do math operations much faster than the 80387, as well as some additional functions. Some motherboards will support both the Weitek and the Intel 80387, but the majority will only support one or the other.

The dual math co-processor support is ideal if you have software that uses one but not the other, and vice versa. If possible, the Weitek unit should be used—but not all software is capable of supporting it.

One final note. Check to see what kind of documentation and support you get with the motherboard you choose. Most vendors supply nothing but a very thin paperback booklet. Manufacturers like Mylex, AMI, and Micronics provide informative and detailed manuals. Intel provides a 200-plus page paperbound book. JDR and Jameco provide technical assistance over the phone. Others like Intel and Mylex will refer you to a local dealer.

## 80386SX Motherboards

Ok, you want an 80386 system, but you just can't stand the price. Well, Intel provided an answer—the 80386SX. As per our discussion in previous chapters, the 80386SX is an 80386 in a 80286's 16-bit world. Internally, the 80386SX works as a 80386. Externally, it has to look at everything in 16-bit chunks instead of 32 bits. Most manufacturers of 80286 motherboards can easily redesign their boards to replace the 80286 with the 80386SX.

Most of the 80386SX motherboards come with the NEAT chip set, and thus they have the shadow ram and interleaved memory features.

They typically have 36 DIP sockets for 256-KB or 1-MB memory chips. There is also room for either four SIPP or four SIMM 256-KB or 1-MB memory modules.

The math co-processor will have to be an 80387SX; however, we have seen some that can use the 80387. As a rule the 80386SX motherboard will require the 80387SX math co-processor.

These motherboards do not come with memory caching mainly because they are designed as a low-entry 80386 machine. Their sole purpose is to provide an economic entry point for the next generation of software that will require the memory management features of the 80386 and follow-on processors.

The 80386SX motherboards make excellent upgrades for old XTs and ATs. Although a 16-MHz 80286 will outperform the 16-MHz 80386SX, the unique memory management feature of the 80386SX will soon overshadow the performance. Through its ability to do more from a software standpoint, it will handle a broader range of tasks both now and in the future.

## 80486 Motherboards

This processor represents another advancement in performance. It claims to be two to four times faster than the 80386. This improvement is due to a fully redesigned register unit, a built-in 8-KB memory cache, and a built-in FPU compatible with the 80387 math co-processor. By having the improved register unit and FPU on the same chip, operations can be performed more quickly. Intel also added hardware and software improvements to facilitate multiprocessing applications.

# MATH CO-PROCESSORS

Most programs that deal with graphics or perform extensive calculations will benefit greatly from the use of a math co-processor. Why? Well, for handling integer math operations, the processor's logic does a fair job. When it comes to floating-point calculations (numbers expressed as a power of 10) and transcendental functions (sine, cosine), the processor must depend on software routines for the math functions. According to Intel's list of reported software, the math co-processor can result in programs running five times faster.

The question is which math co-processor to use. If you are using an Intel processor (8088, 80286, 80386, 80386SX, or 80486), the answer seems apparent—an 80X87 where X is a blank, 2, 3, or 4 depending on the companion processor type. This is a fine choice; but there are others to choose from such as Weitek's 3167, Integrated Information Technology's NP-3C87, and Cyrix Corporation's 83D87 (all for the 80386-class machines).

As for hardware compatibility, the NP-3C87 and 83D87 are hardware compatible with the 80387 and thus a direct replacement. The Weitek math processor is designed to work as a memory mapped device, and thus requires a special interface. Each have unique features that may benefit you for a particular application.

To use these math co-processors, the software you purchase must state which type or types it will support. If you are writing your own programs, there are many high-level compilers that will support some or all of the math co-processors. So again it is important that you select the software products you intend to use before purchasing a math co-processor.

## IEEE 754 Floating-Point Standard

Prior to 1985, computer hardware manufacturers used their own unique form of FPU (floating-point unit), which performed math operations in totally different ways. The result was that programs written in Fortran, for example, would generate different numerical results when run on different machines. The problem was due to the number of significant digits and the method of implementing floating-point numbers.

In 1985 a standard format for representing floating-point numbers was established. It was called the IEEE 754-1985 standard. IEEE stands for the Institute of Electrical and Electronics Engineers. The standard defined the formats of single precision numbers as being 32 bits, double floating-point precision numbers as being 64 bits, and gave a standardized list of math functions to be available for calculation purposes. The standard only established a minimum. Manufacturers were free to add additional bits to the mantissa for increased accuracy, but at least everyone would march to the same beat.

The IEEE floating-point format is shown in the accompanying table. The sign bit is a 1 if the number is negative and a 0 for positive. The number itself is converted to a base 2 number. The number is then divided by 2 until the most significant bit is a 1. The remainder is stored as the significant digit and the number of divisions by 2 becomes the exponent. The basic problem with this methodology is that for each power of 2 represented by the exponent, the significand's precision drops by 50 percent. The result is that many calculations can result in inexact numbers that have to be rounded to the notation's limit to ensure their accuracy at that level.

**The IEEE Floating-Point Formats**

|  | Sign (+/–) | Exponent (power of 2) | Significand (base 2's decimal equivalent) |
|---|---|---|---|
| single real: | 1 bit | 8 bits | 23 bits |
| double real: | 1 bit | 11 bits | 53 bits |

# Intel Co-Processors

Unlike earlier math co-processors for eight-bit microcomputers, Intel designed their math processors to be extension floating-point units (FPU) that would be extensions of the CPU. This way floating-point instructions could be used and executed either by software routines or by a math co-processor, if present. If the co-processor was not present, a software interrupt would be generated. This action would cause the execution of a math co-processor software emulator. By handling math execution in this manner, software development became greatly simplified.

The format of the Intel 80387 math co-processor is shown in the accompanying table. The internal formats of the 8087 and 80287 are nearly identical. The 8087 and 80287 do not have sine and cosine functions but the 80387 does.

### 80387 Internal Format

| Data Register | Sign (+/–) | Exponent (power of 2) | Significand (base 2's decimal equivalent) |
|---|---|---|---|
| R0 | 1 bit | 15 bits | 64 bits |
| R1 | 1 bit | 15 bits | 64 bits |
| . . . | . . . | . . . | . . . |
| R7 | 1 bit | 15 bits | 64 bits |

All the data registers are 80 bits wide and hold numbers in double-extended format to increase the digits of precision. The multiple registers are like the memory storage functions on calculators, which can be used to store intermediate results during a long calculation. Another handy feature of this co-processor series is the ability to handle 16, 32, and 64-bit integers and 18-bit binary coded integers.

The Intel co-processors have continued to improve in performance. The latest versions of the 80387-33 are reported to run faster than a 80387-25 operated at 33 MHz. It is apparent that internal architecture changes have been made to speed things up. Astonishingly, the 80487 processor incorporates a math co-processor directly on the processor itself that is 80387-compatible.

If there were one drawback, it would have to be the inability to use more than one math co-processor in a system. To compete in large-scale number crunching, multiple FPUs are handy if not necessary.

# Intel Compatible

## *NP-3C87*

The NP-3C87 is an 80387 replacement with enhanced features. It is made by Integrated Information Technology. It is claimed by its manufacturer to operate two to three times faster than the 80387 when performing some commonly used math functions. It achieves this increased throughput by wider-interval data paths and improved algorithmic routines. Unique features of the NP-3C87 are the ability to perform a $4 \times 4$ matrix operation and the availability of 32 internal registers. The matrix functions should have great appeal to statistics and other programs that involve linear math operations.

## *83D87*

The 83D87 is also an 80387 replacement with enhanced features. It is made by Cyrix Corporation. Its claim to fame is improved speed in transcendental functions through the use of polynomials and increased accuracy in calculations (10 bits more). Transcendental functions can be calculated an order of magnitude faster than the 80387. It also performs simple math functions such as add, subtract, multiply, and divide much faster than the NP-3C87.

All the other types of math co-processors use algorithms developed by J. E. Volder, a mathematician of the 1950s. The algorithms were written for a computer called the CORDIC. The algorithms were fine for the machines of that day, but today's microcomputers have far greater capability.

Cyrix chose to use polynomials to do transcendental functions. A problem with using polynomials to approximate functions is that the error between the approximated value and the real thing is proportional to the number of terms or elements in the polynomial series used to approximate the functions. Cyrix has proven mathematically that the accuracy of their polynomial approximations are monotonic and correct to the last decimal place of the IEEE standard for double-extended floating-point numbers.

Another interesting feature of the 83D87 is that it can operate as a memory-mapped device. This will do two things for you. First, you have faster access to the math co-processor. Second, multiple math co-processors can exist simultaneously in the same system.

## *Weitek*

Unlike the Integrated Information Technology and Cyrix math co-processors, the Weitek Corporation makes numeric processors for several other CPUs, such as Sun's SPARC and Motorola. The Weitek 3167, probably its best-selling processor, is for the Intel 80386 family of processors.

The 3167 does not use the built-in co-processor interface like the other math co-processors. Instead, it is memory-mapped into a fixed 64-KB block of the memory at hex location C0000000-C000FFFF. This presents a problem to Intel processors that operate in the protected mode, since access above hex FFFFF is denied.

Data is written and read from the data bus as in any memory operation. The difference between this processor and the others is that a specific math function is executed merely by selecting a specific address as opposed to sending a math instruction over the data bus. It is this approach that gives the Weitek the competitive edge.

The Weitek does have some drawbacks. It does not support double-extended format, so there is a loss of precision. This also means that it doesn't conform to the IEEE standard. The instruction set is also smaller in comparison to the other processors; however, the ones that it does implement are lean and mean.

The Weitek does offer special features. Although the instruction set is reduced, it has a class of instructions that are particular to signal processing. If fast Fourier transforms are your thing, the Weitek is a good choice. The other feature of the Weitek is its unique method of encoding instructions by placing the source and destination register numbers in the least significant bits of a memory address. Clever programmers can use the string load-and-store instructions of the 80386 to perform matrix operations with the registers of the Weitek.

# STORAGE

## Floppy Disk Drives

Choosing floppy disk drives is almost as simple as picking an XT motherboard. Your choices are limited to just two sizes and four storage densities. Some brand names claim to be better quality than others; but when you consider that the average price of a floppy drive in mid-1990 was only $80, we don't expect the drive to last forever.

As a rule the better-known brands such as TEAC, Mitsubishi, and Fujitsu, which cost the most, do operate very quietly. This can be interpreted as having a quality design and construction, but this doesn't mean that they work any better than the $50 special that makes a grinding noise as it slides the head back and forth over the floppy disk.

As for size, you have a choice of the older 5.25-inch floppies or the newer 3.5-inch floppies. (See Figure 6.17.) The 5.25-inch drives are available in either 360-KB (360,000 byte) or 1.2-MB (1,200,000 byte) density versions. The 3.5-inch floppies come in 720-KB and 1.44-MB density versions. All drives are half-height drives. The only full-height drives are surplus ones. You will be hard pressed to use full-height floppies, since all cases today come equipped to use half-height floppy disk drives.

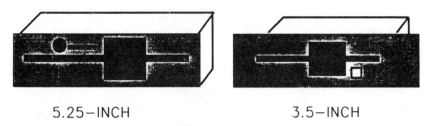

5.25—INCH                          3.5—INCH

**Figure 6.17**   **The two types of floppy disk drives**

## *5.25-Inch Floppy Disk Drives*

The 360-KB floppy disk drive used to be the most common form of data storage for floppies. It is rapidly being replaced by the 3.5-inch 720-KB and 1.44-MB floppies. Still, the 360-KB floppies are extremely cheap. The drives sell for as little as $50 and the diskettes for as little as 10¢.

The 360-KB floppy disk drives can only use the 360-KB density floppies. If you try to use a 1.2-MB floppy in a 360-KB disk drive, it won't work. This is because the 1.2-MB floppy disk requires a stronger magnetic signal to write data onto it. The 360-KB floppy disk drive just can't do it.

The 1.2-MB floppy disk drive can use both the standard 360-KB and 1.2-MB floppy diskettes. It can perform this dual task by being able to switch between high and low signal-strength modes when writing data to the disk.

The reason for the two signal-strength modes is the recording density. To record 1.2 MB of data on the same size floppy as the 360-KB floppy requires two things. First, the number of tracks is doubled from 40 to 80. Second, twice as much data must be packed in each track on the diskette. Since both types of floppy diskettes rotate at the same speed, you must increase the signal strength as you increase data density (bits-per-inch density).

How does the drive know which signal-strength mode to use? When the computer accesses the floppy disk drive, it will read the FAT (file allocation file). The DOS (disk operating system) will immediately recognize the diskette's format. If you are formatting a disk, you must tell DOS the type of diskette being formatted by adding the proper option flag at the end of the format command.

For example, if floppy disk drive A were a 1.2-MB version, you would type FORMAT A: /4 to format a 360-KB floppy diskette. To format a 1.2-MB floppy diskette on the same drive, you would type FORMAT A: with no option flag. DOS would have determined on booting up that the drive was a 1.2-MB disk drive by reading the hardware reference memory. Thus, an option flag would only be necessary for formatting a 360-KB disk. If the disk drive were a 360-KB drive, no option flags would be needed since you can only use 360-KB diskettes.

When using the 1.2-MB floppies, the disk drive will operate in the high signal-strength mode. If a 360-KB floppy is used, it will operate in the low signal-strength mode unless told to do otherwise.

It is possible to operate in the high signal-strength mode with the 360-KB floppy diskette, but long-term effects are unpredictable since the 360-KB floppy diskette's material is not designed to cope with the higher signal strengths.

You will be playing with a data time bomb if you attempt this. Don't be fooled by the fact that the 360-KB floppy disk is formatted to a 1.2-MB capacity. Within a few days or weeks, data and/or programs will disappear as you begin to get data read and write errors.

### 3.5-Inch Floppy Disk Drive

The 3.5-inch floppy disk drive today is a 1.44-MB type that can read and write in both the 1.44-MB and the older 720-KB formats. The portable laptop computers generally come with 3.5-inch 720-KB only floppy disk drives because they are cheap. You will find it hard to purchase a 720-KB only version, and we find it hard to understand why anyone would want too.

Just like its 5.25-inch 1.2-MB counterpart, the 3.5-inch 1.44-MB floppy has two signal-strength modes. The high mode is for the higher-density 1.44-MB disks and the low mode is for the lower-density 720-KB disks. Additionally, you can format the 720-KB disks as if they were 1.44-MB disks just like the 5.25-inch 1.2-MB counterpart can. The results will also be the same—unreliable operation. However, it is difficult to pull this trick on the 3.5-inch disks.

Unlike its 5.25-inch cousin, the 3.5-inch disks are encased in hard plastic shells. (See Figure 6.18.) The 3.5-inch disks also differ in that the higher-density floppies are identified by a hole in the case on the side opposite the write protect switch. To fool the disk drive into thinking the 720-KB is really a 1.44-MB floppy, you have to either punch or drill a hole in the floppy disk's plastic shell. With the prices of floppies getting cheaper every day, we don't understand why anyone would bother making this alteration.

The 3.5-inch floppies are the standard for the future. Several versions are projected to be available in the near future with capacities of 3, 5, and 20 megabytes. It would be wise to have at least one 3.5-inch floppy drive in your system for present and future compatibility reasons.

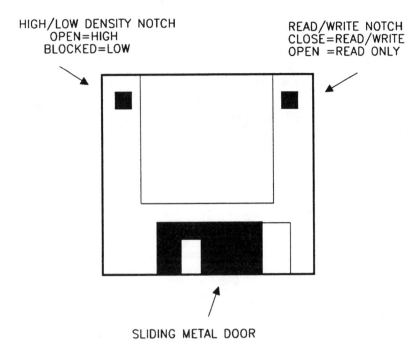

**Figure 6.18**   A 3.5-inch floppy disk

## *Floppy Disk Drive Controllers*

When choosing a floppy disk drive controller, you should make sure that it will support all four floppy types: 360K, 720K, 1.2M, and 1.44M. Even though you may initially use only 360-KB 5.25-inch floppies, don't lock yourself out of future possibilities. A floppy controller that can handle all four types only costs about $20 more.

There is a wide variety of floppy controllers to choose from. Some are just plain A and B drive controllers. Others can control up to four floppy disk drives and can be configured as either the main or secondary controller, as shown in Figure 6.19. You can also purchase a multi-I/O floppy controller board. This board will have a floppy controller, a parallel port, a serial port with an option for a second port, a clock/calendar circuit, and game ports.

Don't be surprised by the fact that all floppy drive controllers come as 8-bit bus cards. Why? Because a floppy drive is a slow device, and a 16-bit bus card won't do a thing toward speeding up operations.

If you plan to upgrade your computer to a larger hard disk, it may be worth your while to use separate floppy and hard disk controllers. The combined

FLOPPY DRIVES A & B

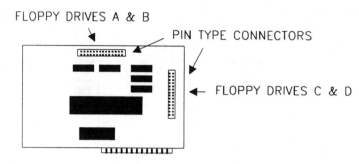

PIN TYPE CONNECTORS

FLOPPY DRIVES C & D

A) FOUR FLOPPY CONTROLLER

FLOPPY DRIVES A & B

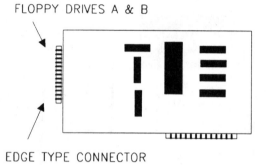

EDGE TYPE CONNECTOR

**Figure 6.19**   Two types of floppy disk drive controllers

hard/floppy drive controller will be more expensive to replace in comparison to just replacing a hard disk only controller. Besides, if you upgrade to an ESDI or SCSI hard disk, you may have to purchase a floppy drive controller anyway.

# Hard Disk Drives

### *Physical Characteristics*

Hard disks presently come in several form sizes. Hard disk drives are referred to as either 5.25-inch or 3.5-inch drives. The size refers to the size of the platters inside the drive unit. The other form factor is height. The drives will come in both half-height and full-height. The half-height drives are usually disk drives that are 100 MB or less in capacity.

Before ordering either size of disk drive, you should carefully examine the available disk drive slots in your computer case to determine which size (3.5-inch or 5.25-inch) and height (half-height, 1.75-inch or full-height, 3.5-inch) disk drive

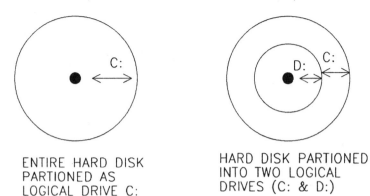

(TOP VIEW OF HARD DISK PLATTER)

ENTIRE HARD DISK
PARTIONED AS
LOGICAL DRIVE C:

HARD DISK PARTIONED
INTO TWO LOGICAL
DRIVES (C: & D:)

**Figure 6.20**  Partitioning of a hard disk

will properly fit. If you should order a full-height drive and find that it doesn't fit, it may cost you a 15 percent restocking fee to return the hard disk.

The 3.5-inch drives are becoming more popular since they are used in laptop and portable computers. The 3.5-inch drives are also nice from the standpoint that you could install them in either a 3.5-inch or 5.25-inch disk drive slot. To mount the drive in the 5.25-inch slot will require extra mounting hardware that costs less than $10.

### Access Times

A hard disk with a specified average access time of 85 ms will actually have access times ranging from 15 ms to 150 ms. The time depends on how far the heads have to move to get to the next track. The advertised access times represent an averaged value, but since everyone measures this parameter the same way, it is a useful tool for comparing different hard disks.

One way to improve the access time is to partition the hard disk into two or more small units, as shown in Figure 6.20. When you select a partition to use, your access will be limited to a subset of the total cylinders. This restriction means that the heads don't have to move as far as they would if the whole hard disk was being used as one partition.

Using a disk with access times less than 80 ms for an XT-class computer will not gain you anything since the XT has its hands full with just an 80-ms disk. On the other hand, an AT-class computer can handle the 40-ms disk drive without any trouble. For the 80386-class computers, a 28-ms disk drive is recommended.

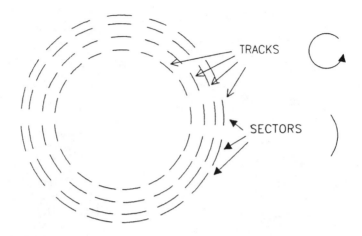

**Figure 6.21**   Tracks and sectors on a typical hard disk

## Interleave Factor

Data on the hard disk is arranged in concentric circles called tracks. The tracks are divided into sectors, as shown in Figure 6.21. Each sector will hold a fixed number of bytes. Depending on the computer's ability to receive data from the hard disk, data may be recorded on the track sectors in one of several sequences.

The controller writes data onto the hard disk a sector at a time. If the computer is fast enough, data will be stored sequentially sector by sector. If the computer or hard disk controller is not able to handle this transfer speed, the data will be stored sequentially on every other sector as the disk spins around. This would require two rotations of the disk to write to all sectors.

This method of writing a sector and then skipping one or more sectors is called interleaving. (See Figure 6.22.) For every sector you skip before writing to another sector, the platter must rotate an additional time for the sectors skipped. In the first method where sectors were written sequentially, a 1-to-1 (1:1) interleave factor was used. The platter only had to rotate one time in order to write all 17 sectors. In the second method where every other sector was written, a 2-to-1 (2:1) interleave factor was used. The platter had to rotate twice in order to write all sectors. Thus the interleave factor defines the sector stepping sequence (number of sectors passing beneath a head) and the number of rotations required to write the entire track.

XT-class computers have an interleave range from 6:1 to 3:1 depending on the speed (4.77 MHz, 8 MHz, or 10 MHz) of the computer and the type of hard disk controller. AT-class computers use either a 2:1 or 1:1 interleave. A 1:1 factor

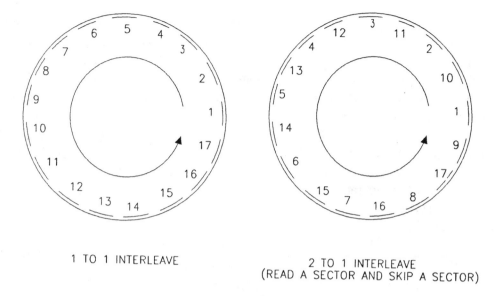

1 TO 1 INTERLEAVE

2 TO 1 INTERLEAVE
(READ A SECTOR AND SKIP A SECTOR)

**Figure 6.22**   **The interleave factor demonstrated**

represents the optimum data transfer rate since all data is read or written in one rotation of the platter.

## *Data Transfer Rate*

Another important characteristic to consider is data transfer rate of the disk controller. For XT computers even a five-megabit (625 KB/sec) transfer rate is overwhelming. In fact a turbo XT with an RLL hard disk (7 megabits/sec) is doing well if it can handle a 3:1 interleave with a data transfer rate of approximately 280 KB/sec. The AT-class machines usually have no problem using a 1:1 interleave at the specified data transfer rate of the controller. Of course the actual data transfer rate is less than the specified data rate since error corrections to the data will occur as it is being retrieved from the hard disk, thus reducing the rate by a small amount.

For an ST-506 controller with a 3:1 interleave and a 3600-RPM (60 revs/sec) hard disk with 17 sectors and 512 bytes per sector, the transfer rate is

$$\text{data transfer rate} = \frac{\text{revs}/\text{sec} \times \text{number of sectors} \times \text{bytes}/\text{sector}}{\text{interleave factor}}$$

$$\text{data transfer rate} = \frac{522{,}240 \, \text{bytes}/\text{sec}}{3} = 174{,}080 \, \text{bytes}/\text{sec}$$

The 2,7 RLL data-encoding method stores 50 percent more data on a disk than the MFM method. The hard disk for an RLL controller must have a higher density capacity than one for an MFM controller. These disks are identified as RLL types by the letter R at the end of the part number. You can use the MFM disk drive with the RLL controller, but it is doubtful if the data will remain on the disk. One day you will try to run a program or access a data file only to find you have disk read errors. The data density of the recording media must match the recording method for reliable operation. Short term, things will appear to work okay, but in the long term (days or weeks), erratic operation will be noted.

The data transfer rates of the different types of controllers are listed in the following table.

|  | Type | Transfer Rate |
|---|---|---|
| (ST-506) | MFM | 5 megabits/second |
|  | RLL | 7 megabits/second |
|  | ESDI | 5 to 15 megabits/second |
|  | SCSI | 16 to 32 megabits/second |

## Type Numbers

When installing a hard disk you will need to know the number of cylinders and heads, and the write precompensation value. These values are stored by the computer in its hardware setup memory so that it will know how to talk to the hard disk. The computer identifies these three values by a type number. The following table lists a few typical values from one PC BIOS.

| Type | Cylinders | Heads | Write Comp | Capacity (megabytes) |
|---|---|---|---|---|
| 1 | 306 | 4 | 128 | 10 |
| 2 | 615 | 4 | 300 | 21 |
| 3 | 615 | 6 | 300 | 32 |
| 4 | 940 | 8 | 512 | 65 |
| 5 | 940 | 6 | 512 | 49 |
| 6 | 615 | 4 | None | 21 |
| 7 | 462 | 8 | 256 | 32 |
| 8 | 733 | 5 | None | 32 |
| 9 | 900 | 15 | None | 32 |
| 10 | 820 | 3 | None | 21 |

| Type | Cylinders | Heads | Write Comp | Capacity (megabytes) |
|------|-----------|-------|------------|----------------------|
| 11 | 855 | 5 | None | 37 |
| 12 | 855 | 7 | None | 52 |
| 13 | 306 | 8 | 128 | 21 |
| 14 | 733 | 7 | None | 44 |
| 16 | 612 | 4 | All | 21 |
| 17 | 977 | 5 | 300 | 42 |
| 18 | 977 | 7 | None | 59 |
| 19 | 1024 | 7 | 512 | 62 |
| 20 | 733 | 5 | 300 | 32 |
| 21 | 733 | 7 | 300 | 44 |
| 22 | 733 | 5 | 300 | 32 |
| 23 | 306 | 4 | None | 10 |
| 24 | 612 | 4 | 305 | 21 |
| 25 | 306 | 4 | None | 10 |
| 26 | 612 | 4 | None | 21 |
| 27 | 698 | 7 | 300 | 85 (ESDI) |
| 28 | 976 | 5 | 488 | 85 (ESDI) |
| 29 | 306 | 4 | All | 10 |
| 30 | 611 | 4 | 306 | 42 (ESDI) |
| 31 | 732 | 7 | 300 | 89 (ESDI) |
| 32 | 1023 | 5 | None | 89 (ESDI) |

Some examples of actual hard disk values and their type numbers are shown in the following table. It is interesting to note that for the ST251 and ST277R drives, a type 10 is specified even though a type 10 is for three heads and not six. As the operating system and software disk drivers are loaded, the head count is corrected in software.

## Type Number for Seagate Drives

| Product number | Capacity (megabytes) | Cylinders | Heads | Drive type # |
|----------------|----------------------|-----------|-------|--------------|
| ST125 | 21 | 615 | 4 | 2 |
| ST138 | 32 | 615 | 6 | 3 |
| ST138R | 32 | 615 | 4 | 2 |

| Product number | Capacity (megabytes) | Cylinders | Heads | Drive type # |
|---|---|---|---|---|
| ST157R | 49 | 615 | 6 | 3 |
| ST225 | 21 | 615 | 4 | 2 |
| ST238R | 31 | 615 | 4 | 2 |
| ST251 | 42 | 820 | 6 | 10* |
| ST277R | 65 | 820 | 6 | 10* |

* Hardware setup ROM stores drive as type 10 but driver software corrects DOS driver to 6 heads.

The write compensation number refers to the cylinder at which the signal level of the write head must increase in order to properly record data. This cylinder position is measured relative to the outside cylinder. This requirement is necessary because the velocity of the platter passing under the heads decreases as the heads move toward the center of the platters. Thus the recording density must increase in order to write the same amount of data on an ever smaller-size track or cylinder.

The setup software that comes with both a hard disk and the motherboard will help you through the setup procedure when the disk type has to be defined. Most hard disk drives come with a diskette containing a hard disk manager.

We purchased a ST-277R-1 (RLL) hard disk drive for our 386SX system. This disk drive has 820 cylinders, six heads, no write compensation, and a 65-MB formatted capacity. The setup software included with the motherboard did not have a hard disk type listed for this combination of cylinders and heads.

Luckily, a Disk Manager/Diagnostics software package by Ontrack was supplied with the Seagate drive. It took care of the whole problem. When we ran the software, it simply asked which of the Seagate drives we were using.

The type number it told the computer system was number 10, but type 10 was for 820 cylinders and three heads. This indicated we had only a 20-MB hard disk, according to the type tables for AT computers; however, everything worked fine. The software low-level formatted the hard disk and marked the bad spots. When it finished, there it was, a formatted 65-MB hard disk.

It then proceeded to ask us if we wanted to partition the disk into smaller logical drives. We told it to split the disk into two partitions of 30 and 35 MB. It couldn't have been simpler.

## Hard Disk Controllers

The MFM and RLL controllers can control a maximum of two hard disk drives and two floppy disk drives, if the floppy drive controller is present. (See Figure

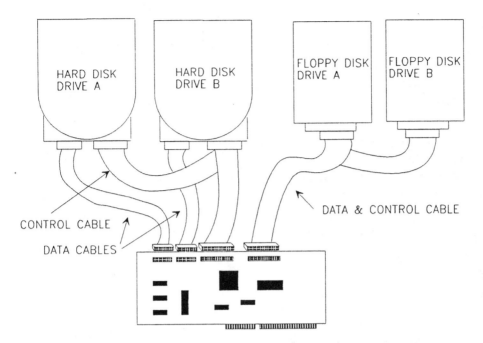

**Figure 6.23** Cable connections between controller and disk drives

6.23.) As mentioned previously, the MFM has a transfer rate of five megabits/second and the RLL has a transfer rate of seven megabits/second. They are available in either eight-bit or 16-bit versions.

The ESDI specification is really three in one: the enhanced small-disk interface (magnetic), the enhanced small-tape interface, and the enhanced small-disk interface (optical). The ESDI controller can talk to as many as seven devices, although current designs limit it to two devices.

The MFM, RLL, and ESDI controllers use a separate 20-pin data cable for each device and a common 34-pin control cable connected to each device. Cable lengths are limited to three meters.

The SCSI controller by itself is not a device interface. SCSI is a specification for the physical and electrical characteristics of a bus for interconnection of devices. It acts as a coordinator for the devices connected on the bus.

The SCSI controller is able to operate a total of eight devices using one 50-pin cable daisy-chained between the devices. Recall that the MFM, RLL, and ESDI use a separate data and control cable with a maximum cable length of three meters. The maximum cable length for the SCSI is six meters.

When the processor needs information from the hard disk, the SCSI controller has to first convert the processor's commands into SCSI bus commands and then send them to the SCSI hard disk on the bus. The hard disk has to interpret the commands. Data is then passed from the SCSI hard disk to the SCSI controller and to the processor.

These extra steps to retrieve data is why the ESDI controller has a speed advantage even though its data transfer rate is less than that of the SCSI interface. Since the ESDI controller only has to execute a one-step process of moving the heads and then reading the data, it can process information more quickly even though it is at a slower rate.

There are several advantages to the SCSI type of controller. The fundamental advantage of the SCSI is that it is composed of intelligent devices. The computer can command a device to do something and then leave. The device will then operate on its own without further assistance from the processor.

The design burden of the SCSI controller is relegated to the devices themselves and not the controller. This way the designer can select the best device controller for each device.

Another advantage is that the data lines of the SCSI bus are less susceptible to interference.

An MFM controller is cheap. Some go for as little as $50. The RLL controller is in the $100 range. An ESDI controller will set you back $200 or more. A SCSI controller will cost $400 or more.

Almost all hard disk controllers come with an onboard ROM BIOS. Its function is to perform the low-level formatting, mark bad sectors, and do disk partitioning. To access the ROM BIOS you will have to use the DOS Debug software. The sequence will usually go something like this:

```
A:>        (the DOS prompt will be on the screen)
A:>DEBUG   (you type the debug command)
-          (the debug prompt appears)
-G=C800:X  (execute ROM BIOS program)
```

The X value is 5 for the WD1002S-WX2 Western Digital controller and CCC (hex) for the Adaptec ACB-2070A controller. Both controllers are for XT-class computers.

The ROM BIOS program will ask you questions about your hard disk and computer, and then proceed to initialize and set up your hard disk. You do not have to use the ROM BIOS. In fact you can set a jumper on the controller card to disable it.

The Adaptec controllers and some others come with ROM BIOS. The Adaptec has a provision on the controller to either enable or disable the ROM BIOS. If ordering another brand, be sure to check and see if the ROM BIOS can be disabled. The OS/2 operating system will not function properly with the ROM activated, so keep this in mind should you encounter problems when trying to install OS/2 or any of the new operating systems when they become available.

Why choose a controller with a ROM BIOS on it? Well, the principal reason would be that the BIOS is tailored to take advantage of the enhanced design features of the controller. The controller may be able to perform faster-than-normal data transfers, thus requiring special optimization testing of the computer and hard disk. There could also be other reasons known only to the designer of the controller card. Regardless of the reason, you shouldn't buy a controller card that will not allow you to disable the ROM BIOS function if you so desire.

## *Selecting a Controller*

When looking for a hard disk controller, there are a list of things that you will have to know. You need to know the format type, whether you want floppy control or not, interleave factor, data transfer rate, and whether it is for an eight-bit or 16-bit computer.

First, what type of format are you going to use? Remember that there are four types: MFM, RLL, ESDI, and SCSI. The MFM will be the least expensive. The RLL will cost just a little more, and will give you 50 percent more storage capacity and data transfer capacity. The ESDI and SCSI are expensive, but they are fast.

Second, do you want the hard disk controller to control your floppies as well? Each model of controller has nonfloppy and floppy versions. If you need the floppy capability, check to see if it will support all four versions of floppies: 360 KB, 720 KB, 1.2 MB, and 1.44 MB. This way, you can have any mix of 5.25-inch and 3.5-inch floppy disk drives.

If you plan to add more than two floppies to your system, you would be better off buying a hard-disk-only controller and a separate four-floppy controller. Otherwise, when you decide to add a third floppy drive, you may have to buy a new hard disk controller and a new floppy drive controller.

There are floppy drive controllers that are capable of being added to the system as a secondary floppy drive controller, but some hard/floppy drive controllers will not work with an additional floppy drive controller installed.

We have used a secondary floppy drive controller with a system that had a hard/floppy drive controller with no side effects. The secondary floppy controller came with two ROM BIOS chips. This controller was unique in that it could be configured to act as either the primary or secondary floppy drive controller by simply inserting the correct ROM BIOS chip and changing a jumper on the floppy drive controller. The moral of the story is "check to see if the controller can be configured as either a primary or secondary controller."

A word of caution about adding the third and fourth floppies. When the computer performs its hardware configuration analysis as to what disk drives are in the system, it will assign logic letters to the floppies first and then to the hard disk drives. For example, if you had three floppies and a hard disk, the setup program would assign letters A, B, and C to the floppies. The hard disk and its partitions would be assigned the letters D and up.

So what is the problem? There is no problem unless you are trying to use MS-DOS 4.01. It seems that the setup program for installing MS-DOS 4.01 has decided that only two floppies can or should exist, and they will be assigned the logic drive letters A and B. Hard disk drives will begin with the logic designator C. In the case of our A, B, and C floppies and our D hard disk, MS-DOS 4.01 will try to install itself on the C floppy when the hard disk install option is picked.

It will be almost impossible to install MS-DOS 4.01 on a system with more than two floppies. There is a way to do it, but it is not very straightforward. Go back to the chapter on software (Chapter 4) and look under DOS 4.01 for some tricks on how to do it.

If you do plan to add more than two floppies, it is recommended that you use DOS 3.3 instead of DOS 4.01 on the computer. It will allow you to install the DOS system for booting the computer on any drive you desire. It is also easier to install.

Third, if your computer is capable of operating at 12 MHz or greater, you should look for controllers capable of a 1:1 interleave factor for optimum performance.

To help assist you on your hunt for a hard disk and controller, we have included an extensive table of the more commonly found items in the magazines and different computer suppliers. Not all advertisements list the information needed to fully determine specifications. They will list the manufacturer's part number but not the specifics of the product. It is assumed that you know what you are looking for or that you will fully trust them to pick the right components for you.

**Hard Disk Drive Listing**

## Partial Listing of Available Hard Disk Drives

| Model | Type | Capacity (MBits) | Access Time (averaged) | Size | Height |
|---|---|---|---|---|---|
| Seagate ST225 | MFM | 21 | 70 | 5.25 | Half |
| Seagate ST225N | SCSI | 21 | 65 | 5.25 | Half |
| Seagate ST125 | MFM | 21 | 28 | 3.5 | Half |
| Seagate ST125A | IDE | 21 | 28 | 3.5 | Half |
| Seagate ST138-0 | MFM | 32 | 40 | 3.5 | Half |
| Seagate ST138-1 | MFM | 32 | 28 | 3.5 | Half |
| Seagate ST138A | IDE | 32 | 28 | 3.5 | Half |
| Seagate ST138N | SCSI | 32 | 28 | 3.5 | Half |
| Seagate ST238R | RLL | 32 | 65 | 5.25 | Half |
| Seagate ST138R-0 | RLL | 32 | 40 | 3.5 | Half |
| Seagate ST138R-1 | RLL | 32 | 28 | 3.5 | Half |
| Seagate ST250R | RLL | 42 | 70 | 5.25 | Half |
| Seagate ST250N | SCSI | 42 | 70 | 5.25 | Half |
| Seagate ST251 | MFM | 42 | 40 | 5.25 | Half |
| Seagate ST251-1 | MFM | 42 | 28 | 5.25 | Half |
| Seagate ST251N | SCSI | 43 | 28 | 5.25 | Half |
| Seagate ST157A | IDE | 44 | 28 | 3.5 | Half |
| Seagate ST157N-0 | SCSI | 48 | 40 | 3.5 | Half |
| Seagate ST157N-1 | SCSI | 48 | 28 | 3.5 | Half |
| Seagate ST157R-0 | RLL | 49 | 40 | 3.5 | Half |
| Seagate ST157R-1 | RLL | 49 | 28 | 3.5 | Half |
| Seagate ST177N | SCSI | 60 | 24 | 3.5 | Half |
| Seagate ST277R-1 | RLL | 65 | 28 | 5.25 | Half |
| Seagate ST277N-1 | SCSI | 65 | 28 | 5.25 | Half |
| Seagate ST278R | RLL | 65 | 40 | 5.25 | Half |
| Seagate 4096 | MFM | 80 | 28 | 5.25 | Half |
| Seagate 1096N | SCSI | 84 | 24 | 5.25 | Half |
| Seagate 4144R | RLL | 122 | 28 | 5.25 | Half |

| Model | Type | Capacity (MBits) | Access Time (averaged) | Size | Height |
|---|---|---|---|---|---|
| Micropolis 1355 | ESDI | 158 | 23 | 5.25 | Full |
| Micropolis 1375 | SCSI | 158 | 23 | 5.25 | Full |
| Micropolis 1558 | ESDI | 338 | 18 | 5.25 | Full |
| Micropolis 1578 | SCSI | 332 | 18 | 5.25 | Full |
| Micropolis 1568 | ESDI | 677 | 16 | 5.25 | Full |
| Micropolis 1588 | SCSI | 668 | 16 | 5.25 | Full |
| MiniScribe 8425 | MFM | 20 | 68 | 3.5 | Half |
| MiniScribe 8425F | MFM | 20 | 40 | 3.5 | Half |
| MiniScribe 8438 | RLL | 30 | 68 | 3.5 | Half |
| MiniScribe 8450 | RLL | 40 | 46 | 3.5 | Half |
| MiniScribe 8051A | IDE | 42 | 28 | 3.5 | Half |
| MiniScribe 3085 | MFM | 70 | 20 | 5.25 | Half |
| MiniScribe 3180E | ESDI | 150 | 17 | 5.25 | Half |
| MiniScribe 9380E | ESDI | 330 | 16 | 5.25 | Full |

## Hard Disk Controller Listing

## Popular Hard Disk Controllers

| Part number | Computer type | Optimum interleave factor | Format type (Mbits) | Data rate | Floppy control | Number hard disks |
|---|---|---|---|---|---|---|
| **Western Digital** | | | | | | |
| WD1002A-WX1 | XT | 3:1 | MFM | 5.0 | NO | 2 |
| WD1003V-MM1 | AT | 2:1 | MFM | 5.0 | NO | 2 |
| WD1003V-MM2 | AT | 2:1 | MFM | 5.0 | YES | 2 |
| WD1004-27X | XT | 3:1 | RLL | 7.5 | NO | 2 |
| WD1004-WX1 | XT | 3:1 | RLL | 7.5 | NO | 2 |
| WD1006V-MM1 | AT | 1:1 | MFM | 5.0 | NO | 2 |
| WD1006V-MM2 | AT | 1:1 | MFM | 5.0 | YES | 2 |
| WD1006V-SR1 | AT | 1:1 | RLL | 7.5 | NO | 2 |
| WD1006V-SR2 | AT | 1:1 | RLL | 7.5 | YES | 2 |
| WD1007-WAH | AT | 1:1 | ESDI | 10.0 | NO | 2 |
| WD1007-WA2 | AT | 1:1 | ESDI | 10.0 | YES | 2 |

| Part number | Computer type | Optimum interleave factor | Format type (Mbits) | Data rate | Floppy control | Number hard disks |
|---|---|---|---|---|---|---|
| WD1007A-SE1 | AT | 1:1 | ESDI | 15.0 | NO | 2 |
| WD1007A-SE2 | AT | 1:1 | ESDI | 15.0 | YES | 2 |
| 7000-FASST2 | AT | NA | SCSI | 16/32 | NA | 7 |
| **Adaptec** | | | | | | |
| 2370 | XT | 3:1 | RLL | 7.5 | NO | 2 |
| 2372 | AT | 1:1 | RLL | 7.5 | YES | 2 |
| 2310 | AT | 1:1 | MFM | 5.0 | NO | 2 |
| 2312 | AT | 1:1 | MFM | 5.0 | YES | 2 |
| 2320 | AT | 1:1 | ESDI | 10.0 | NO | 2 |
| 2322 | AT | 1:1 | ESDI | 10.0 | YES | 2 |
| AHA1540 | AT | NA | SCSI | 10.0 | NO | 2 |
| AHA1542 | AT | NA | SCSI | 10.0 | YES | 2 |

## *Reliability*

Whatever your application, disk drive reliability is important. It is important to manufacturers, too, because they have to determine what kind of warranty to offer; they have to estimate costs of support and balance that against manufacturing costs in a highly competitive market.

One figure frequently used in the industry to assess longevity and reliability is MTBF, mean time between failures. Years ago this figure was relatively low for mechanical devices such as disk drives. Today, however, manufacturers are quoting MTBF figures between 40,000 and 150,000 hours. At the high end, that's the equivalent of nearly 17 years.

In a hardware market with technology only a couple of years old, how can we know a drive will last an average of 17 years? It is a statistical question that can be answered in a couple of ways.

The most common method is to select a random sample from a drive production line and submit the sample to a series of laboratory tests that compress time, perhaps giving drives months' worth of usage in a single day. If enough drives are selected, and the sample is scientifically random, then the resulting data is highly accurate.

That means that a given series of tests must include drives that all use the same motor, the same platters, the same electronics. It also means that all factors including time of day, day of the week, and time of the year must be considered when selecting the random sample.

Although such compressed tests may seem unnatural and inaccurate compared to actual, online usage, statistically it doesn't matter. For esthetic reasons you may prefer to consider purchasing a used car that accumulated 50,000 miles in one year as opposed to one that has the same mileage but is several years old, but statistically your chances of problems with a given model are the same.

Very large manufacturers may conduct these tests themselves, or they may hire a reputable engineering or consulting firm from outside to make the MTBF projections for them.

There is another way to make MTBF projections using computer models. A number of engineering service companies use computers to calculate hardware reliability by entering each individual component along with reliability information about them and circuit-board design data into a computer. A program analyzes the design and predicts failure rates.

Computer projections are particularly helpful on very large or expensive systems, but they also are used on smaller products such as video displays and disk drives.

# Tape Drives

One method of making a copy of your hard disk contents is to dump or record it onto floppy disks. To copy a 20-MB hard disk will require approximately fifty-six 360-KB floppy disks and about one hour of time. Even using 1.44-MB floppies will require 14 floppies and about 45 minutes. This is a long time to sit there and feed the computer.

An alternate method is a tape drive. A tape storage unit like the one in Figure 6.24 offers a convenient method for backing up a hard disk's contents. All you have to do is insert a tape and run the backup utility software. You can go have coffee or tea while it does its thing.

Two primary tape standards are the 3M Data Cartridge 600 (DC-600) and 2000 (DC-2000). The DC-600 is the most commonly used. It can store data in 60, 125, 150, and 320-MB capacities. The DC-2000 only comes in a 40-MB capacity.

When selecting a tape drive size, select one large enough to hold the entire contents of the hard disk; otherwise, you will have to change tapes in the middle of the backup process. This means you have to sit and wait for the moment to come.

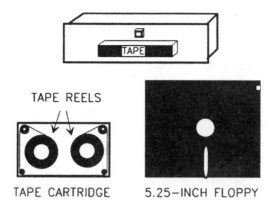

TAPE REELS

TAPE CARTRIDGE      5.25-INCH FLOPPY

**Figure 6.24**  A typical data tape storage unit

It is not recommend to use VCR or small audio-cassette-size tape units since they are slow and prone to errors. Also avoid streaming tape units because they are very inflexible in how you can use them.

Only two hardware interfaces are recommended: the QIC-02 (Quarter-Inch Committee 02) or the SCSI. You can get units that will connect to the floppy drive controller, but they operate at less than half the speed of the QIC and SCSI. The data transfer rate will be less than two megabytes/second. Both the QIC and SCSI have a data transfer rate of five megabytes/second for tape devices.

A basic problem with tape backup units is software. Even though the tape controller interface can be either QIC or SCSI, the software for a particular vendor's tape product in all probability will not work with another vendor's tape unit. So don't expect to be able to use your DC-600 tape in just any tape unit.

A standard is emerging. It is called SyTOS (Sytron Tape Operating System). It has been selected by IBM as the standard software for its units. Remember, IBM carries a heavy influence in the marketplace, whether it be good or bad. In this case it is good since some standard is needed.

The software for the tape unit should be capable of performing several functions. It should be able to back up a single hard disk partition or selected partitions.

Selective file backup would also be very convenient. A selective file restoration feature is handy also, since only those files that have been damaged or erased on the hard disk need to be restored and not the whole hard disk.

In the case of tapes that are smaller than the hard disk being backed up, the software should be able to handle multiple tape backups. Most important of all, the software should be able to absolutely verify the accuracy of the data on the tape as well as having a method for recovering potentially bad data on read-back from the tape.

# VIDEO GRAPHICS

One of the most obvious and important pieces of your computer system is the display system, which consists of a bus-level adapter card and a monitor. A number of video display standards are in use across many computer platforms, but given the state of today's software, some form of graphics-compatible system is the only thing that makes much sense.

## Graphics and Text Standards

### *Mono Text (MDA)*

The first type of video display available for the PC was the MDA (monochrome display adapter) display. It can display 80 characters by 25 lines of high-resolution text. The characters are formed from a seven-dot wide by 11-dot high character cell configuration. The character box is nine dots by 14 dots. The character box is wider so that a guard spacing will surround the character. This is to make the characters more readable on the video screen. Figure 6.25 illustrates a character box and Figure 6.26 shows the standard screen format for text.

The MDA video adapter is able to display a total of 255 characters. In addition to the normal upper and lower-case letters of the alphabet, numbers, and standard typing symbols, a set of 126 graphic symbols is included. The graphic symbols let you do simple line and box drawings, some math representations, and a few other types of graphical illustrations.

The biggest drawback to the MDA display is that it cannot do addressable dot graphics. With addressable dot graphics, you could draw anything that you desired on the video screen. The answer to this problem came from a non-IBM company. They developed a video board that quickly became a standard that exists to this day. It is called the Hercules Graphics Adapter.

It is almost impossible to find an MDA-only display adapter today. The reason is that the monochrome graphics adapter (Hercules graphics standard) is commonly available for less than $40.

### *Hercules Graphics Adapter*

The Hercules graphics adapter provided two modes of monochrome operation. One mode was the standard 80 by 25 text format of the MDA display. The other mode was a high-resolution dot-addressable graphics mode of 720 dots horizontal by 348 lines, as shown in Figure 6.27.

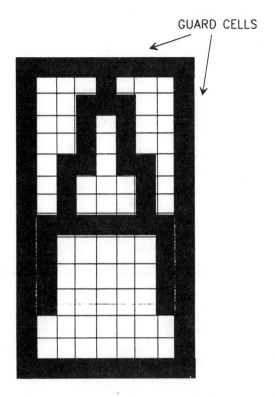

**Figure 6.26**   Character box and cell representation of the letter A

The vertical and horizontal relationship of the number of dots is directly related to the text box size. Here is the relationship:

720 dots horizontal = 9 text box dots × 80 characters
348 dot vertical lines = (14 text box dots × 25 lines) − 2

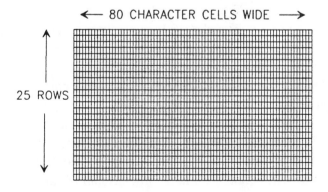

**Figure 6.25**   Standard screen format for high-resolution text

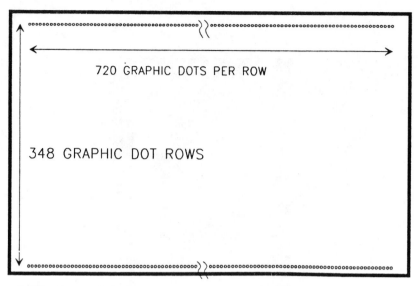

**Figure 6.27**   Screen format of the Hercules graphics adapter

To use this high-resolution capability, a special software driver is needed. The driver is required for proper control and addressing of the graphics controller on the Hercules graphics adapter.

For low-cost monochrome (black and white) operation, the Hercules graphic adapter is almost always used. You will find it advertised as a monochrome graphics adapter.

## Color Graphics Adapter

This is the turkey of graphic's displays. The CGA (color graphics adapter) display was the first attempt at a color graphics display for the IBM PC. In the text mode, it can display the standard 80 columns by 25 lines of text; however, the text cells are formed from an 8 by 8 dot cell. (See Figure 6.28.) In addition, there is no cell box guard as in the case of the monochrome display adapter; thus, characters like 8 and 0 are hard to distinguish.

On most monitors you can actually see the individual dots that compose each character. You will find that you have to defocus your eyes to get the dots to blend together to form a solid and readable character. The text also has a very coarse look which becomes tiring over a long period of time.

As for its graphics capability, there are two modes: low resolution and high resolution, as shown in Figure 6.29. In the low-resolution mode, you can display

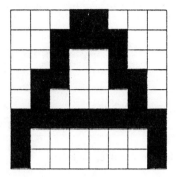

**Figure 6.28**   CGA representation of the letter A

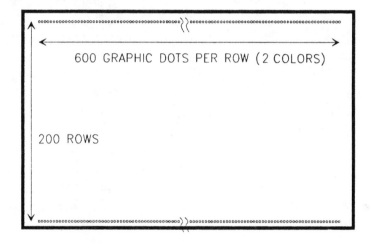

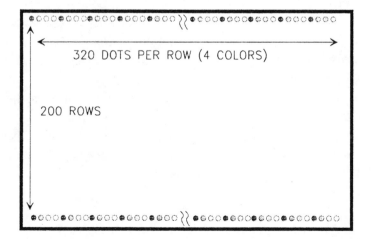

**Figure 6.29**   The two display modes of CGA

COLOR PALETTES

| | | 1 | 2 | 3 | 4 |
|---|---|---|---|---|---|
| | 1 | BACKGROUND | BACKGROUND | BACKGROUND | BACKGROUND |
| COLORS | 2 | GREEN | CYAN | LIGHT GREEN | LIGHT CYAN |
| | 3 | RED | MAGENTA | LIGHT RED | LIGHT MAGENTA |
| | 4 | BROWN | LIGHT GREY | YELLOW | WHITE |

**Figure 6.30**   CGA palette and color choices

320 dots on a horizontal line by 200 lines vertically in four colors. In the high resolution, you can display 600 dots per horizontal line and 200 lines vertically in two colors.

Your total choice of colors is 16, but you can only use two or four colors from the set of 16, depending on the graphics resolution. Your choice of colors applies to the whole screen and not each dot. In other words, the entire graphics screen will appear in only two or four colors. And one of those colors has to be a background color.

For the four-color mode, the three remaining foreground colors (colors to draw with) have to be adjacent colors from the 16-color list, shown in Figure 6.30. Thus you are limited to four sets of colors. The result is a rather pitiful color display, but it was really something for a while, when it first came out.

For the two-color mode, the one remaining foreground color could be any one of the 16 palette colors. The display was reasonably sharp, but you could only draw one foreground color over another background color.

The CGA mode is not used at all any more except in some laptop computers with flat screens, but that is changing quickly to the EGA mode. Most software will support the CGA mode because there are so many laptop computers out there that have only the CGA mode as a means of displaying graphics. A lot of game software also supports CGA mode; but they, too, are quickly converting to the EGA and VGA modes.

With the drop in prices, it makes absolutely no sense at all to buy a CGA graphics card. You can purchase EGA and VGA multigraphics adapter cards that will emulate the CGA mode if you need it. We recently purchased just such an EGA card for $68. Why would you want to buy a limited CGA graphics card for $40?

| TYPE | TEXT FORMAT | BOX SIZE | RESOLUTION | COLORS |
|------|-------------|----------|------------|--------|
| ALPHA | 40 x 25 | 8 x 8 | 320 x 200 | 16 |
| ALPHA | 80 x 25 | 8 x 8 | 640 x 200 | 16 |
| GRAPHIC | 40 x 25 | 8 x 8 | 320 x 200 | 4 |
| GRAPHIC | 80 x 25 | 8 x 8 | 640 x 200 | 4 |
| ALPHA | 80 x 25 | 9 x 14 | 720 x 350 | 3 |
| GRAPHIC | 40 x 25 | 8 x 8 | 320 x 200 | 16 |
| GRAPHIC | 80 x 25 | 8 x 8 | 640 x 200 | 16 |
| GRAPHIC | 80 x 25 | 8 x 14 | 640 x 350 | 16 |

**Figure 6.31**  Possible display modes of EGA

## EGA

The EGA (enhanced graphics adapter) display was the first step toward a decent text and color graphics display. It has two text-display sizes and several graphics and color resolutions.

The text cell size is 8 by 14, which is very close to the MDA's 9 by 14 size. The EGA graphics adapter can also change to an 8 by 8 cell text size to display 43 lines of text instead of 25 lines. The capabilities of the EGA display are shown in Figure 6.31.

The EGA adapter has three graphics resolutions. The first two are compatible with the CGA mode (320 by 200 and 600 by 200). It also is capable of a high-resolution 600 by 350 display. The number of colors available for each mode depends on the amount of memory on the EGA adapter. With the full 256 KB of memory, you can do 16 color displays in all three modes, and the 600 by 350 mode offers a choice of 16 colors from a palette of 64 total colors. Every EGA adapter card available today comes with 256 KB installed, but this was not the case several years ago.

Another mode supported by some EGA cards is called EGA Plus. This is a 640 by 480 graphics mode in 16 colors. You will require a special graphics software driver to use the card.

A wide variety of EGA graphic adapters are available today. Nearly all of them will emulate the MDA, Hercules, and CGA modes. Better yet, they will work with either a monochrome, CGA, or EGA monitor.

One thing you need to check on before ordering one of these multimode cards is whether they require a multisync monitor to emulate the different modes. Some adapters require a multisync monitor because the scanning frequencies for the various modes are different. Some cards will do a scan conversion so that one type of monitor will work in all the different modes. Others will generate the actual scanning values; thus, the monitor must be able to sense the scanning rate change (multisync).

Some cards will only operate in the MDA and Hercules modes when a monochrome monitor is used. Others will operate in all four modes when a monochrome monitor is attached. The different colors are represented as different shades of grey (intensity level varies). So it is possible to start off with an EGA graphics adapter card and a monochrome monitor; then, at a later time when money permits, you can purchase an EGA monitor.

Before you commit to an EGA display card and monitor, you need to know that EGA is going the way of the CGA mode. With the falling prices of VGA monitors and video display adapters, it really doesn't make any sense to use EGA unless you are really on a tight budget.

The EGA mode is reasonably sharp, and you can sometimes find a monitor/adapter combination at a deeply discounted price, or as a used set from someone who has upgraded to VGA. In this case, if your budget is tight, the EGA combination could be a good choice. However, you eventually will switch over to VGA. So take the EGA plunge cautiously.

## VGA

The VGA (video graphics array) display does everything that all the previous display adapters do and more. It uses a 9 by 14 text box just as the MDA adapter. It has a resolution of 640 dots per horizontal line by 480 lines vertically. It is capable of displaying 256 colors from a palette of 262,144 colors.

Two other special modes are also provided on nearly all VGA cards. A mode called Super VGA constitutes an 800-horizontal dot line by 600 lines vertically in 16 colors. Some are also offering a 1024 by 768 mode in 16 colors. VGA display capabilities are shown in Figure 6.32.

These special modes require software written specifically for that video card. Nearly all will supply a variety of software driver to let you use these "hi-res" color modes with a variety of today's software packages.

Today's VGA cards can do the same emulations as the EGA multifunction card. It will support the MDA, CGA, Hercules, and EGA modes with a variety of monitors. However, not all VGA cards can use the wide range of monitors, so you need to check before buying.

| TYPE | TEXT FORMAT | BOX SIZE | RESOLUTION |
|---|---|---|---|
| TEXT | 40 x 25 | 9 x 16 | 360 x 400 |
| TEXT | 80 x 25 | 9 x 16 | 720 x 400 |
| GRAPHIC | SPLIT | 8 x 8 | 320 x 200 |
| GRAPHIC | SPLIT | 8 x 8 | 640 x 200 |
| TEXT | 80 x 25 | 9 x 16 | 720 x 400 |
| GRAPHIC | LINEAR | 8 x 8 | 320 x 200 |
| GRAPHIC | LINEAR | 8 x 8 | 640 x 200 |
| GRAPHIC | LINEAR | 8 x 16 | 640 x 350 |
| GRAPHIC | LINEAR | 8 x 16 | 640 x 350 |
| GRAPHIC | LINEAR | 8 x 16 | 640 x 480 |
| GRAPHIC | LINEAR | 8 x 16 | 640 x 480 |
| GRAPHIC | LINEAR | 8 x 8 | 320 x 200 |

**Figure 6.32**  Graphics-text modes available with VGA display

Just as mentioned for the case of multimode EGA cards, you should check on the requirements of the VGA card for operation in the different modes. You may or may not need a multisync monitor.

Another advantage of the VGA cards is that they are usually 16-bit data bus devices, which translates into faster graphics operation. Better yet, some cards use the special graphic's engines (special video controller chips) such as those available from Texas Instruments. These graphic cards can draw or paint the video screen five to 10 times faster than a regular VGA graphics controller; however, they require special software to use this capability.

In reference to software drivers, you need to see what software support drivers come with the card. It may or may not have the required graphics driver that will support a particular software package that you are using or plan to use.

It used to be that the only drawback to VGA was price, but not any more. In fact, some VGA cards sell for less than some brands of EGA cards. You can obtain a VGA card for less than $100. It will usually come with only 256 KB of memory. You will need to add another 256 KB of memory to use the 800 by 600 and 1024 by 748 modes.

### *Beyond VGA*

In the never-ending march toward better display capability, the next horizon for color graphics adapters is for 256 colors in both the 800 by 600 and the 1024 by 768 modes. This means that you can have a high-resolution color text display of up to 130 columns by 60 lines. Several of the presently available VGA cards offer these resolutions, but only in 16 colors and four colors depending on the amount of memory installed on the video card.

The biggest cost factor in going to these higher resolutions is the cost of the video monitor. In 1989 a color monitor capable of meeting these display qualifications would have cost over $1000. In 1990 the cost dropped to $600. As these high-resolution modes catch on, the price of the hardware will drop even more, and more software developers will make use of these features.

## Video Graphics Cards Technology Considerations

### *EGA*

What should you look for in an EGA video card?

**1**  Foremost would be the ability to emulate MDA, Hercules, CGA, EGA, and EGA Plus.

**2**  The ability to emulate these modes with a nonmultisync monitor would also be nice since the price of a multisync monitor is a couple of hundred dollars more than a regular EGA color monitor.

Additionally, see if it will work with a monochrome monitor in these different modes (shades of gray).

**3**  Ensure that the card comes with 256 KB of video memory and not 128 K; otherwise, you will not be able to do a full 16 colors in the 600 by 350 and 640 by 480 modes.

**4**  Last on the list would be software drivers. Make sure that drivers are included for the software you will be using. These drivers are required to let you take advantage of the special display modes.

What else should you look for? One item that is important to know but hard to determine is compatibility. Not all EGA cards correctly emulate the register-level functions of the original IBM EGA video card. The result could be improper operation with software packages for which software drivers are not supplied by the board's manufacturer.

How can you determine this compatibility problem? Magazine reviews are the best source. Since EGA cards are disappearing like the CGA cards, you want to find current magazine reviews of EGA cards. Back issues should be available from the local library.

However, as we have said before, consider carefully whether you want an EGA card at all. The price difference between an eight-bit EGA and VGA card is almost nothing—$10 or so for many companies. In fact, we have seen a few companies offering VGA adapters at a cheaper price than a comparable EGA card.

## VGA

What was said for EGA holds equally true for VGA with the following additions:

1   Make sure it supports $800 \times 600$ and $1024 \times 748$ graphic modes.
2   Make sure you get 512 KB of video memory if you intend to use these two high-resolution modes.

Also check to see if the card uses standard DRAM or the higher-performance VRAM. VRAM (video ram) costs more, but yields a significantly higher screen-writing speed. This would be most beneficial for graphics oriented software.

The VRAM chip differs from its DRAM counterpart in that it has two data I/O ports. The processor can read and write to it just as a normal DRAM. The video controller can also read data from it, but the controller does it through a separate serial data port.

The result is that both the processor and video controller can use the memory at the same time. This enables the processor to more quickly change the video memory contents, without having to wait for the video controller.
3   Select a card that is compatible with the VGA register standards.
4   Don't buy an eight-bit data bus version. Go for the 16-bit AT versions. The card will work much faster when doing graphic displays.

If you are interested in using the card to display computer-generated color graphic displays for use with standard TVs and video recorders (see Figure 6.33), you may want to consider using the following special VGA video graphics cards:

Publishers' VGA and VGA-TV
Targa 16 Video
U.S. Video VGA/NTSC Recordable Video
Vision Technologies' Vision VGA

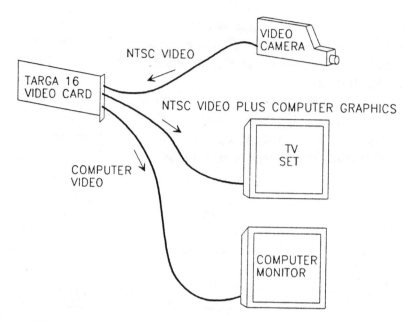

**Figure 6.33**   VGA interface connections with camera, TV, and computer

This is a new feature that a few companies are offering. Currently you pay a relatively high premium for standard TV video capability, and the units can be relatively difficult to configure for your system. However as the computer and video markets move closer and closer together—witness the interest in interactive video and the rise in popularity of image databases—we will see more of these products. And, as usual, the price will come down as features improve.

## Video Monitors

There is more to selecting a video monitor than simply deciding whether you want monochrome (black and white) or color. Since nearly all EGA and VGA video graphic adapters support multiple modes, you have to be careful in selecting the right monitor to go with a particular manufacturer's card.

The basic problem is the scanning frequencies required for the different modes of operation. If you attempt to use a monitor with a card that generates scanning frequencies different from what the monitor was designed for, the monitor could be damaged or destroyed. Most cards can be set by means of switches for a particular monitor so that this catastrophe will not happen unless you incorrectly set the switches.

## Table of Scanning Rates

| Video Mode | Horizontal Scanning Rate (KHz) | Vertical Scanning Rate (Hz) |
|---|---|---|
| MDA | 18.432 | 50 |
| CGA | 15.750 | 60 |
| EGA (600x350) | 21.800 | 60 |
| VGA (640x480) | 31.500 | 60 |
| VGA (800x600) | 31.500 | 70 |
| (1024x748) | | |

Another specification most people overlook or just plain don't understand is the pixel resolution of color monitors. Pixel resolution is controlled by five factors: dot pitch, dot size, dot shape, brightness, and purity. Of the five, dot pitch is the only physically defined specification. (See Figure 6.34.) It specifies the separation distance between the individual color dots or stripes on the video monitor's display tube. Monochrome monitors don't have this problem.

To form one graphic display dot out of the many that compose a single scan line requires three adjoining red, blue, and green color dots on the display tube's face. The closer together these individual dots are, the sharper the resolution.

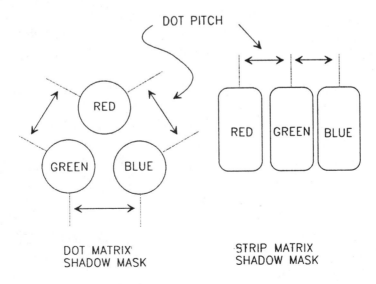

**Figure 6.34**   Two methods of dot composition in video display

An EGA or VGA color monitor with a dot pitch of 0.41 mm will appear to look fine unless it is compared against a standard 0.31-mm dot pitch tube or 0.26-mm dot pitch Sony Trinitron tube. So it is important to note this characteristic when looking at color monitors.

The other four parameters are a function of the monitor's electronic design. And this is an area where no real standards exist. Only the eye of the potential buyer can distinguish which monitor has the best focus and dynamic brightness range.

Magazine reviews can give you comparisons of the different monitors and their characteristics, and you should review advertisements in the major computer journals. But remember that it is mostly a judgment call, depending on whether the monitor is correctly adjusted and whether the reviewer or advertiser is biased for or against a particular brand of monitor.

## *Monochrome*

These display monitors represent the bottom of the line for displays. They are intended for use with the MDA and Hercules display modes. Their display screens come in one of three colors: green, amber, or white. Their task in life is simple, provide a low-cost text-entry workstation, with monotonic graphics if needed.

You will also find a choice of the regular curved-faced display tube or a flat-face display tube. The curved face is the most commonly found display tube. It can be easily seen over a wide angle of view. The flat display tube is a more recent occurrence. Its claim to fame is reduced glare. This type of display can be easily adjusted to eliminate glare caused by lights in a room. This is an impossible feat with curved tubes.

These monitors operate at an 18.432-KHz horizontal and 50-Hz vertical scanning rate. The video and sync (horizontal and vertical scanning signals) are TTL logic-level compatible. The video line simply turns the display tube's scanning beam on and off as it scans across the screen.

Monochrome monitors cost between $50 and $100.

## *EGA*

These monitors are a good choice for low-end color text and graphic displays. They are capable of displaying 16 colors. As with their monochrome cousins, they require TTL logic sync and video signals.

Unlike the monochrome monitors, these guys require red, blue, and green video lines. Remember that each displayed graphic's dot is a composition of red, green, and blue colors. By using the three colors in different combinations you can generate a near infinite number of possible colors, almost.

Since EGA is a TTL or digitally controlled display, the red, blue, and green colors can only be turned on or off. This limits the number of possible combinations to eight. To obtain the other eight colors for a total of 16 colors, a video intensity control line is used. This line is responsible for what is called the high and low intensity signal.

To show how it works, we will give you an example. If the blue, and green signal lines are turned off and only the red signal line is turned on, you should see red. Well, maybe. If the intensity signal line is in the high mode, yes you will see red. If it is in the low-intensity mode, the red will appear to be brown. The same coloration effect occurs with the other colors.

Because of this coloration effect, it is important that the contrast or video level control be set properly on the EGA display monitor or else colors will not be correctly represented. The best way to do this is by running the color setup program that comes with most EGA graphics cards. All 16 colors will be displayed on the screen so that you can best adjust the contrast and brightness controls for the correct and best color appearances.

If there was a limitation of the EGA color display, it would be the limited number of colors.

EGA color monitors sell for as little as $270 refurbished or $300 new. These lower-priced monitors are usually the 0.41-mm dot pitch displays. For $30 to $50 more, you can get a 0.31-mm dot pitch display.

Again we don't recommend going with the EGA choice simply because the prices on VGA have fallen to the point that you can buy a VGA graphics adapter and VGA monitor for about the same price as the EGA.

## VGA

Although VGA is a high-resolution color graphics mode, it does not necessarily mean you have to use a color display. You now have a choice of either a very sharp VGA monochrome or a sharp VGA color monitor. The difference in price is about $200; but price does not totally describe the difference.

The distinguishing characteristic of VGA over EGA is the number of colors that can be displayed. EGA can only display a total of 16 colors. A VGA monitor can display over 200,000 different colors. The VGA monitor is able to perform this feat because it uses analog video signal lines instead of the digital lines. Recall that with digital or TTL lines, you can only have one of two conditions, on or off. With analog you have an infinite number of possibilities between fully on (max) and fully off (min).

**Monochrome**   The VGA monochrome is a recent addition to the marketplace. It was intended to provide a low-cost alternative to a VGA graphics display. The surprise comes when you compare a VGA monochrome display to a VGA color display.

Of course the shades of amber or white are bland in comparison to the dazzling colors of the color display, but if you look past the colors, you will notice the extremely crisp and sharp display of the monochrome monitor. The reason for this condition is that a monochrome display tube is one continuous coating of phosphorous as opposed to the red, blue, and green color dots of the color display tube.

The VGA monochrome monitor offers an outstanding display for very little money. One can be purchased for as little as $150.

**Color**   The VGA color monitor is the color monitor to have. Once you have used one, you will never look at a CGA or EGA color screen again. With a resolution of 640 × 480 in 256 colors it makes the other color displays look pitiful.

About the only unique thing to mention about VGA color displays is the size of the display tube and its dot pitch. To comfortably read the dense and sharp display of 640 × 480 and 800 × 600 graphics, the screen should be a minimum of 14 inches in size as measured diagonally from opposing corners of the tube. A 16-inch or larger tube is highly recommended.

The dot pitch should be a minimum of 0.31 mm. We have seen some cheap 0.41 mm VGA monitors advertised—it is not recommended that you buy one —the displayed text and graphics will appear soft or slightly out of focus at the higher graphics resolutions, because of the large dot pitch.

One particular feature that may be of interest to you is the Zenith flat-screen color tube. Zenith developed the first truly flat screen color tube. Not only does it eliminate the annoying glare problem, it also allows the tube to display a much brighter image while maintaining true color dynamics. Nearly all color monitors suffer from color shifting (slight color changes) as the brightness is turned up to compensate for a room's bright lighting.

## Multisync

If you want a monitor that will handle everything you can throw at it, a multisync monitor is for you. These guys automatically sense the frequencies of the horizontal and vertical synchronization signals. Once they determine what video mode you are trying to operate in, they adjust their scanning to present the proper-sized display.

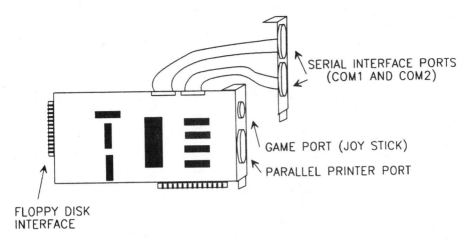

SERIAL INTERFACE PORTS
(COM1 AND COM2)

GAME PORT (JOY STICK)

PARALLEL PRINTER PORT

FLOPPY DISK
INTERFACE

**Figure 6.35**  Diagram of a typical input/output board

The TTL or digital versions of the multisync color monitors will work in the MDA, CGA, Hercules, and EGA modes with all the proper color or monochrome functions. The multisync monitors cost a little more than a regular EGA or VGA color monitor, but they provide you with a piece of equipment that probably won't become obsolete after a few years of use. Several of the newer multisync monitors already have the capability to support the next generation of super high-resolution displays.

# EXPANSION CARDS

## Multi-I/O

### *Parallel*

To communicate with the outside world, the computer needs I/O (input/output) ports. These I/O ports consist of parallel and serial channels. Since communication is done a byte at a time, nearly all I/O boards will be eight-bit. A typical I/O board (see Figure 6.35) will have one parallel port and two serial ports (second serial port will be optional).

The parallel port's electrical design and software compatibility is constant among all the classes of computers from the XT to the 80486. Life has remained stable for this interface port with the exception of the IBM's PS/2 series. The standard configurations are LPT1 and LPT2. Within the last few years LPT3 and

LPT4 have been added to the I/O configuration, but it is not supported by DOS. You will have to use software that can specifically utilize these additional I/O connections.

The IBM PS/2's parallel ports are capable of bi-directional communications. This enables them to perform high-speed communications. This capability is found only in the MicroChannel bus I/O cards.

The parallel port is almost always used as a printer output port. This port is unidirectional, meaning that data only flows one way, which is out. With the proper software, transfers of 100 KB/second or greater are possible through this port. When used as the standard parallel print port, data transfers at about 10 KB/second.

Other devices can be attached transparently to this port while it is being used as a printer port. One type of software protection requires that a special device (security key) be attached to the parallel port. The printer cable then attaches to the security device. Only the protected software knows that it is there. There is no indication that the operation of the printer is affected in any way. One company makes a voice synthesizer that attaches to the parallel port and works in the same manner as the security key. These transparent taps are accomplished by using the extra control lines available on the parallel port.

One basic problem with the parallel port is that cable runs should not be over 15 feet. Because of the relatively low noise-rejection level of the TTL signals on the parallel interface, the cable becomes susceptible to electrical interference when it is very long. Also, since high-speed data signals are present on the cable, the cable will act as an antenna and radiate a broad range of signals that will interfere with a number of devices such as radios and TVs.

### Serial

The serial port or ports are the more versatile of the two I/O ports. DOS will support asynchronous serial communications through the serial ports from 300 baud to 9600 baud. There are numerous communications packages that will enable you to use the serial port at 19.2K and 38K baud, but this is really pushing the performance of the serial I/O port.

The two most common uses of the serial port is for modems and mouse devices. DOS only supports the use of COM1 and COM2. Communications ports COM3 and COM4 can be used also, but it requires software that supports it.

Although you can use an external modem and attach it to the serial port on the I/O card, typically the modem will mount inside the computer case with the serial interface built right on it. Most modems and their accompanying software will support operation on either COM1, COM2, COM3, or COM4.

The only problem with these additional comm ports is that the even ports share a common interrupt line and the odd ports share a common interrupt line to the interrupt controller. Thus you must be careful when assigning these ports to different devices.

For instance, if you have a mouse connected to COM1, you shouldn't connect a modem or other type of device to COM3 that requires the use of the interrupt controller. This is because the mouse will generate a great number of interrupts as it is rolled across the table. The software servicing the common interrupt will have to do double duty trying to determine the source of the interrupt (mouse, modem, or other device).

Mouse devices can use the serial port because of the numerous control lines that are available, but not in a way you can imagine. The mouse device connects to several of the handshake or control lines on the serial interface port. As the mouse is moved around on the table, it triggers the serial interface's interrupt request line. This action causes a special software mouse driver to check which control lines are changing so that it can determine the direction and amount of motion of the mouse.

Printers can also use the serial port, although their operation will be slower than when used with the parallel port. An advantage to using the serial port would be that the printer could be placed more than 15 feet away from the computer. In fact, this is the advantage of the serial port—long cable runs.

The reason long cable runs are possible is due to the high noise-rejection level of the RS-232 signals. Unlike the parallel port's 0 to 5-volt TTL logic levels, the serial port's voltage level goes from −12 to +12. This wide voltage-swing capability for representing logic 1s and 0s gives it a high immunity to electrical interference.

All is not rosy with the serial interface design for all the classes of computers. The earlier serial interfaces used the Intel 8250 chip. This chip had a known hardware problem (extraneous interrupt). Early PC and PC-XT computers designed their ROM BIOS to handle this problem. When the 8250A came out, it corrected several of the earlier problems including the extraneous interrupt; but PCs wouldn't work properly with it because the ROM BIOS was designed to live with this particular problem. This chip should not be used, since operation is unpredictable.

The latest version, 8250B, fixed the remainder of the problems with the chip, but it incorporated the earlier 8250 problem that the ROM BIOS was designed to correct. This deliberate incorporation of a bug (problem) allowed the 8250B to properly work with PCs while correcting other known problems with the chip. If you use a serial interface card, make sure it uses the 8250B, or else you may experience a strange problem at some point in time that will not be repeatable or explainable.

If this wasn't confusing enough, along came the AT class of computers and its particular quirks with the serial port. Since the AT class is so fast, a faster response serial interface chip was needed. The 16450 is the fast version of the 8250.

The 16450 chip is required for high-speed operation (9600 baud or greater) of the serial interface port. The 8250B can be used, but operation is unreliable at the higher data-transmission speeds. If you plan to use the OS/2 operating system, you will have to use the 16450 chip.

Another version of the chip is the 16550. It is similar to the 16450, but it has a large I/O data buffer built into it. This chip will not work as a replacement for the 16450.

When looking for a serial interface card, you need to determine what class of computer you intend to use it on. If you intend to use it only for the XT (8088) or AT (80286) class of computers you can use the 8250B, although the AT will not be able to use it at 9600 baud. If you intend to use it in an AT (80286) or higher class (80386, 80386SX, or 80486), please ensure that the 16450 chip is installed and not the 8250B.

The XT cannot use the 16450 because its ROM BIOS will not support it. So if you have an XT computer with intentions of upgrading to an AT or higher class machine, don't try and be smart by ordering the serial interface with the 16450 thinking that you can use it later. You will drive yourself crazy trying to make it work.

One last thought on the serial interface. When ordering the card, order the optional second serial port. It will only cost you about $10 more. When you do decide to add it, you will spend $20 in phone calls just trying to find the parts.

## Game Ports

Most multi-I/O cards come with one game port. This port allows you to connect a joy stick device like the ones used with model airplanes. It is very handy for use with games. It serves as a supplement for using the cursor movement keys on the keyboard. Instead of having to push the up and down cursor keys, you simply push the joy stick forward or back to accomplish the same thing. The same goes for left and right movement. If you are into games, a game port and a joy stick are essential.

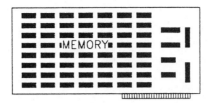

**Figure 6.36**   Expanded memory board

## *Clock/Calendar*

The XT class of computers do not have a built-in clock for tracking time and date when the computer's power is turned off. Some multi-I/O boards come with a clock/calendar to make up for this original design flaw. The AT and higher class of computers have a clock/calendar built on the motherboard with a battery source for keeping it alive.

To use the clock/calendar requires a special software driver that is usually supplied with the card. As the computer is booting up, the special software driver will read the clock/calendar on the multi-I/O card and will set the computer's clock/calendar automatically for you. You will also have to use their special software to set their clock/calendar.

Even though the clock/calendar is on the multi-I/O board, you don't have to use it. So don't reject a multi-I/O board for use in an AT or higher class computer just because it may have a clock/calendar. You will probably be surprised to find that multi-I/O boards with and without the clock/calendars cost just about the same.

# Memory Boards

### *Expanded Memory*

As discussed in earlier chapters, expanded memory is a way to have fast memory-storage capability. The standard by which expanded memory works has been changed several times. The latest version is LIM 4.0 (Lotus, Intel, and Microsoft collaborated standard). A typical eight-bit expanded memory card is shown in Figure 6.36.

Earlier versions of the LIM standard had compatibility problems between several programs and hardware designs. The latest version has incorporated fixes to these problems. Thus, when ordering an expanded memory board for use with either an XT or an AT computer, ensure that it conforms to the LIM 4.0 standard.

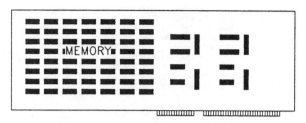

**Figure 6.37**    Extended memory board

In case you have forgotten, expanded memory works on the principle of memory blocks that can be accessed through a memory window located just above where the video RAM resides in the 640-KB to 1-MB memory range of the PC. Since this memory window is above the 640-KB main memory, it is out of the control of DOS, and thus its use is unpredictable without the LIM 4.0 software driver.

The memory window and the LIM 4.0 driver allows programs to store and retrieve data in the expanded memory area, which is located above the 1-M memory boundary of the XT-class computers. By specifying a particular 64-KB segment on the expanded memory board, you can write four continuous 16-KB memory pages before having to select another 64-KB segment. The LIM 4.0 standard will allow up to 32-MB of expanded memory.

If you have an AT or higher class of computer, you really shouldn't use the expanded memory card. Instead, you should use extended memory configured for use as expanded memory.

### *Extended Memory*

Extended memory differs from expanded memory in that it can be directly addressed by the 80286 and other 16-bit processors when operated in the real mode (non-8088/8086 mode). The linear address range of the 80286 goes from 0K to 16M continuously. The extended memory starts at the 1-M boundary where the 8088/8086 stops. A typical 16-bit extended memory card is shown in Figure 6.37.

Since this memory can be directly addressed just as any memory location in the 640 KB range, it will operate much faster when used as expanded memory with a LIM 4.0 driver. Additionally, by using some of the new memory management utilities such as QEMM386 and MAX386, you can divide up your extended memory and use part of it for expanded and part for extended.

If you need to use the LIM 4.0 expanded memory function for software that you have, it makes no sense to purchase an expanded memory card for use in a

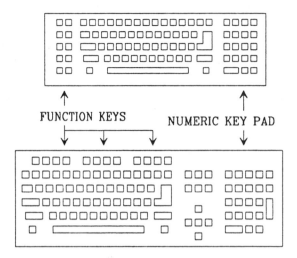

**Figure 6.38** Typical keyboard layouts

16-bit computer, since the expanded memory card is an eight-bit type memory card that can only be used as expanded memory.

With the advent of Windows, OS/2, and other high-level multitasking software, it is inevitable that you will need extended memory for your computer. So again, don't buy an expanded memory card for your 16-bit machine.

# I/O DEVICES

## Keyboards

The number of available keyboards is truly amazing. There are more than 10 different sizes, shapes, keyboard layouts, and touch control. It can be a most difficult job. Two standard types of keyboards are shown in Figure 6.38.

So where do you start? Well first of all, you need to determine the number of function keys needed. Most software uses the standard F1 through F10 function keys. Some of the newer software can use function keys F11 and F12. Some keyboards have as many as 22 function keys.

The next consideration may or may not be important to you. The physical size of the keyboard could be of concern. Some people find the long keyboards awkward, since the main part of the keyboard occupies the left two-thirds of the keyboard. It feels like you are working on the edge of it. If this is a problem, look for a keyboard with the function keys on the left side and the numeric keypad on the right. This arrangement will give you a sense of balance.

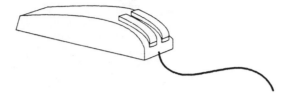

**Figure 6.39**   A mouse pointing device

Now you have to decide how many keys you want. Sounds silly, but it is true. There are 84, 101, 104, and 111-key versions. The reason for the different numbers is that some dual functions on the 84-key version are separated out to separate keys on the larger keyboards. The cursor control, insert, delete, home, end, page up, page down are just a few of the keys that are reassigned to special single-function keys of their own.

Probably one of the most overlooked features is the tactical feel of the keyboard. Some keyboards have a mushy feel when you type, others are stiff. Some have a clicking sound and the feel you would find on a typewriter.

Another option available these days is a trackball. A trackball operates like a mouse device. Instead of rolling it around on the table, you use your hand to roll a ball protruding from the keyboard. The motion of the ball mimics the mouse movements.

If all this wasn't enough, some keyboards come equipped as a calculator and/or alarm clock.

# Mouse

A mouse (see Figure 6.39) is a very popular device for moving a cursor or pointer around the video screen as opposed to using the function keys and cursor control keys.

The standard is the Microsoft serial-interface mouse. It fits very comfortably in your hand as you move it around on the desk top.

There are two basic types of mice. One is a mechanical mouse that has a hard rubber ball in it. This mouse can be used on any clean flat surface. The other type is an optical mouse. It has photocells that pick up reflections from a special optical pad that it moves over. The choice between the two is purely personal.

Some mice come with two control buttons, others have three. You will find that nearly all software supports the left/right buttons. A few software packages support the third or middle button.

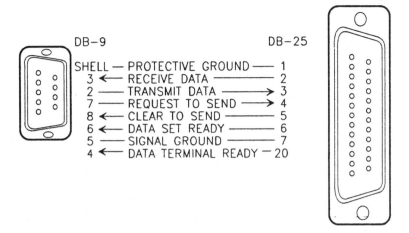

**Figure 6.40**   DB-9 to DB-25 connector cable

When choosing a mouse, you will have to determine how you want to connect it to your computer. As mentioned, the serial-interface type of mouse is the most common. The other type of mouse uses a special mouse bus card.

In the case of the serial version, you will need to be sure that you have enough serial ports to support the mouse and other devices that you want to add. Also, remember from our discussion on multi-I/O cards, the mouse should not be connected to the same even or odd port that is occupied by a modem or other device that depends on the common interrupt-request line.

When purchasing a low-cost mouse, be sure to see if it comes with a DB-9 to DB-25 conversion cable. (See Figure 6.40.) Nearly all serial-interface mouses come with a DB-9 connector; however, the DB-25 connector is the most common serial-interface type connector. Thus, you will need the conversion cable if you are going to use the mouse.

Some mice come with the conversion cable and others don't. You can usually purchase the conversion cable along with the mouse for about $5. If you don't, you could spend $7 to $10 at a Radio Shack store to purchase the same thing.

The bus-controlled mouse also presents the problem of being able to fit into your computer. If you don't have any room for an eight-bit mouse bus card, you can forget this mouse interface option.

## Scanners

A new thing to have these days is a scanner. It has an interface card of its own that plugs into one of the eight-bit expansion slots on the motherboard.

**Figure 6.41**   Flat bed or page scanner

These devices come in two versions. One is the flat-bed type that scans a whole 8.5 by 11-inch piece of paper at one time, as in Figure 6.41. The other type is the popular hand-held scanner, shown in Figure 6.42. These can scan a 4-inch swath up to 11-inches long.

Through the use of software supplied with them, you can scan almost anything into one of the popular paint or draw programs. This can save a tremendous amount of hand-drawing time.

Scanners can also scan text and read it directly into the computer. This function, which can save you lots of typing time, requires OCR scanner software.

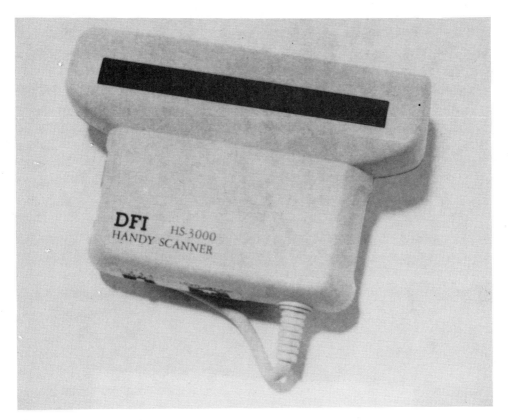

**Figure 6.42**    **Hand-held scanner**

Scanners are like mice and keyboards—you will just have to shop around and find the one right for your particular tastes.

# Modems

A modem is an expected part of today's computer. It is relatively easy to dial into a bulletin board locally or nationally. There are more bulletin boards than you can possibly imagine. There are also numerous public information services available by telephone with the use of a modem.

**Figure 6.43a**   **An internal modem**

Modems come as either external or internal devices. (See Figures 6.43a and 6.43b.) Most people opt for the internal version, since it is out of sight and doesn't take up valuable desk space. The external version requires a serial interface port for connection. Of course some users much prefer to have an external model complete with on/off switch and status lights that relay configuration information. An external modem is a good choice if you use more than one computer and you want to be able to move easily between hardware.

When looking for a modem, it should say "Hayes compatible." Hayes modems became the standard by which everyone was judged years ago. Nearly all modem

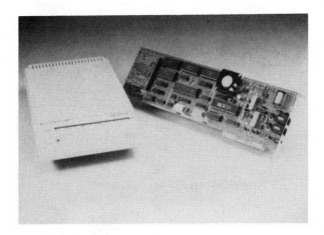

**Figure 6.43b** An external modem

software support packages come with default settings for the Hayes modem standard. You will save yourself a lot of headaches if you go this route.

One word of caution, however. Not all modems fully implement the Hayes modem command set of instructions. The only suggestions that we can offer is to go to the library and search back through past computer magazines for reviews of modems. These comparison articles do a thorough job of testing and comparing the products.

As for data transmission speed, 1200 baud was common just a few years ago, but with the dramatic drop in prices, 2400 baud modems are quickly becoming standard. For $80 you can get a Hayes compatible modem which is capable of operating manually or automatically at 300/1200/2400 baud. Seven years ago, a 300 baud only modem would have cost $400.

# Printers

Printers today fall into one of two types: dot matrix or laser. The dot-matrix printer can usually print in several different sizes, densities, and fonts with amazing resolution. In fact the newer printers are capable of 300 dots-per-inch resolution in the graphics printing mode. This is equivalent to a laser printer. But alas, the laser's quality and speed is no match for the dot-matrix. The dot-matrix

**Figure 6.44a**   **A narrow carriage dot-matrix printer**

printer used to have a competitive price edge over the laser, but that is rapidly changing.

A whole book could be written on printers. It is not our intent to describe all the unique features and capabilities. If you desire a detailed comparison of all the available printers, it is suggested that you obtain back copies of PC Magazine's yearly reviews of printers. They review hundreds of dot-matrix, laser, and color printers each year. There is no better way to review the market of printers.

**Figure 6.44b**   **A wide carriage dot-matrix printer**

## *Dot-Matrix*

Dot-matrix printers come in two basic sizes and versions. The narrow-carriage size is for standard 8.5 by 11-inch paper and the wide-carriage size is for handling paper up to 15.5 inches in width. (See Figures 6.44a and 6.44b.) Both types can be found in 9-pin and 24-pin print head versions.

Unless you are an account, it is hard to justify buying a wide-carriage printer. There are times when it is handy, but for probably 99.9 percent of your printing needs, the narrow-carriage version will do the job.

**Figure 6.45** A laser printer

As for print heads, the 9-pin printers are very cheap, but the 24-pin print heads yield outstanding print quality. The 9-pin is adequate for most printing needs including printing letters. In the NLQ (near-letter-quality) mode, they do a respectable job of generating print close to that of a typewriter. If quality and graphics printing resolution is required, the 24-pin print head versions is the only way to go. They can generate near perfect letter quality text and their graphics resolution can rival a laser printer.

When shopping for a dot-matrix printer, it is important to find out which versions of printers they can emulate. This is important because software packages cannot support all the hundreds of types of printers on the market. Epson and IBM printers have become a standard by which most software packages have been written, thus the printer you pick should emulate one of these two popular printers.

## *Laser*

Laser printers are quiet, fast (eight pages per minute), and have near perfect print quality (300 dots-per-inch resolution). The standard of the laser printing world is the HP-II, shown in Figure 6.45.

With the laser printer you can print either lengthwise or sideways. The software drivers that come with software packages today support this function along with many others.

If you require professional looking letters and graphs, and need quick printing, the laser is the only way to go.

One thing you should be aware of is the cost of operating a laser printer. It will cost you about 5 to 7 cents per printed page. You can get the toner cartridges refilled for about one third the cost of a new one, thus saving 2 to 3 cents per printed page, but it is still an expensive way to print. A dot-matrix by comparison only costs a few tenths of a cent to print a page.

It is suggested that you have a cheap dot-matrix printer on hand to do rough-draft printing. You can then do the final version on the laser.

## CHAPTER SEVEN

# BLUEPRINTING YOUR COMPUTING NEEDS

Before you start to build, you have to learn how to shop.

Why? Because the whole purpose of building your own computer from scratch is to get the most system for the least amount of money. You can always pay someone else to build your "perfect" system; this book is for someone who would rather pay himself.

Now, all that said, we need to expand the definition of the "most computer." This does not always mean the fastest or the biggest or the most capable: sometimes the "most computer" is the one that is the most personalized to your particular needs and wants.

Right from the start, let's recognize that building your own computer is not going to give you a free machine. Typical savings are 10 to 20 percent lower than mail order prices for assembled systems, and perhaps 20 to 30 percent below the prices of comparable systems in retail stores.

## THE PURCHASING PROCESS

But we need to put a value on the fact that the system you build should be exactly tailored to your present and future needs. And finally, there does come a certain satisfaction to be able to answer an envious question about your PC system by saying, "I built it myself."

We're going to start our expedition by establishing a systematic approach to purchasing. Here are the separate steps we want to work through:

1   Define your needs.
2   Define a "soft" system.
3   Create a parts list.
4   Go shopping for components.
5   Shop for assembled systems.
6   Comparing oranges and oranges.
7   The make or buy decision.

## YOU'RE IN THE SAME BUSINESS

One of the most interesting elements of the computer system industry today is that almost nobody makes anything. Mighty IBM purchases its motherboards from one source, its disk drives from another, and keyboards from a third. The tiny storefront PC "maker" merely screws together elements it purchases from a wide range of domestic and Asian sources. So will you when you build your own machine.

Think of it as a competition. It's you, with your own handiwork and creativity, against the packaging and marketing skills of computer companies.

There is simply no way for you to pay less for a single motherboard than IBM does, because Big Blue buys by the shipload. You're not going to get a better price on a disk drive than Compaq because Compaq goes right to the manufacturer, while you will be buying from a retailer who buys from a distributor who buys from the manufacturer.

But you can avoid paying the "value added" profit margin that goes on top of the assembled parts.

## WHAT ARE YOUR NEEDS?

There are two ways to buy almost anything, and the same principles apply here:

1   Determine what you want, and then see how little you can spend to get it; or
2   Determine how much money you have to spend, and then see how much it will buy.

From our point of view we think most business users will be in the first group, and most hobbyists will fall into the second group. But few decisions are that pure—many business buyers will be operating within a tight budget, and some hobbyists may find that their wants will take the bottom line above their budget goal.

In either case, it really is necessary to start with a look at the big picture. Think of this part of the process as deciding whether the new car you want should be a zippy sports car, a Mack dump truck, or something in between. We'll worry about whether it has rack-and-pinion or recirculating ball steering later.

Today's PCs can be generally divided into three classes, based on the capacity of their microprocessor. The classes have followed an evolutionary pattern, with the second and third stages building upon—and improving upon—the previous. We've already discussed the relative merits of the XT, AT, and 80386-class computer systems. Now, as part of the buying process, you will need to decide how your needs match up with the capability of the available hardware.

Unless your needs are very basic—and, perhaps more important, not likely to change—the XT class of machine is almost certainly too slow and limited for modern computing. Very little in the way of new software is being written for this class.

And, for purposes of this book, the XT class does not offer much in the way of opportunity for do-it-yourselfers. This group of computers has become a commodity item, with the assembled price almost always cheaper than the sum of its individual parts. Of course, we'll show you how to build such a basic model in this book, but we'd recommend you set your goals a little higher.

The AT class. The true workhorse of the contemporary PC industry has been the Intel 80286 chip, at the heart of IBM's original PC-AT machine.

The 80286 chip is a true 16-bit CPU, capable of computing on blocks of 16 bits at a time as well as moving those blocks around inside the computer's bus. The original clock speed for the 80286 was 8 MHz, but that was quickly supplanted by 12-MHz versions and more recently by chips that can operate at speeds of up to 16 MHz.

The third class of modern computers are based on Intel's 32-bit processors, the 80386 and 80486. It is worth noting that many of the 80386 and 80486 machines use an "AT bus" structure for the physical layout of their motherboards. This lets you construct your system using many of the same basic building-block boards and peripherals used in 80286-based machines. Such boards usually add either a special section of the motherboard or a special noncompatible bus slot for a bank of 32-bit memory chips.

There is also a hybrid form, the 80386SX, which we also have discussed previously.

If you are looking toward the future, there is no question but that an 80386 or 80486-based system is the way to go. The present capabilities are stunning, but the future possibilities are astounding. Prices have dropped sharply on 80386 machines, but the margins still remain considerably above the levels of XT and AT-class machines. For the build-it-yourselfer, the 80386 may offer the greatest opportunity to get the most for the (comparatively) least.

# BASIC SYSTEM NEEDS

As today's software products get more sophisticated, a fast and powerful computer becomes necessary. Word processors have grown from simple text editors to powerful document editors capable of doing a complete publishing job. Simple spreadsheets of 256 columns by 521 lines have given way to 1000 by 9000 spreadsheets that can do a wide assortment of things. Databases of today offer an almost unlimited way to file data and generate reports with the simplest of ease. Like it or not, the days of simple software are gone.

With multitasking, the computer operator can have the computer do several jobs at the same time. For example, the accounts receivable program could be selected to initiate invoice printing. After it starts printing, the operator can switch to another memory partition and initiate another task, such as inventory analysis for reordering. Finally, the operator can then switch to another memory partition to do word processing. Thus the machine is running three programs all at the same time.

Networking of PCs in a business setting has become imperative these days. Networking allows all the PCs connected to the net to act as extensions of each other. You can transfer files, send and receive electronic mail, and do a host of other things that will increase office productivity by reducing the need for physically carrying interoffice files, documents, and memos. Networking allows one or two large storage-capacity PCs to act as the central data banks for the other PCs connected to the system, thereby saving the cost of having to provide every PC with large data-storage capability.

All these advanced features of today's business and office environment cry out for powerful processors like the 80386 and 80486.

# DEFINE YOUR APPLICATIONS

Far too many computer shoppers go looking for a computer before they have determined what they really intend to use a computer for. This applies to both the neophyte and the experienced business person. The motive may be to have the latest and greatest hardware or to stay one step ahead of the competition. The result is still the same, overkill or insufficient capability.

Regardless of whether you are buying for your own personal use or for the company, take the time to understand why you are buying a computer. What are the major applications you will be using? Will you be the only user or will several people access the machine you are building? How important is the computer to the overall set of tasks you plan to do?

# THE "SOFT" SYSTEM

We need to describe the system you are designing for yourself in the broadest of terms before we can get down to the purchase of the individual parts. For purposes of this "soft system" we need only start with the most basic of building blocks. Every personal computer consists of the following:

**CPU**      The "brain" of the computer, almost always located on a "motherboard." As we have discussed, you will have to choose among three classes of CPUs: 8-bit, 16-bit, and 32-bit.

**Memory**   The "scratch pad" of the computer, where programs and data take up temporary residence while the brain is in use. Decisions here include the amount of memory and its speed rating.

**Storage**  This is the "library" of the computer, where permanent copies of programs and data are kept. Most computers use disk drives—either smaller capacity "floppy disk" drives or larger "hard disk" drives for storage. Like books on the shelf, information stored here is "nonvolatile" and, barring an accident, cannot be forgotten by the brain.

**Display**  This is the user's window into the computer. You'll need to choose a display card.

**Input**      Keyboards . . . mice . . . other.

**Output**    Printers . . .

# THE SPEC SHEET

The first step in ordering your system is the creation of a spec sheet (in the industry, this is called a "build sheet").

Include on your spec sheet some alternatives. For example, under Display you may want to list the items needed for both color and monochrome VGA and EGA systems. Display cards and disk drives are relatively inexpensive elements of the system; if you must find a way to save money, we'd suggest you look into buying as capable a basic system as you can get and scrimp a little on the add-in parts. You can always upgrade later.

As part of the shopping and systems design process we have divided computer system components into two categories: Microprocessor-dependent and Microprocessor-independent. As you think about system design, consider these aspects of your individual system. (Chapter 8 expands on this idea as we help you select the components you need to build a system.)

Within each category there are a number of major subcategories. We've taken a pass at something near to an all-inclusive chart:

Motherboard
        XT
        AT
        80286/80386/80486
                AT bus (ISA bus)
                Proprietary bus
                MicroChannel bus
                EISA bus

Memory
        Motherboard
        Add-in card
        Extended/expanded

Controller
- Floppy disk
- Hard disk
  - MFM
  - RLL
  - IDE (built-in)
- Combination

Storage
- Floppy disk drive
- Hard disk drive
- Specialty storage
  - CD-ROM
  - WORM
  - RAM cards

I/O
- Serial ports
- Parallel ports
- Bus mouse

Display
- Adapter
  - TTL
  - CGA
  - EGA
  - VGA
  - Super VGA
- Monitor
  - Color
    - CGA
    - EGA
    - VGA
    - Multisync
  - Monochrome
    - TTL
    - VGA

Printer
>   Impact
>   Nonimpact

Input
>   Keyboard
>   Mouse

Case
>   XT
>   AT
>>       Full size
>>       Tower
>>       Baby
>>       Baby Tower

Power supply

Software
>   Operating system
>>       DOS version
>>       OS/2
>   Applications
>>       Word processor
>>       Database
>>       Spreadsheet
>>       Graphics
>>       Utilities

In addition to the system subcategories, we'd like to suggest you include a special category—call it The Future.

Consider as best you can your future needs as you design your dream system. You don't have to buy everything at once, but do make sure that what you do buy is capable of expansion and enhancement.

And finally, you need to collect information about the vendors with whom you may end up doing business. Besides the obvious things like company name, telephone, and address, you need also to record—and later compare—such items as terms of payment, guarantees and warranties, service policies and support.

From our point of view, we are quite willing to pay a reasonable premium for the assurance that there will be a company standing behind the products we have purchased.

(You may have noticed that we have spoken only of writing down notes on a legal pad. Obviously, this data collection could be done with the help of a computer—a spreadsheet program may be the perfect vehicle for some users. The important thing is to do the work in the manner that makes you most comfortable. Don't let the computer stand between you and your creativity.)

If you have little or no computer experience, it would be advisable to contact two different computer consultants to make recommendations as to how you should proceed and what you should be buying in terms of software and computer hardware, particularly for business applications. Having a couple of knowledgeable people confer on what your current and future business needs are can help you get started in the right direction. This will save some backtracking later.

If you are an experienced user with an existing system, you should be examining ways to upgrade or enhance the computer operation. If you do not have a network installed, maybe you should look into what it could do for you. See if you could get double or triple duty from each computer by upgrading the present systems with 80386 motherboards that will allow multiple jobs to be run at the same time.

As to type or types of printers to use, match the right printer to the right job. Laser printers are fast and give typeset quality print, but they are expensive to use (about 5¢ a copy). Dot-matrix printers can also produce excellent quality and fair speed, and they cost less than a penny a page to operate.

# STRATEGY

With the mission objectives defined, you are now ready to develop a strategy for executing your mission. A good strategy consists of several different plans of action to cover the contingencies that arise during the execution of a plan. Money usually becomes the first problem that alters the initial course of action. Another stumbling block is finding exactly what you need in both hardware and software. Finally, gaining approval for your choices may become difficult.

Ultimately the best assurance of success is to plan carefully what you need a system for, then set about a systematic approach to finding the most economical system that fits all of your needs and objectives. We will discuss the process of narrowing down the selection in the next chapter.

## Upgrading or Replacement?

If you already have a computer, you may want to consider upgrading parts of it instead of trashing the whole system for a new one. You can remove that old 80286 8-MHz motherboard and replace it with either an 80386SX 16 MHz or a true 80386 20 MHz. Everything else can remain the same. The results of this upgrade is a computer that will operate two to three times faster in addition to being able to use the new 386 software. If data storage is a problem, a 60-MB hard disk and controller only cost about $500 in mid-1990 dollars.

If you need a faster machine, more storage, and would like to have the VGA display capability, you better go for a new system. By the time you make all the changes, the chances are that you will have spent more than the negotiated cost of a complete replacement system. In fact, you can probably negotiate a trade-in deal to help reduce the cost.

We were able to trade in an old 80286 12-MHz system toward a new 80386 20-MHz system at a local discount store, regaining some of the value of our 80286 parts. The price for the 80386 was almost identical to the magazine ads, and we received the added benefit of getting credit for the 80286 parts we were trading as well as local service and support. The thing that sold us was the substantial trade-in that they were willing to give us for the old system. The mail order places don't do this kind of horse trading. This incident also brought to our attention the fact that you don't have to go to the magazine ads to find good prices. Besides, if we have problems, we can go see these people face to face for help.

## Leasing or Rental?

You may want to consider leasing instead of purchasing, but you should consult your accountant to see if it makes sense for you. In general, purchasing a system will probably turn out to be the best choice, particularly given the savings you can realize by building it yourself.

In general you should start the computer selection process by deciding what you want to do with a computer. Defining carefully what applications you need will set certain limits on the hardware requirements. Next, narrow down the two or three hardware alternatives you may have and, finally, select a vendor and buy the parts. The next chapter offers some hints on purchasing the hardware you need, and Chapter 9 shows you how to put it all together.

## CHAPTER EIGHT SHOPPING AND PURCHASING

## INTRODUCTION: BUILDING VERSUS BUYING

Now that you have decided what you want in the way of a computer system, it is time to rush to the magazine advertisements or mail order catalog and start buying, right? WRONG! The whole purpose of building your own computer from scratch is to get the best system for the least amount of money and to customize the system to your own personal wants and needs; therefore, you need to establish a systematic approach to purchasing.

Although the basic idea is to build your computer from separately purchased components, you may want to keep a side list of assembled generic computer systems that you find as you scan through the magazine advertisements. There are two reason for doing this.

First, you will have a comparison price by which to judge your savings. You should be able to save approximately 20 percent or more over that of a readily assembled computer system (computer, printer, and monitor).

Second, you may find a system like the one you want to build, and the price may be acceptable to you. Thus you may decide to buy instead of build.

Given the small price differential (20 percent), why would you want to do it yourself? Well, basically for three reasons. First, you want to save money.

Second, the satisfaction and experience of doing it yourself. Third, you can tailor the system to your needs.

In the preassembled systems, you have no control over the motherboard brand, types of cards, disk drives, or power supply used in them. If you purchased one of these systems and decided to add an extra floppy or hard disk drive, modem, joystick, printer, extended or expanded memory board, or other computer accessory, you may find that you are in trouble. Here are some possible problems:

1  No room to add the extra interface cards.
2  Incompatibility between the cards you want to add and those in the computer.
3  The case will not hold the additional disk drive or drives that you want to add.
4  Power supply may not handle the additional power requirements for the accessories you intend to add.

There are many more points we could make, but we believe you now understand why you may want to build your own system from scratch.

Given all these problems, why would you ever want to order a preassembled system? One important reason is that the computer was assembled and tested by experienced personnel. If you have a problem, you can get it repaired or replaced with a minimum of inconvenience to you.

If you simply order the parts and assemble it yourself, you are likely to encounter resistance from vendors in returning defective items and/or items that don't appear to work. After all, did you damage it, connect it incorrectly, was it defective to begin with, or did you order the incorrect part for the application? We don't blame them for giving you a difficult time, since they are working on thin profit margins to begin with. They can't afford your problems!

Another point to be made about ordering a completely assembled system is that the vendor can offer a hard price to beat. They are in the unique position of buying in quantity.

By bundling a computer, monitor, keyboard, printer, and low-cost software together as a package, they can sell a lump sum of products as just one product. This packaging allows them to discount all the items in the package, since they are now selling only one product as opposed to five. The administrative and sales cost reductions is the reason they can offer the discount without losing any profit.

Don't become discouraged. The odds are in your favor that you can beat any advertised assembled computer system price. Unless you are a real mechanical klutz, you should have no problem assembling your own system.

```
Processor Independent       Processor Dependent (XT or AT)

1. Floppy Disk Drives       1. Mother Board
2. Hard Disk Drive          2. Disk Drive Controller
3. Display Monitor          3. Memory Expansion Boards
4. Printer
5. Keyboard
6. I/O cards
7. Cables
8. Case/Power Supply
9. Software
```

**Figure 8.1**   Suggested list of processor independent and dependent items

# BASICS

We recommend an itemized listing of all the computer components (separate sheet for each component) going into your system along with prices from different vendors. From these lists, you can identify the best prices and who is selling the items. Additionally, you can better see trends as to which vendor offers the best overall prices for certain categories of products.

It is also suggested that you group the components into two categories, as shown in Figure 8.1. By first dividing the computer system components into two categories (microprocessor-dependent and nonmicroprocessor-dependent) you can determine the fixed cost of your system. The difference between the fixed cost and the amount you can spend will define the expenditure restrictions on the purchase of a motherboard, hard disk controller, memory boards, and the video graphics controller.

In addition to the components lists, you should also keep a vendor list, with information such as shown in Figure 8.2. It will provide valuable data as to who

```
Vendor: XYZ Computer Store
Address: 123 Caroline St., Fredericksburg, VA 22401
Telephone:   1-800-123-4567   (Sales)
             1-800-123-4568   (Support)
Terms: Cash, Check, COD, Charge Card (No Surcharge)
Policy: 30 day return with no restocking fee
Warranty: 1 year on all computer systems
             90 days on individual parts
```

**Figure 8.2**   Suggested vendors information form

offers the best purchasing options and after-purchase support, as well as other information.

You may also want to keep a side list of items you find interesting along with comments as to where you found the information. You will have a quick reference source that will save you lots of time by not having to search back through the magazines and catalogs.

# SHOPPING

One of the most important things to do is determine the maximum dollar amount you are willing to spend. It is very easy to fall into the trap of over buying once you get started.

Buying a computer is similar to buying a car. You start off looking for a certain basic model with specific features, but before you leave the car lot, you have added every option that the dealer can pile on.

What are the sources for locating computer components? The local book store is a good place to start. Most all have a large magazine selection. Try to locate a monthly publication called Computer Shopper. It is the granddaddy of all the computer advertisements.

Computer Shopper is a monthly publication with about 700 pages. As the name implies, it is a shopper's paradise of hardware and software. It also has many excellent articles.

Other recommended publications are PC Magazine, Personal Computing, and Byte. There are many other excellent publications, but these are among the most popular.

It would also be advisable to scan through the local paper's personal ads section. You may run across a real deal on a system that someone is looking to sell.

After you have all your resource material, find a quiet place with a large work surface where you can spread everything out in front of you, such as a library table or a kitchen table. Once you have decided where you want to work, collect all your sales information material together, along with paper clips and a yellow highlighter, and get started.

Start by scanning through your material and locate what to buy and where to buy it (maybe several places). Rather than writing items down as you find them, we suggest that you tag the pages with paper clips and highlight the items with a yellow marker or the color marker of your choice.

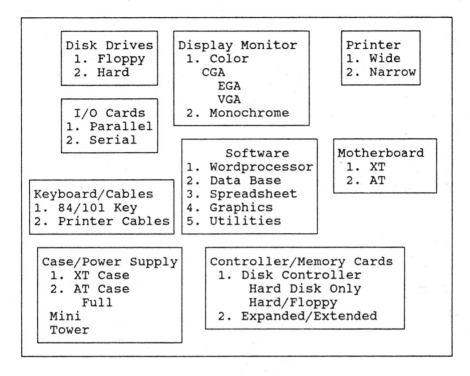

**Figure 8.3** Breakdown of component details

Once you have accomplished this task, go back and locate the paper-clipped pages. Now record the prices onto the individual component lists that you made earlier, or make a detailed breakdown of components as shown in Figure 8.3. It would also be a good idea to make general notes as you record the items (choices, options, and warranties). Each entry on the component list form should include: source (catalog or magazine), page number, vendor, and the item or items of interest, including prices.

Don't forget to note packaged items such as hard disk plus controller or monitor plus video card. Vendors will usually offer combinations of standard computer components at a discount over individually purchased items.

Also remember to record general information about the vendors. Things to note are

1   Toll-free 800 numbers for sales, service, and technical support
2   Surcharges for using charge cards
3   Shipping and handling charges
4   Return policies

**5**   Warranty support
**6**   Disclaimers
**7**   Product support

Free telephone access is imperative to saving you money. Some vendors don't have 800 numbers; however, this reason should not rule them out, since they may offer superior support. Some offer 800 numbers only for ordering. If you need to trace your order, return an item, or ask general purchasing questions concerning your order, you may have to call them on a non-800 number at your expense. If both sales and support 800 numbers are provided, place a star beside that vendor's name.

Make the most of the 800 numbers. If you have a question about the vendor's products, call and ask. Just remember, you are not obligated to buy. In fact this first contact may help you in deciding if they are the kind of people you want to do business with.

Don't forget to examine the fine print in the sales adds. This area of the ad will describe the additional costs that you might incur. Some vendors charge you a surcharge fee of up to 6 percent for using a charge card. Those that do not charge extra for charge cards will display this fact in large type. Charges for handling (preparing items for shipment) vary from $10 per item to no charge at all.

One of the more important things to look for is restocking fee charges. Should you decide to return an item for whatever reason, you may be faced with a restocking fee. This fee can be as high as 20 percent of the cost of the returned merchandise.

If the vendor determines the item is not suitable for restocking, you are now stuck with the item plus having to pay shipping charges again to have it returned to you. A very small number of vendors offer 30-day return privileges at no charge. Some vendors operate on an "all sales final" policy, which means you are stuck with what you buy (good, bad, or indifferent).

Check for warranty information. Some vendors don't handle warranties. You have to deal with the manufacturer of the product. Other warranties vary from 30 days to five years with various restrictions. Shipping, and/or labor, and/or replacement parts may or may not be covered.

If all this preparation seems like a lot of work, you are right. However, to put things into perspective, look at it this way. You will probably spend several weeks collecting and analyzing information. And you can count on at least 20 hours spent doing this work. If you take the difference between the cost of the system you are building versus a readily assembled system, then divide it by the 20 hours or whatever time you spend, you will find that the time was worth $30 to $50 per hour in savings.

| Disk Drives | | | | | |
|---|---|---|---|---|---|
| Item/Notes | Price | Vendor | Warranty | Source | Page |
| 360K floppy                             * | $   70 | A | 1 yr | P | 25 |
| 360K floppy | $   90 | B | 60 day | P | 11 |
| 360K floppy                             * | $   70 | C | 1 yr | P | 8 |
| 20Meg hard disk                         * | $  200 | A | 1 yr | P | 23 |
| 20Meg hard disk | $  225 | B | 60 day | P | 13 |
| 20Meg hard disk | $  220 | C | 1 yr | P | 11 |
| Disk Controller Cards | | | | | |
| Item/Notes | Price | Vendor | Warranty | Source | Page |
| 8 bit hard/floppy controller (XT) | $  140 | A | 1 yr | P | 27 |
| 16 bit hard/floppy controller (AT) | $  150 | A | 1 yr | P | 28 |
| 8 bit hard/floppy controller (XT) | $  110 | B | 60 day | P | 12 |
| 16 bit hard/floppy controller (AT) | $  150 | B | 60 day | P | 12 |
| 8 bit hard/floppy controller (XT) * | $   90 | C | 1 yr | P | 8 |
| 16 bit hard/floppy controller       * | $  100 | C | 1 yr | P | 11 |

Vendor:   A = ABC Microdevices   B = AMCORE Electronics   C = TINEX

Source:   M = Computer Shopper   N = PC Magazine   O = Byte Magazine
          P = Catalog

**Figure 8.4**   Floppy/hard disk drive and controller listing

Another benefit of all this work is that you are learning the nuts and bolts of computers. The only way to really learn is simply to do it. You can read all the books you want, but you really won't fully understand until you start applying what you read.

By shopping for the individual items, you will begin to understand what the specifications mean since the differences between similar products may be small in price but big in performance. Things that used to appear to be basically the same will now appear as different as night and day.

# SHOPPING EXAMPLE

To help you get started, we will go through an example of what you should do. Please keep in mind that your lists should contain more entries than the examples to follow. (See Figures 8.4 through 8.10.)

| I/O Card and Printer Cable | | | | | |
|---|---|---|---|---|---|
| Item/Notes | Price | Vendor | Warranty | Source | Page |
| Parallel/Serial/Clock | $ 60 | A | 1 yr | P | 30 |
| 6 foot cable | $ 10 | A | 1 yr | P | 44 |
| Parallel/Serial/Clock | $ 60 | B | 60 day | P | 10 |
| 6 foot cable * | $ 7 | B | 60 day | P | 31 |
| Parallel/Serial/Clock * | $ 50 | C | 1 yr | P | 17 |
| 6 foot cable | $ 13 | C | 1 yr | P | 45 |

Vendor: A = ABC Microdevices   B = AMCORE Electronics   C = TINEX

Source: M = Computer Shopper   N = PC Magazine   O = Byte Magazine
P = Catalog

**Figure 8.5**   **Parallel/serial I/O listing**

We have keep the lists short for the sake of the demonstration. The information for the lists was obtained from three current catalogs that were available. Please note that even with only three sources, you can get a lot of information. Also note that one sheet of paper will fill up quickly, even when it is restricted to just one particular component of the system.

Before getting started, we need to review how to set up the component listing sheets. The first thing to note is that vendor and source are referenced by a single

| Monitor and Graphics Card | | | | | |
|---|---|---|---|---|---|
| Item/Notes | Price | Vendor | Warranty | Source | Page |
| Monochrome * | $ 120 | A | 1 yr | P | 16 |
| RGB * | $ 285 | A | 1 yr | P | 16 |
| EGA | $ 490 | A | 1 yr | P | 16 |
| Monochrome | $ 160 | B | 60 day | P | 8/9 |
| RGB | $ 320 | B | 60 day | P | 8/9 |
| EGA * | $ 460 | B | 60 day | P | 8/9 |
| Monochrome | $ 160 | C | 1 yr | P | 50 |
| RGB | $ 300 | C | 1 yr | P | 50 |
| EGA | $ 480 | C | 1 yr | P | 50 |

Vendor: A = ABC Microdevices   B = AMCORE Electronics   C = TINEX

Source: M = Computer Shopper   N = PC Magazine   O = Byte Magazine
P = Catalog

**Figure 8.6**   **Video monitor and card listing**

letter of the alphabet. This notation allows quick referencing without having to write the names each time an item is recorded.

One suggestion is to assign vendors the letters A through L and information sources such as magazines the letters M through Z. Just so you don't forget, record the full names with referenced letters at the bottom of each listing page.

The remainder of the sheet should be self explanatory. The asterisk denotes the lowest-priced item for its type. We suggest you make one blank listing sheet as a master. Using the master, make 10 or 15 copies and use them to write on.

Study each of the sample component listings and note the range of prices.

Ok, lets collect those items that have an asterisk beside them to see what kind of system we can build, and what it will cost. The asterisk indicates the lowest-cost items in each list. In the case of equal costs, the warranty factor determined the winner. The minimum-cost system is shown in Figure 8.11.

Now that a base system has been established, you can change and/or add items to arrive at other more powerful system configurations according to your budget constraints.

# Shopping

Armed with your list of items to order, the vendor's information listing, a notepad, and the telephone, let's get ready to shop. Notice we said shop and not order. What you are going to do now is call those 800 numbers and get current prices. Remember that those advertised prices are already two to three months old by the time you read them.

Why not just go ahead and order? For one thing, you are looking for a good deal. Let the salesperson know that up front. Let them know you are doing comparative shopping. If they give you static or seem uncooperative, cross them

| Case / Power Supply | | | | | |
|---|---|---|---|---|---|
| Item/Notes | Price | Vendor | Warranty | Source | Page |
| XT Case / 200 watt supply | $ 130 | A | 1 yr | P | 12/78 |
| AT Case (full size) / 200 watt | $ 180 | A | 1 yr | P | 12/78 |
| XT Case / 200 watt supply     * | $ 100 | C | 1 yr | P | 16 |
| AT Case (baby size) / 200 watt  * | $ 160 | C | 1 yr | P | 16 |
| Vendor:  A = ABC Microdevices  B = AMCORE Electronics   C = TINEX | | | | | |
| Source:  M = Computer Shopper  N = PC Magazine   O = Byte Magazine<br>P = Catalog | | | | | |

**Figure 8.7**   Case/power supply listing

| Mother Boards | | | | | |
|---|---|---|---|---|---|
| Item/Notes | Price | Vendor | Warranty | Source | Page |
| XT, 8088, 8MHz, 640K memory     * | $ 140 | A | 1 yr | P | 6 |
| AT, 80286, 12MHz, 640K memory    * | $ 250 | A | 1 yr | P | 8 |
| XT, 8088, 8MHz, 640K memory | $ 168 | B | 60 day | P | 6 |
| AT, 80286, 12MHz, 640K memory | $ 278 | B | 60 day | P | 6 |
| Vendor:  A = ABC Microdevices   B = AMCORE Electronics   C = TINEX | | | | | |
| Source:  M = Computer Shopper  N = PC Magazine   O = Byte Magazine<br>         P = Catalog | | | | | |

**Figure 8.8**   Motherboard and math co-processor listing

off your list and forget their unbelievable prices because trouble may lie ahead for you. If they are friendly, cooperative, and say that they will be waiting to hear back from you, put a big star beside their name. Oh yes, don't forget to get the salesperson's name and telephone extension.

Once you have decided on one or more vendors, you can place your order or orders. The big question is how do you intend to pay for it. Your options are COD (cash), check, money order, credit card, or other form of guaranteed cash. Our advice is to use a major credit card and pay the credit card company off at the end of the month. Hopefully, your card has a 30-day no interest charge, which means you have up to 30 billing days to pay for the charge after it has been made; otherwise, it will cost you 1 percent to 1.5 percent on the unpaid balance.

| Keyboards | | | | | |
|---|---|---|---|---|---|
| Item/Notes | Price | Vendor | Warranty | Source | Page |
| 84 keys | $ 60 | A | 1 yr | P | 15 |
| 101 keys                        * | $ 70 | A | 1 yr | P | 15 |
| 84 keys | $ 60 | B | 60 day | P | 37 |
| 101 keys | $ 70 | B | 60 day | P | 37 |
| 84 keys                         * | $ 50 | C | 1 yr | P | 12 |
| 101 keys                        * | $ 70 | C | 1 yr | P | 12 |
| Vendor:  A = ABC Microdevices   B = AMCORE Electronics   C = TINEX | | | | | |
| Source:  M = Computer Shopper  N = PC Magazine   O = Byte Magazine<br>         P = Catalog | | | | | |

**Figure 8.9**   Keyboard listing

| Printers | | | | | | | |
|---|---|---|---|---|---|---|---|
| Item/Notes | | | Price | Vendor | Warranty | Source | Page |
| # pins | draft speed | NLQ speed | | | | | |
| 9 | 192 | 40 | $ 200 | B | 1 yr | P | 49 |
| 24 | 240 | 80 | $ 370 | B | 1 yr | P | 49 |
| 9 | 192 | 38 | $ 200 | C | 2 yr | P | 23 |
| 24 | 240 | 80 | $ 314 | C | 2 yr | P | 22 |
| 9 | 180 | 45 | * $ 170 | C | 1 yr | P | 24 |
| 24 | 180 | 60 | * $ 300 | C | 1 yr | P | 25 |
| Vendor:  A = ABC Microdevices   B = AMCORE Electronics   C = TINEX | | | | | | | |
| Source:  M = Computer Shopper   N = PC Magazine   O = Byte Magazine   P = Catalog | | | | | | | |

**Figure 8.10**   Printer and cable listing

Why use a credit card when you have cash? There are three reasons. First, cash transactions are hard to trace and prove; this includes payments by check. Second, the credit card company is your friend, believe it or not; they can provide an audit trace of charges and can act as a mediator between you and the vendor.

In summary, plastic money is fantastic if used correctly. Unfortunately, most people use it to live beyond their means. This is why you should have your shopping list in front of you when you order. Buy only what you have listed and don't let the salesperson talk you into anything else; otherwise, you have defeated this whole process that we have just gone through.

If you really want more than you can afford, get a small loan from the bank and pay the credit card off. It will cost you less in the long run, as well as establishing good credit locally.

```
Case:          XT Case / 200 Watt Power Supply  $ 100
Floppy:        One floppy disk drive            $  70
Monitor:       Monochrome with graphics card    $ 120
Keyboard:      84 key                           $  50
I/O Card:      Parallel/Serial/Clock            $  50
Printer:       9 pin                            $ 170
Cable:         6 foot                           $   7
Mother Board:  Turbo XT                         $ 170
```

**Figure 8.11**   Selected components and cost

# RETURNS

## Return Expenses—Shipping and Insurance

Returning merchandise to the vendor can be costly. First of all, you will have to pay the return shipping cost. Don't forget to add sufficient insurance to cover the package in case it gets lost since you are still liable for it. If you are returning the item for replacement or exchange, the vendor will usually pay the return shipping to you.

## Return Expenses—Restocking Fee

If you return an item within 30 days for one of the following reasons, you may have to pay a restocking fee:

1   You return an item as defective, but the vendor determines that it is not defective.
2   You return an item because you ordered the item incorrectly.
3   You changed your mind, and you no longer want the item.
4   You ordered two or more of the same item, and you are returning the extra item.
5   You refused to take delivery of the shipment. Let's say you got mad because they took so long to ship it to you.

What is a restocking fee? To cover the labor and overhead costs of accepting an item back into inventory, the vendor usually has to charge you. This fee is usually charged by vendors who offer good prices on their products, since they are operating on a low profit margin and operating cost, and being a former business person, you really can't blame them.

How much will the restocking fee cost you? The typical fee is 15 percent. This means you would lose $75 on $500 of returned merchandise in addition to the shipping, insurance, and telephone expense.

The best advice we can offer is be sure of what you are ordering, understand the terms of shipment—when it will be shipped, method of shipment, approximate time when it should arrive, and the vendor's policy of notifying you of delays in shipment such as out-of-stock.

# Conditions for Returns

Most vendors allow up to 30 days to return defective or incorrectly shipped items. PLEASE NOTE: If you discover that any packages are damaged when you receive them, don't open them! Notify the carrier and file for a damage claim. Let the carrier open and inspect the package because they will be totally responsible for the expenses. If you open the package, you may have to share the blame.

How can you determine if there is shipping damage? The obvious damage is a crushed box or large puncture holes. Another fairly obvious sign of damage is loose items in the box. Shake each box after receiving it. If you hear things rattling around, there is a good possibility that damage has occurred. Less noticeable damage is slightly crushed corners, edges, or a mushy feeling when the sides of the box are depressed. In this event, it is better to open the box in the presence of the carrier. It may be that the package was just improperly packed; however, the package could have been dropped.

We had this happen to us when an EGA color monitor was ordered through a discount center. When it arrived, everything looked fine. When the box was opened, the monitor case was cracked severely. The vendor took the blame, since it had been packed using slabs of foam instead of the original shipping material.

The monitor that was purchased was a refurbished unit, and the original material was not available. We were lucky, since the carrier did not want to accept blame because there was no visible signs of damage to the box.

We informed the vendor of their report of no damage to the box, and how poorly it was packed. They apologized and immediately sent us another unit without waiting for the damaged unit to be returned first. Not all vendors will do this. Oh yes, we knew that it was a refurbished unit, that is why we ordered it. It was an excellent buy.

# Returning an Item

Before returning anything to the vendor, you must call or write and request a return authorization number. This number should be clearly visible on the return address; otherwise, the returned merchandise might get lost or misplaced when the shipping department receives it. The people in the receiving department have no idea why the package came to them unless there is a reference number on the outside.

When you do ship items back for whatever reason, it is important that the item or items be returned in the original shipping container and packing material. If not, the vendor may reject it and claim that improper shipping may have damaged the item. Additionally, all items should be returned in the original packages, just as you received it; this includes warranty cards.

What about software products? If a software package has been opened (shrink wrap removed), you are out of luck. No one is going to take it back regardless of who is at fault. If you receive software and decide to reject it (wrong software, not what you wanted, or changed your mind), don't open it! Call the vendor; explain the problem; ask for a return authorization number; and ship it back.

## CHAPTER NINE

# ASSEMBLY AND TEST OF THE COMPUTER COMPONENTS

Building your own PC from individual components is not very difficult at all. Most of the components either snap or slide into place. Once in position, a couple of screws will secure it from any further movement.

Probably the most difficult and possibly harmful part of the whole process is connecting the cables. The two power cables from the power supply can be connected backwards on the motherboard, with the possibility of permanently damaging it. The cable connections to the hard and floppy disk drives have a key insert in the connector to prevent you from incorrectly plugging them in. Connecting the other end of the cable to the floppy/hard disk controller is another story. It can be plugged in backwards.

We will take you through each part of the assembly process. The critical areas of assembly and cable connections will be explained and illustrated.

## PREPARATION

You will need to prepare a clean work area for assembling your computer. We suggest using a table with several bath towels spread out over the table. This will protect the table, prevent scratching of the computer case, and most important of all, it will prevent screws and other small hardware from bouncing off the table onto the carpet or the floor.

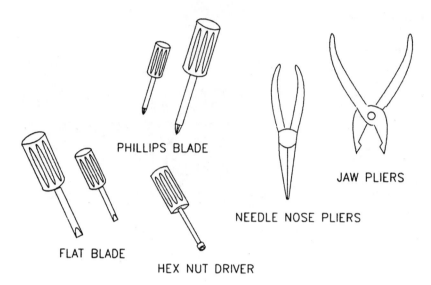

PHILLIPS BLADE

JAW PLIERS

NEEDLE NOSE PLIERS

FLAT BLADE

HEX NUT DRIVER

**Figure 9.1**   Basic tools for assembling your computer

Good lighting is essential. A 75-watt to 100-watt overhead light and a high-intensity desk lamp are recommended. You should also have a flashlight handy for peering into small places to find accidentally dropped screws. It is easy to drop screws and other items into the computer while you are assembling it.

A small tool kit is recommended. It should consist of several sizes of flat-blade screwdrivers and at least two sizes of Phillips screwdrivers. The shafts should be, at a minimum, 4 inches in length. You may also find it handy to have a 1/8, 1/4, and a 3/8-inch hex socket. A pair of needlenose pliers and a pair of small jaw pliers are needed, too. Figure 9.1 shows a suggested selection of basic tools.

Don't unpack everything and put it in a pile. Open the boxes and examine the contents, but keep everything together. Misplaced screws and documentation can be a real headache. Read the instructions that come with each item before you start assembling or installing it. Some items may have key instructions on installation.

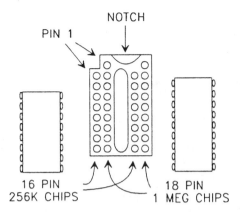

**Figure 9.2**  Memory sockets and correct positions for chips

# INSTALLING THE MOTHERBOARD

## Preinstallation

### *Memory*

The first step of the assembly process is installation of the motherboard. Prior to its installation, all memory chips and the math co-processor, if you are using one, should be installed.

Installing memory and the math co-processor on the motherboard requires special handling. First you need to lay the motherboard on a flat surface with a large piece of cardboard beneath the motherboard. The flat surface is to keep the motherboard from flexing as you install the memory components. The cardboard is to prevent the component wire leads that protrude from the bottom of the board from bending. If the leads are long enough, they may bend over and make connection (short circuit) to an inappropriate point on the board.

As you insert the memory chips, the motherboard will flex. If it flexes too much, you can damage it by breaking some of the copper interconnection traces on the board. It will be nearly impossible to find and repair the broken traces, so be careful.

The manual or documentation that comes with the motherboard should have an illustration of how and where to install the memory chips. (See Figure 9.2.) Study it well, because almost all 80286, 80386SX, and 80386 motherboards come with dual-function memory sockets that can accept either 1M × 1, 256K × 1, or 256K

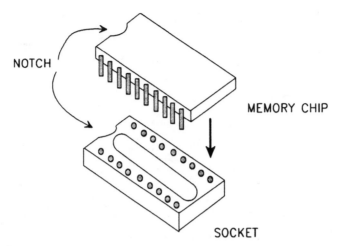

NOTCH

MEMORY CHIP

SOCKET

**Figure 9.3**   Memory chip reference mark and socket reference mark

× 4 memory chips. The sockets are so close together that it is possible to cross plug a memory chip so that part of it is plugged in one socket and the other half is in the other socket. You will know that you have done this when you get to the end of a row and find that the legs on the last chip have nothing to plug into.

There is only one correct way to insert the memory chips. The memory chips have a reference mark on them to identify where pin 1 is located. Pin 1 of the chip must be matched to the corresponding pin 1 on the memory socket on the motherboard. The socket on the motherboard also has a reference mark. The mark on the memory chip is either a notch or a dot. The socket usually has a notch, as shown in Figure 9.3.

To install the memory, you can use one of two methods. The first method requires an IC insertion tool, shown in Figure 9.4. The second method is done by hand.

An IC insertion and extraction tool is not difficult to use. Most Radio Shack stores carry them. Instructions on how to use them should be on the back of the card. If not, store personnel can show you how.

Installing memory chips with your fingers can be dangerous. If you are not careful, the chip can roll over as you try to press it into the socket. The result is 18 to 20 pin punctures in your finger, or bent leads that can't be repaired.

Most IC (integrated circuit) chips come with their legs slightly extended. This is to ensure a snug fit once they are inserted into a socket. The trouble is that it is difficult to insert them without using an insertion tool.

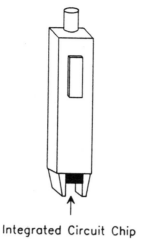

Integrated Circuit Chip

**Figure 9.4**  Integrated-circuit insertion tool

What you want to do is straighten the legs so that it will be easier to insert them by hand. To do this, you need the needlenose pliers. (See Figure 9.5.)

**1**  Grasp the body of the IC with the needlenose pliers.
**2**  Hold the IC against a flat surface (one row of legs).
**3**  Slightly rotate the IC to straighten the legs.
**4**  Repeat the process for the other side.

Now it is time to insert the IC into the motherboard. Ensure that the notch or mark on the end of the IC is aligned with the notch or mark on the sockets. Insert the IC as per the illustration in the documentation that came with your motherboard.

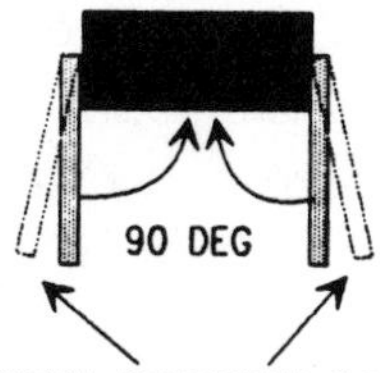

(END VIEW OF MEMORY CHIP)

90 DEG

ORIGINAL POSITION OF PINS

**Figure 9.5**  How to bend the IC's legs

## *Math Co-Processor*

You don't have to install the math co-processor before installing the motherboard, but it is easier to do it now.

**CAUTION!!**     Don't remove the math co-processor from its carrier or black foam until instructed to.

**PLEASE!**     Make sure that you don't have a static electricity problem. Plug some small metal appliance with a three-wire power cord into a wall outlet and put it on your work table. Now sit in a chair and don't shuffle your feet over the carpet on the floor. Touch the appliance to drain off any static buildup on your body. Now you can remove the math co-processor from its carrying case.

If you have an 8087 or and 80287 co-processor, it will be a long 40-pin IC. It has a notch just like the memory chips to identify where pin 1 is located. Locate the math co-processor socket on the motherboard. The motherboard's documentation should help you find it. Align the notch on the co-processor with the notch on the socket and plug it in. You may have to bend the legs just as you did the memory chip. Please be gentle.

**DON'T FORCE IT!!**     If you force it into the socket and discover that it is wrong, you will have a difficult time trying to remove it. In fact, you will need a special tool to get it out and you have to get out an improperly installed math co-processor before you can apply power to the system.

If you have an 80387SX or 80387 co-processor, it will be a 1.5-inch square IC. If you look carefully, you will find one corner has been beveled, as shown in

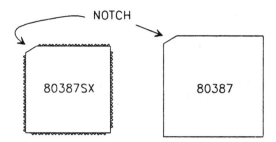

**Figure 9.6** 80387SX and 80387 co-processor IC, showing beveled corners

Figure 9.6. Carefully examine the math co-processor's socket to find the identical beveled edge.

Gently place the math co-processor over the socket. Ensure that the beveled edge of the co-processor and the beveled edge of the socket are aligned with each other. Gently press on the middle of the co-processor. It should gingerly snap into place.

# Installation

### *Standoff Supports*

Before installing the motherboard you will have to insert standoffs into it. The standoffs are to support the board so that it doesn't rest against the metal surface of the case and short out the board's electrical connections.

First, you will have to identify where to place the standoffs. Examine the case to identify where the securing screws will go. Figure 9.7 should help.

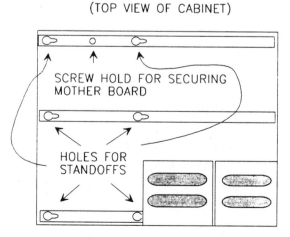

**Figure 9.7** Top view of case, identifying screw hole

Now position the motherboard in the case so that the identified screw hole can be seen. Examine the holes around the motherboard to identify where standoffs could be used (no blockage of the holes). If you see any holes that cannot be used, make a note of them. Now remove the board and insert the standoffs in the holes on the motherboard that were not blocked. Don't insert a standoff in the identified screw hole position, because a screw will go there. Refer to Figure 9.8.

To install the motherboard you have to lower it into place and snap it into its permanent position inside the case. Examine the mounting holes in the case. Notice that the holes have slits adjacent to them. The motherboard will have to be lowered into position so that the standoffs fit into the large mounting holes, as shown in Figure 9.9.

Once in place, you slide the motherboard toward the side where the slits where located. This should lock the motherboard into place. The securing screw hole should be visible. To check your placement of the board, gently try to lift each side and corner of the motherboard. It should not lift up. If it does, slide it back toward the large holes; realign the board; slide it back toward the slits; and check positioning again. Don't be surprised if it takes you several tries.

Now find the appropriate small screw and screw it into the securing screw hole.

If you are assembling an XT computer (8088), you will need to set the dip switches for memory size and number of disk drives. It will be easier to do it now rather than later. If you wait until everything is installed, you will have to push a mass of cables out of the way to access the dip switches. In fact, in some designs the disk drives cover up these configuration switches.

**WARNING!**   Don't use a pencil to set the switches. The graphite can cause a short circuit if it gets onto the motherboard.

# INSTALLING THE POWER SUPPLY

## Horizontal or Standard Cases

The power supply usually mounts to the right of the motherboard, just behind the disk drive cage. Note that there are two triangular-shaped fingers on the bottom of the power supply. These fingers slide into two slots on the chassis. (See Figure 9.10.)

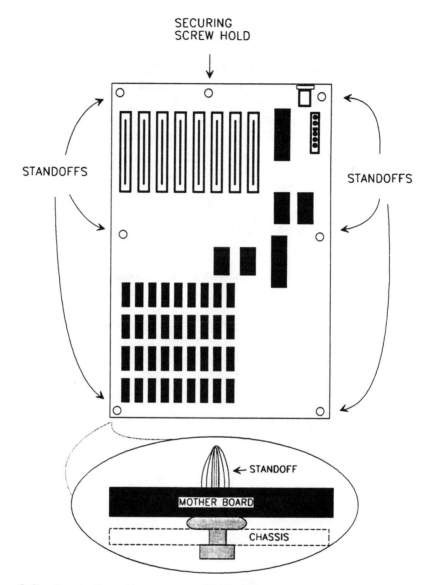

**Figure 9.8**   Standoffs and how they should look when inserted

Place the power supply in the chassis about one inch from the back of the chassis. (See Figure 9.10.) The multicolored power connector cables should be hanging out over the motherboard, as in Figure 9.11.

Slide the power supply toward the back of the chassis. You should feel a little resistance as the fingers lock into place. Try to lift the power supply. You shouldn't be able to if the fingers properly locked into place.

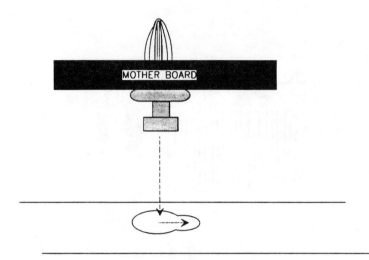

**Figure 9.9**   Motherboard over mounting holes

With the power supply locked into position, go around to the back of the chassis and locate the screw holes for securing the power supply. (See Figure 9.12.) Find the appropriate screws and secure the power supply to the chassis with the screws.

Now locate the two power connectors for the motherboard. These are two six-pin connectors. Note that each connector has two black wires, along with some wires of other colors. (See Figure 9.13.) When these connectors are plugged

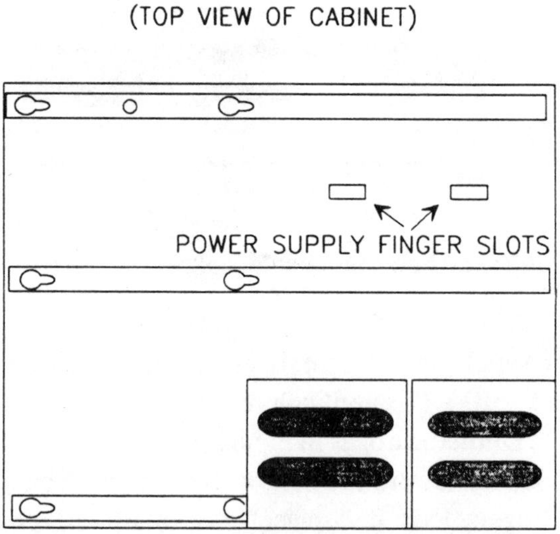

(TOP VIEW OF CABINET)

POWER SUPPLY FINGER SLOTS

**Figure 9.10**   Hole positions for mounting power supply

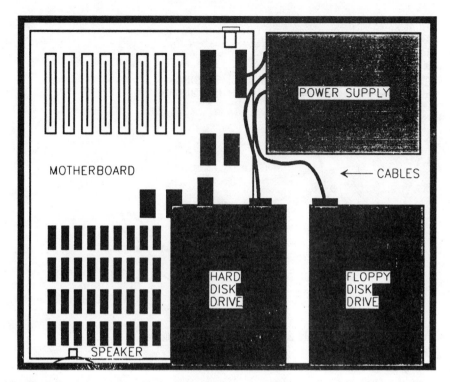

**Figure 9.11**   **Placement of power supply**

into the power strip on the motherboard the black wire pairs should be together in the center of the connector, so you end up with four black wires adjacent to each other.

The remaining four-wire (orange, black, black, red) power connectors are for the floppy and hard disk drives. There is only one way to plug them in. A key on the connector allows them to go in just one way, as shown in Figure 9.14.

The long, black power cord plugs into the back of the power supply. Set it aside for now.

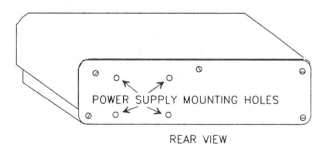

**Figure 9.12**   **Mounting screw holes for securing power supply**

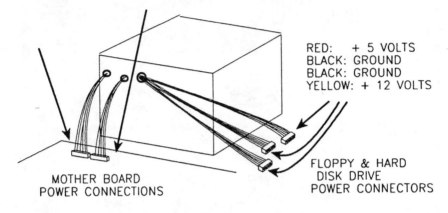

BLACK: GROUND
BLACK: GROUND
BLUE:   −12 VOLTS
YELLOW: +12 VOLTS
RED:    +5  VOLTS
ORANGE: SIGNAL GOOD

RED:    + 5 VOLTS
RED:    + 5 VOLTS
RED:    + 5 VOLTS
WHITE: + 5 VOLTS
BLACK: GROUND
BLACK: GROUND

RED:    + 5 VOLTS
BLACK: GROUND
BLACK: GROUND
YELLOW: + 12 VOLTS

FLOPPY & HARD
DISK DRIVE
POWER CONNECTORS

MOTHER BOARD
POWER CONNECTIONS

**Figure 9.13**  **Power supply connections and color codes**

If your case has indicator lights, a turbo speed switch, or a reset switch, connect them to the appropriate points on the motherboard if it supports such connections. Also plug in the speaker at this time.

Refer to the motherboard's documentation for guidance.

## Vertical or Tower Cases

Tower cases will either have a chassis plate configuration similar to the horizontal case or it will have a shallow power supply cage that the power supply slides into. (See Figure 9.15.)

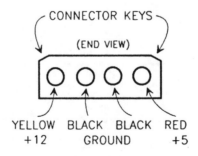

CONNECTOR KEYS

(END VIEW)

YELLOW    BLACK    BLACK    RED
+12            GROUND            +5

**Figure 9.14**  **Power connector with beveled edges**

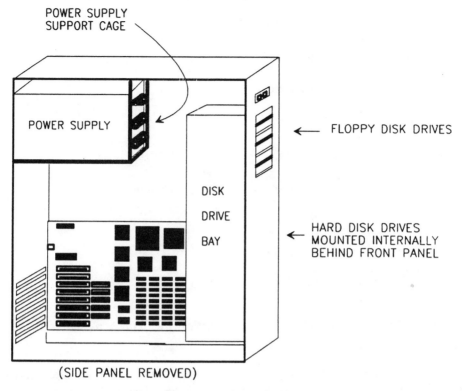

**Figure 9.15**   The cage-type mount for the power supply

The motherboard will mount in the vertical case similar to the way it mounts in the horizontal case, with the exception of plastic hook standoffs for supporting the board vertically, as shown in Figure 9.16.

# INSTALLING DISK DRIVES

The only difficult part about installing the hard and floppy disk drives is ensuring that they are correctly oriented (right side up).

The floppy disk drives will have a little lever that you rotate to lock the floppy disk hub in place. The correct orientation of the drive is with the lever to your left and the circuit board facing up, as in Figure 9.17.

The correct orientation of the hard disk drive is with the circuit board facing the bottom, as in Figure 9.18.

Most disk drive packages come with mounting hardware and instructions on how to assemble the pieces. Many floppy drive assemblies use permanent screw

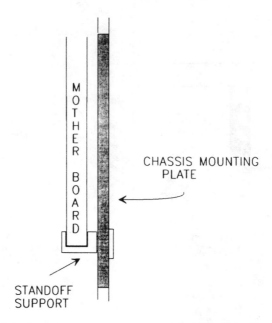

**Figure 9.16** The motherboard mounted vertically with the hook standoffs

mounts, while the hard drives generally use sliding rails with a set screw to hold them in place. The newest mounting technique uses plastic sliding rails for hard and floppy drives. These rails clip into place so you can remove an individual drive by pressing on each side of the mount and pulling forward.

## XT Cases

XT computer cases differ from the AT and tower case in that the floppy and hard disk drives are held in place by screws. The drives are suspended between the

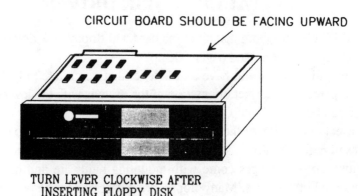

**Figure 9.17** The floppy disk drive orientation

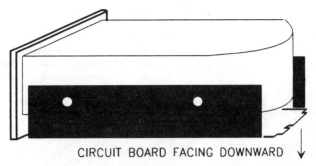

**Figure 9.18** The hard disk drive orientation

mounting plates on the left and right sides of the drives. (See Figure 9.19.) Screws are then inserted through the openings on the plate and screwed in until snug.

There is only one problem with this mounting procedure. Depending on whether you first mount drives in the left or right compartment, you will only be able to secure screws on both sides of the first installed compartment. When you mount drives in the other compartment, you will only be able to mount screws on one side.

It is recommended that you mount the floppies in the right compartment first on a standard side-by-side case. Use screws on both the left and right sides to secure the drives. Now slide the hard disk into the left compartment (see Figure 9.20) and secure it with two screws on the left-hand side.

## AT and Tower Cases

Disk drives are easier to mount in the AT and tower cases. Rails are first attached to the drives and the drives are then slid into the disk drive compartments using

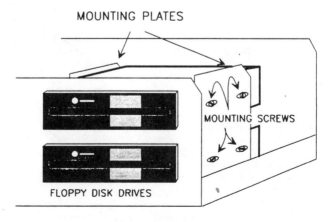

**Figure 9.19** XT floppy disk drive mounting

MOUNTING PLATES

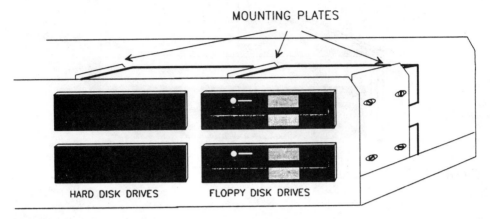

Figure 9.20 XT case mounting of hard and floppy disk drives

the guide rails. (See Figure 9.21.) Right-angle clips are then used to secure them in place so that they don't come out.

## Connecting Power

After you have mounted the drives, locate the four-wire power connectors from the power supply. Locate the corresponding connections on the disk drives. Make the connections, being careful to note the beveled edges—they are your key to the correct way to plug in the connectors.

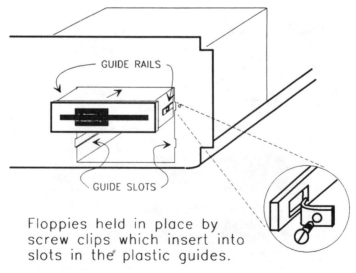

Floppies held in place by screw clips which insert into slots in the plastic guides.

Figure 9.21 AT case mounting of drives

# INSTALLING SYSTEM CARDS

Now it is time to install the expansion cards. If you have a parallel/serial I/O card, install it in the first eight-bit expansion socket on the motherboard, closest to the power supply. Short cards are mounted in the expansion sockets closest to the power supply because of the hard disk drive. Follow the instructions in the supplied documentation as to how to connect the serial interface cable.

The next card to mount is the hard/floppy disk controller. Before mounting the controller, locate pin 1 on the controller's board for the data and control sockets. Use the controller's documentation to help you, and refer to Figure 9.22. The cables plug into the sockets so that the colored edge (usually red) is adjacent to pin 1 of the socket.

The controller should mount in the next expansion socket closest to the power supply. Be sure to plug it into a 16-bit expansion socket if it is a 16-bit controller.

If you have separate floppy and hard disk controllers, mount the hard disk controller first. This will help to minimize the cabling mess, since the hard disk controller and the hard disk will be next to each other.

Now mount the floppy disk controller. Since it is an eight-bit device, you need to find an eight-bit slot. You can plug it into a 16-bit slot, but depending on the manufacturer of the motherboard, it may or may not work correctly.

There is a data bus control line that the expansion cards can control. This line enables the cards to identify themselves as either eight-bit or 16-bit devices; therefore, it really shouldn't matter whether the eight-bit card plugs into either an eight-bit or 16-bit expansion socket.

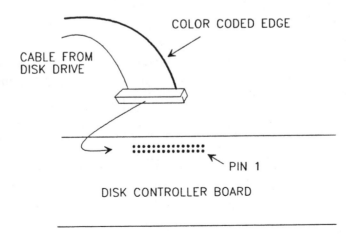

**Figure 9.22**   **Connector and cable alignment for disk controller card**

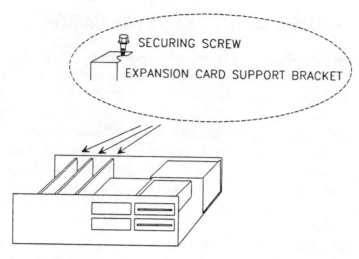

**Figure 9.23**   Retaining screw positions

Now mate the controller cables to the edge connectors on the disk drives. You can only connect them one way because there is a key guide in the socket to ensure a correct connection.

Make sure that the floppy data/control cable goes to the floppies and not the hard disk. The floppy control cable has two connectors. One is mounted on the end and the other is about six inches away from it. The floppy that you connect the end connector to will become the A disk drive.

Note that some disk drives require that a jumper be set to identify the A: drive and the B: drive. Check the documentation that came with your units to find out whether you have to set a jumper for these drives.

With hard drives, particularly, a terminating resistor pack usually is required in the final drive in the chain. If you are using two hard drives the first drive must have this resistor pack removed and you have to make sure the second (or final) drive in the chain has its terminating resistor in place. Again, the instructions we have seen with most of these drives are fairly clear. Simply follow the steps recommended by the manufacturer.

Now mount the video graphics card and any other expansion cards that you have. Once all cards are mounted, screw them into place with the retaining screws, as shown in Figure 9.23.

# CHECKOUT OF THE SYSTEM

Before we proceed any further, turn the computer upside down and shake it. If there are any loose screws or other metallic objects in the computer, let's get them out now.

Make sure the power switch is in the off position on the power supply. Now connect the keyboard, video monitor, and the printer. Plug in the power cord to the power supply.

Turn the power on. The hard disk should spin up. The floppy disk drives will momentarily come on and then power off. Within a few seconds the video monitor should display the POST (power on self test) of the ROM BIOS as it goes about checking for the presence of I/O devices and bad memory. That is, of course, if you remembered to turn on the video monitor.

The monitor screen will clear and the floppies will come on one at a time and then go out. The hard disk drive light should then momentarily come on. The ROM BIOS is trying to find some software to load into the computer and execute.

If the disk drives fail to come on, go back and check all cabling. It is important to get the floppies working, since they are needed to initialize the hard disk and for installing software on it.

If the cabling checks out, unplug all the cables from the hard disk drive and try powering up again. If things still don't work, try reversing the floppy cable connection on the floppy controller. The colored mark may be on the wrong side. If you still have trouble, either call the vendor that you ordered from or get someone technically competent to help you.

Now find an operating system disk and insert it in floppy disk drive A. Simultaneously hold down the CTRL, ALT, and DEL keys. The computer will then proceed to do a quick check followed by an activation of the A floppy disk drive. The ROM BIOS boot routine should now load the operating system from the DOS diskette into the computer's memory. The familiar DOS prompt >A: should appear.

Type DIR and ENTER for directory and watch a listing of the directory on the screen. Insert another program disk in the B floppy disk drive, or remove the floppy from A and insert it into B. Now type B:DIR to display a directory from the B floppy.

Now get the disk manager/diagnostics disk that probably came with the hard disk and insert it in the A floppy disk drive. Make sure the screen shows A> prompt. Follow the documentation that came with the hard disk as to how to low-level format, partition, and set type number if using a 16-bit computer.

If everything checks out, turn off the power and get ready to put the cover on. If you can load from the floppy but you have trouble accessing the hard disk, don't panic.

Continue the troubleshooting process by determining if the disk drive is spinning. Look for LED lights and listen for fans and motors. If all is quiet it may simply mean a disconnected power cord. Is everything else working? If you can still boot from a floppy drive, then you have basic power, and the floppy side of your controller (if it is a combined unit) is working, at least.

Sometimes it is hard to tell whether a hard disk is spinning when everything else appears to work normally. Place your hand on top of the hard drive and turn on the power. You should be able to feel the drive vibrate as the disk comes up to speed. If in doubt, disconnect the power cable (a three-wire, colored cable that attaches through a plastic connector) from the rear of the drive and repeat the experiment. If you still can't tell a difference between power on and power off, there's a good chance the hard disk isn't spinning.

Finally, remove the power cable from your A: floppy drive and replace it with the power cable that came off of the hard disk. Now see if you can still boot from the floppy. If you can, power is getting to the hard drive Ok, and the problem is inside. But before you take the unit in for service, plug the power cable that came off of the floppy drive into the hard drive and give it one more try. A poor connection, or the inate perversity of inanimate objects can join together to keep things from working properly. You have nothing to lose by giving it one more shot.

But what if the hard disk seems to spin Ok, but it still won't work? If you have access to another computer that uses the same type of drive—not the same model, necessarily, but the same type of controller, ST-506, ESDI, etc.—then swap out the drive. Remove all of the cables from the drive and slide the hard drive assembly out of its case. Disconnect the power and data cables from the drive in the second machine and attach them to your malfunctioning drive. IF YOU ARE REASONABLY CAREFUL you don't even have to install the drive. Simply prop it carefully on its side on top of the hard drive cage, making sure that none of its electrical components is touching anything else and that it is reasonably stable. Attach the cables and turn on the power.

If the drive works, you have a controller problem. To make sure, remove the controller from the second machine and use it to replace the controller in your original machine. If the second controller works with your original machine and your troublesome hard disk, you have found the problem. If the second controller doesn't work in your original machine, the problem is more difficult—either a bus problem, a subtle power supply difficulty, or another module that has failed and is dragging down the address or data bus.

In this case, remove everything you can from the bus. This includes any multifunction cards, extra memory, network controllers, mouse or scanner ports, modems, and the like. All you should have in the system is a video card and the hard disk controller. Now try bringing up the hard disk again. If it works this time, try plugging in the cards you removed one at a time until you find the culprit.

If the hard disk still doesn't work, seek professional help; but at least you know you have done everything you can before you bring in the cavalry.

# FINAL ASSEMBLY

The only thing left to do is put the covers on. For an XT and vertical cabinet, this is not a difficult process. The full size horizontal AT case is a bit tricky.

If you examine the inside of the front of the AT's cover you will discover two 1-inch pins sticking out. They mate into sockets on the front of the chassis. If you try and force the cover onto the chassis, you may bend the pins. Just have a little patience. Just like mounting the motherboard, it may take several tries.

# INSTALLING THE OPERATING SYSTEM

With the covers on and everything connected, power up the computer with a DOS operating system disk in the A floppy disk drive. Now turn to the hard disk installation section of your DOS manual and follow it.

Good luck and happy computing.

# SUMMARY

You now have the background knowledge to understand basic computer terminology and technology. You also have the skills to shop wisely. There is absolutely nothing to stop you from building the system of your dreams at an affordable price. Furthermore, you should also be able to upgrade and repair your own computer system.

Good luck. Now let's build a computer!

# GLOSSARY

**Access Time**   The response time of a component in relation to a request from the processor. Access time is normally less than the time duration of one clock cycle. It can be defined as: 1/clock speed = access time in nanoseconds.

**Address Bus**   Means of selecting a specific memory location.

**Address Lines**   On a computer system bus, the lines used to define memory and I/O address locations. Used by the CPU to know where to send and receive specific information.

**Binary Number System**   The base 2 number system of the computer.

**Bit**   A single digit that can be either a logic 1 or a logic 0. This is the computer's principal means of counting.

**Bus**   Multiple pathways of signals for carrying information or specifying a location in memory.

**Byte**   Eight bits make a byte. One byte equals two hex digits. This is the smallest information block of a processor operation. A processor instruction is one byte in size. Data may be either one or two bytes in size.

**Central Processor Unit (CPU)**   The brain of the computer. This is the microprocessor on the motherboard of personal computers.

**Clock**   A solid state timer that provides a standard interval for the CPU and other system components.

**Clock Cycle**   One beat or pulsation of the master oscillator or clock. It is expressed in hertz (10 MHz, 20 MHz . . .).

**Clock Speed**   The reference frequency of the processor's clock expressed in MHz (megahertz).

**Color Monitor**   A multicolor device where black is only one of the many colors. Used for text and graphics displays.

**Compiler**   A special computer program for translating text and math statements understood by humans into special hex codes that are understood by the computer.

**CPS**   Characters Per Second. The number of characters that can be printed in one second on a single line.

**CPU**    (See Central Processor Unit.)

**Cycles per second**    (See hertz.)

**Data Bus Width**    Information capacity of the bus (8, 16, 32 bits).

**Data Bus**   The information highway responsible for carrying information to and from the processor and a particular device that has been addressed, such as memory or I/O.

**DIP**   Dual In-Line Plug. A configuration for solid state chips that includes a parallel line of connector pins along either side of the device. Commonly used for memory expansion and other computer chips.

**Direct Memory Access Controller**   A chip or chips that control direct memory access by the CPU and peripherals. See DMA.

**Discrete Components**    The individual parts on the computer boards, such as resistors, capacitors, and integrated circuits.

**DMA**    Direct Memory Access. A technique for the CPU and other devices, such as disk drives, to retrieve information from computer memory.

**DOS**    Disk Operating System. The low-level software or operating instructions that enable the computer to perform basic functions such as keyboard entry and video output, printing, and interface with applications software. In the PC world the most common operating system is PC-DOS or MS-DOS.

**Dot-Matrix**   A printer that prints by forming dot patterns into characters.

**DRAM**   Dynamic Random Access Memory. The most common kind of computer memory. These chips are "dynamic" because they must undergo repeated refresh through reading and writing to retain their memory contents.

**Execution Time**   Amount of time required to complete one processor function, such as add or subtract. It is measured in clock cycles and expressed in time units of nanoseconds.

**FAT**   File Access Table. On a disk drive, the small database that shows the computer where to access files on the disk.

**Floppy Disk**   A flexible type of storage media. Can be found in 5.25-inch and 3.5-inch sizes with storage capacities of 360 KB to 1.44 MB.

**Hard Disk**   A rigid type of storage media. Storage media is normally enclosed permanently inside the hard disk unit. It has faster data access times and much higher storage density than floppy disks.

**Hertz**   Term that describes the frequency of a clock for a one-second time period. One cycle per second equals one hertz (Hz).

**Hexadecimal**   The base 16 number system (0–F). One hex number equals four bits in binary.

**Keyboard**   The device used by a human to input information to the computer.

**KHz**   1,000 Hz = 1 KHz.

**Laser**   A printer that works very similarly to a copier. The computer uses a laser to write onto the copier's drum.

**LPM**   Lines Per Minute. The number of lines that a printer can print in one minute.

**Latency**   In a disk drive, the time required for the desired data to rotate under the read/write head once the head has been positioned over the proper track or cylinder. This time must be added to the arm movement or access time to derive an accurate time to data figure.

**Math Co-Processor**   A CPU support chip that takes over certain math operations. A math co-processor can speed up overall system operation by a factor of five or more, depending on the applications being used.

**MHz**   1,000,000 Hz = 1 MHz.

**MIPS**   Millions of Instructions Per Second. The number of times a computer can execute a particular function in one second. It is expressed in units of one million.

**Module**   A collection of discrete components working together to perform a specific function such as a disk drive controller or a video graphics card.

**Monochrome Monitor**   A two-color video display in which one of the colors is black. Used primarily for text-only displays.

**Motherboard**   The main computer circuit board. It contains all of the operational components of the computer, including CPU and memory. I/O, display, and other computer components typically reside on separate expansion cards, though some modern motherboards include the entire computer system.

**Nibble**   Four bits make a nibble. A nibble is equal to one hex digit.

**ns**   Nanosecond. One billionth of a second.

**Operating System**   The software that is initially loaded into the computer to prepare the system for operation as a personal computer as we know it.

**PPM**   Pages per minute. The number of pages that a laser printer can print in one minute.

**Printer**   A device used to make permanent visual copies of the computer's output.

**RAM**   Random Access Memory. This is the main memory used for storing and executing programs and manipulating data.

**ROM**   Read Only Memory. A solid state memory device used in computer systems for boot-level and other system instructions.

**Settling Time**   In a disk drive, the time required for the read/write head to settle over the desired disk location. This time must be added to the arm movement or access time to derive an accurate time-to-data figure.

**SIMM**   Single Inline Memory Module. A small circuit board with edge connectors most commonly used to hold memory expansion chips for the motherboard or a dedicated memory expansion card.

**SIPP**   Single Inline Pin Plug. A small circuit board with a number of vertical pins most commonly used to hold memory expansion chips for the motherboard.

**SRAM**   Static Ram. Nonvolatile random access memory used in some computer systems.

**Storage**   A nonvolatile place where computer information can be stored for use at a later time.

**Switching Power Supply**   A transformerless power supply that uses a charge/discharge switching action to generate the required voltages. Switching supplies are lighter and smaller than conventional devices, and are almost always used in computer systems.

**Time Interval**   Clock cycles expressed in nanoseconds. The reciprocal of clock speed in megahertz.

**Transfer Rate**   The speed at which information can be transferred over the data bus.

**Video Display**   A fast text and graphical device used by the computer to communicate to a human.

**Volatile Memory**   Memory whose contents will be lost when power is removed.

**Winchester**   The original name given to hard disks.

**Word**   A two-byte binary number or a 16-bit binary number. One word equals four hex digits. Data is normally stored in word or byte (half-word) sizes.

# INDEX

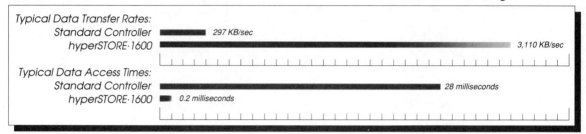

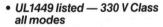

# STABILINE® Uninterruptible Power Supplies

UPSY Series STABILINE® Uninterruptible Power Supplies provide a reliable source of clean, continuous, sine wave AC power for computers and other voltage sensitive equipment. These true on-line UPS systems regulate voltage, protect equipment from noise and provide battery backup in event of utility power failure. Operate at extremely high frequency and utilize MOSFET semiconductor components. Typical operating times for 120 V, 60 Hz types range from 5, 10 or 30 minutes at full load; 10, 25 or 60 minutes at half load. Times can be extended by turning off non-critical devices. Have RS232 signal level interface DB-9 connector to interact with commercial computer operating systems to facilitate orderly system shutdown. Feature low velocity forced air cooling, low audible noise, protection from short circuits, overloads and excessive battery discharge. Input connection on 120 V, 60 Hz types is by an 8-foot cordset with a NEMA 5-15P plug and a UPS input plug IEC-320 connector. Operating temperature range is 0°C to 40°C. Assemblies do not draw from battery power until voltage drops below 96 VAC for longer battery run time and overall system life. Use of pulse width modulation (PWM) concept results in small size, light weight, quiet operation and high efficiency. Cabinet versions are UL listed and CSA approved.

| AC Input Single Phase | | Output | | | Internal Battery Backup Time (Min.) | | Cabinet Models | | Rack Mount Models | |
| AC Voltage | Current (Amps.) | Voltage (±)3% | Max. Amps. | Max. Load (VA) | Full Load | Half Load | Type | Each | Type | Each |
|---|---|---|---|---|---|---|---|---|---|---|
| 96-132 | 5 | 120 | 3.3 | 400 | 5 | 10 | UPSY61004 | 1150.00 | UPSY61004R | 1250.00 |
| 96-132 | 5 | 120 | 3.3 | 400 | 30 | 60 | UPSY61004L | 1295.00 | UPSY61004LR | 1395.00 |
| 96-132 | 10 | 120 | 6.7 | 800 | 10 | 25 | UPSY61008 | 1695.00 | UPSY61008R | 1795.00 |
| 96-132 | 12 | 120 | 10.4 | 1250 | 10 | 25 | UPSY61012 | 2695.00 | UPSY61012R | 2795.00 |

# PQI Series STABILINE® Power Quality Interfaces

PQI Series STABILINE® Power Quality Interfaces divert and attenuate electromagnetic interference, spikes and transients before they can reach sensitive electronic equipment. Unique, state-of-the-art multi-stage suppression/filtration design utilizes hybrid technology to offer a choice of "Good", "Better" and "Superior" performance levels. All units are lightweight and packaged in attractive, fire-rated ABS plastic housing with convenient access to AC and telephone line input and output connections. Circuit allows bidirectional protection from source or load power disturbances. Feature 205 V peak clamping level; 95 joule energy dissipation capability; less than 1 ns single stage response time; 3000 A surge withstand. Types with "D" suffix have telephone line multi-stage transient protection for use with FAX/modems. Let-through voltage for normal/metallic (line-to-line) and common longitudinal (line-to-ground) is 200 V peak, 200 mA maximum (steady state condition). Response time is less than 1 ns; withstand FCC part 68 metallic waveforms without failure.

All types except those with "D" suffix have circuit breakers. All Series 2000 and 3000 types have on/off pilot light. All PQI Series units are CSA approved and UL 1449 listed (clamping level 330 V).

| | | | | Receptacles | | | | |
| | | Nom. | Max. | NEMA AC | | RJ11 | Circuit | |
| | Type | Volt. | Amps. | Qty. | Style | Qty. | Breaker | Each |
|---|---|---|---|---|---|---|---|---|
| **Series 1000 — Good Performance** | | | | | | | | |
| | PQI-1115 | 120 | 15 | 4 | 5-15R | — | Yes | 75.00 |
| | PQI-1115D | 120 | 15 | 2 | 5-15R | 2 | No | 89.00 |
| **Series 2000 — Better Performance** | | | | | | | | |
| | PQI-2115 | 120 | 15 | 4 | 5-15R | — | Yes | 149.00 |
| | PQI-2115D | 120 | 15 | 2 | 5-15R | 2 | No | 179.00 |
| **Series 3000 — Superior Performance** | | | | | | | | |
| | PQI-3115 | 120 | 15 | 4 | 5-15R | — | Yes | 199.00 |
| | PQI-3115D | 120 | 15 | 2 | 5-15R | 2 | No | 229.00 |